THE
CHRISTIAN
WORDSWORTH,
1798–1805

William A. Ulmer

STATE UNIVERSITY OF NEW YORK PRESS

Cover illustration: a detail from "Salisbury Cathedral from the Meadows" by John Constable. Courtesy of the Tate Gallery.

Published by
State University of New York Press, Albany

For information, address State University of New York Press, 90 State Street, Suite 700, Albany, NY 12207

Production by Christine L. Hamel
Marketing by Michael Campochiaro

Library of Congress Cataloging-in-Publication Data

Ulmer, William Andrew.
  The Christian Wordsworth, 1798–1805 / by William A. Ulmer.
    p. cm.
  Includes bibliographical references and index.
  ISBN 0-7914-5153-4 (hardcover) — ISBN 0-7914-5154-2 (pbk.)
    1. Wordsworth, William, 1770–1850—Religion. 2. Christianity and literature—England—History—19th century. 3. Christian poetry, English—History and criticism. I. Title.

PR5892.R4 U46 2001
821'.7—dc21

                                                              2001020006

10 9 8 7 6 5 4 3 2 1

CONTENTS

For Andrew Benjamin,
Best Philosopher,

And Jeffrey Paul,
Child of Joy

PREFACE

This book undertakes two closely related projects. First, it reconstructs the evolution of William Wordsworth's religious attitudes during the years 1798–1805. Second, it presents detailed readings of the Immortality Ode and Thirteen-Book *Prelude* as religious poems. These projects are related but distinct because Wordsworth's religious poetics allowed his private faith to inform but not dominate his public statements—or, in the case of *The Prelude*, his statements intended eventually for publication. The Wordsworth this study envisions could have avowed with Shelley, "Didactic poetry is my abhorrence." The preponderance of the evidence suggests that Wordsworth regarded his spiritual beliefs as a form of Christianity by the time he wrote the great achievements of 1804–1805. But the faith of the poet and the religious vision of the poetry do not fully coincide. As a result, the motives and meaning of Wordsworth's imaginative recourse to Christianity can appear teasingly ambiguous.

They have unquestionably been interpreted in very different ways: over the years scholars have alternately defended and denied the Christian character of Wordsworth's poetry with equal insistence. For me, all such moves and countermoves finally just reinscribe their enabling assumptions about what constitutes Christianity—and that fray it seemed pointless to enter. Yet it seemed equally pointless to endorse the common contemporary opinion that Wordsworth's most compelling work is radically humanistic, radically secular, and thereby to deny honorific force to the poetry's persistent evocations of Christianity. Through allusions to Christian paradigms, the Immortality Ode and Thirteen-Book *Prelude* deliberately establish Christian analogues for their prophetic claims. The Victorian reception of Wordsworth shows how the resulting mix of tradition and innovation could signify as powerfully Christian in its own cultural milieu; and my conclusion speculates that Wordsworth himself construed the Ode and *The Prelude* as vehicles of a revisionary Christianity. But offering that speculation is a far cry from appropriating the poetry for orthodoxy. Let me reassure readers that nowhere do I characterize Wordsworth's poems as forthright endorsements of Anglican doctrine. In reading the Immortality Ode and Thirteen-Book *Prelude*, I simply point at moments to a displaced Christianity shaping the text's spiritual outlook more thoroughly than the criticism ordinarily allows. We misconstrue the imaginative endeavor of both poems, it seems fair to say, if we slight either the seriousness of their religious commitments or the Christian affinities of their religious perspective.

The book proceeds towards the Ode and the 1805 *Prelude* by tracing Wordsworth's own developmental progress towards them. My genealogy of Wordsworth's faith begins with certain Coleridge letters frequently cited in accounts of Wordsworth as a skeptically inclined humanist. This skeptical figure—to me his existence has come to seem a sort of scholarly urban legend—differs dramatically from the Wordsworth who emerges from my own analysis of Coleridge's correspondence. I argue for a 1798 Wordsworth who surely believed in God, whose theism seemingly assumed the inadequacy of natural religion (despite his poetry's focus on nature), and whose respect for Christianity probably included elements of intellectual assent. We cannot say that Wordsworth's early Christian affiliations extended without question into outright belief, and that is an important point not to be forgotten. But it is also important that those affiliations independently placed him on the margins of Christianity even in 1798. For Wordsworth's underlying Christian sympathies set the terms for his reception of the One Life, the Coleridgean theological postulate which prompted his later commitment to Christianity by forcing him to rethink his own religious position. So Wordsworth's 1798–1805 spiritual development involves the transformation of early Christian "sympathies" into the determined if stubbornly individualistic Christian "commitments" of sometime between 1802–1804.

For plotting that transformation my crucial coordinates are the terms "death" and "soul." Wordsworth scholarship often attributes the poet's Christian reorientation to the trauma caused by John Wordsworth's 1805 drowning. Wordsworth's poetry lingers anxiously over the prospect of death, however, from at least the time of *Salisbury Plain*. With his *Ruined Cottage* revisions of 1798, Wordsworth obligated himself to contemplate Margaret's death within the ontological context of the One Life. So human mortality became, in part, a specifically religious problem and a problem best resolved by the traditional notion of an immortal soul. Wordsworth's 1804 identification of "soul" and "imagination"— implied in the Ode and reaffirmed in the Thirteen-Book *Prelude*— allowed him to reauthenticate the idea of personal immortality, to feel it on his pulses with renewed conviction. That conviction, I argue, completed his progress to Christian faith. No real crises occasioned this progress. It was slowly cumulative, an effect of gradually emergent tendencies long in place, and as such it was emphatically a return. Home at last at Grasmere, the Anglican Wordsworth of 1804 held a faith he had come increasingly to value as a familial and national heritage. For Wordsworth, in short, the way of the soul was a conservative way.

That claim touches on perhaps my greatest challenge to established conceptions of Wordsworth. Asked to defend my book's pertinence to contemporary students of Romanticism, I would respond, "the book concerns Wordsworth!" Asked to elaborate, I would answer that scholars from the Victorian period onwards have stressed the centrality of religion for the cultural enterprise of British Romanticism. But I would then quickly add that this study presents the religious side of the case for Wordsworth's early conservatism. This case was opened in 1984 by James Chandler, who argued that "Wordsworth's major work, his programmatic poetry of second nature, is conservative from the start"; more recently Kenneth Johnston has similarly raised the possibility that Wordsworth's "poetry existed much more within the confines of established social and cultural norms that the traditional romanticizing of his poetical revolution acknowledges."[1] In its broader implications, my argument moves in this same direction. In the Romantic period some forms of religious partisanship promoted political radicalism: Coleridge's Unitarianism provides an obvious example. The more religious we find the early Wordsworth, however, the more conservative a figure we encounter. For all the aporias and estrangements of Wordsworth's poetry, his repeated and profoundly characteristic recuperation of the unfamiliar may mean that his poems are dedicated, in their ultimate ideological import, to a reinscription of the socially conventional and normative. My account of Wordsworth's evolving Romantic Anglicanism over the years 1798–1805 strengthens the possibility that his imaginative orientation and political viewpoint were both more conservative, early on, than has often been believed.

Parts of my argument were published as "The Christian Wordsworth, 1798–1800" in *JEGP* 95 (1996): 335–58, and as "Wordsworth, the One Life, and *The Ruined Cottage*" in *SP* 93 (1996): 304–31. I am indebted to my *JEGP* and *SP* readers for their authoritative and helpful responses, and to both journals for their permission to reprint revised versions of those essays. My thanks also to the University of Alabama for the sabbatical leave during which this project was formulated and for support afforded by the University Research Grants Committee (RGC 2–67873). At SUNY Press, James Peltz, Katie Leonard, and Christine Hamel helped steer the book to port; nearer to home, Myron Tuman, Sydney Sowers, and Tonya Beasley provided invaluable help with computer problems: my thanks to all. I also thank John Patrick Herman and Kurt Fosso for their attentive readings of my manuscript; while I doubt they learned much or became better Wordsworthians for the experience, I know they became my closer friends. My greatest debt is to my closest friend, my wife Kelly Brennan—but she received the dedication to my previous book. Here the dedication goes to my two temperamentally very different boys, my reflective eldest son, with his talent for asking difficult questions, and his more carefree younger brother, with his talent for contenting himself in any situation. This book is for them, with love.

ABBREVIATIONS

As my parenthetical identifications will remind readers, citations of Wordsworth's poetry are ordinarily from the reading texts presented in the Cornell Wordsworth Series, with exceptions noted. Unless otherwise indicated, references to *The Prelude* are to the 1805 version as it appears in the AB-Stage reading text established by Mark Reed in his Cornell Series volume; and citations from Coleridge's poetry, from William Keach's *STC Poems*. References to Ode or the Immortality Ode of course indicate Wordsworth's "Ode: Intimations of Immortality from Recollections of Early Childhood."

CLSTC	Samuel Taylor Coleridge, *Collected Letters of Samuel Taylor Coleridge*, Ed. Earl Leslie Griggs. 6 vols. Oxford: Clarendon Press, 1956–71.
CWSTC	Samuel Taylor Coleridge, *The Collected Works of Samuel Taylor Coleridge*. Gen. ed. Kathleen Coburn. 16 vols. Bollingen Series 75 Princeton: Princeton University Press, 1971– .
DS	William Wordsworth, *Descriptive Sketches*. Ed. Eric Birdsall. The Cornell Wordsworth. Ithaca: Cornell University Press, 1984.
EW	William Wordsworth, *An Evening Walk*. Ed. James Averill. The Cornell Wordsworth. Ithaca: Cornell University Press, 1977.
FBP	William Wordsworth, *The Five-Book Prelude*. Ed. Duncan Wu. Oxford and Cambridge, Massachusetts: Blackwell Publishers, 1997.

HCR   *Henry Crabb Robinson on Books and Their Writers.* Ed. Edith J. Morley. 3 vols. London: J. M. Dent and Sons Limited, 1938.

HG   William Wordsworth, *"Home at Grasmere": Part First, Book First of "The Recluse."* Ed. Beth Darlington. The Cornell Wordsworth. Ithaca: Cornell University Press, 1977.

HNF   Hoxie Neal Fairchild, *Religious Trends in English Poetry.* 6 vols. New York: Columbia University Press, 1939–68.

LB   William Wordsworth, *"Lyrical Ballads," and Other Poems, 1797–1800.* Ed. James Butler and Karen Green. The Cornell Wordsworth. Ithaca: Cornell University Press, 1992.

LEY   *The Letters of William and Dorothy Wordsworth: The Early Years, 1787–1805.* Ed. Ernest de Selincourt, rev. Chester L. Shaver. Oxford: Clarendon Press, 1967.

LMY   *The Letters of William and Dorothy Wordsworth: The Middle Years.* Ed. Ernest de Selincourt, rev. Mary Moorman and Alan G. Hill. 2 Parts. Oxford: Clarendon Press, 1969–70.

LLY   *The Letters of William and Dorothy Wordsworth: The Later Years.* Ed. Ernest de Selincourt, rev. Alan G. Hill. 4 Parts. Oxford: Clarendon Press, 1978–88.

MH   Jonathan Wordsworth, *The Music of Humanity: A Critical Study of Wordsworth's "Ruined Cottage" incorporating texts from a manuscript of 1799–1800.* New York: Harper and Row, 1969.

NCP   William Wordsworth, *The Prelude: 1799, 1805, 1850.* Ed. Jonathan Wordsworth, M. H. Abrams, and Stephen Gill. Norton Critical Edition. New York: W. W. Norton, 1979.

NS   M. H. Abrams, *Natural Supernaturalism: Tradition and Revolution in Romantic Literature.* New York: W. W. Norton, 1971

1805 *Prelude*   William Wordsworth, *The Thirteen-Book "Pre-lude."* Ed. Mark L. Reed. 2 vols. The Cornell Wordsworth. Ithaca: Cornell University Press, 1991.

1850 *Prelude*   William Wordsworth, *The Fourteen-Book "Pre-lude."* Ed. W. J. B. Owen. The Cornell Wordsworth. Ithaca: Cornell University Press, 1985.

PTV   William Wordsworth, *Poems, in Two Volumes, and Other Poems.* Ed. Jared Curtis. The Cornell Wordsworth. Ithaca: Cornell University Press, 1983.

PW   *The Poetical Works of William Wordsworth.* Ed. Ernest de Selincourt and Helen Darbishire. 5 vols. Oxford: Clarendon Press, 1940–49.

PrW   *The Prose Works of William Wordsworth.* Ed. W. J. B. Owen and Jane Smyser. 3 vols. Oxford: Clarendon Press, 1974.

RC&P   William Wordsworth, *"The Ruined Cottage" and "The Pedlar."* Ed. James Butler. The Cornell Wordsworth. Ithaca: Cornell University Press, 1977.

RR   Robert Ryan, *The Romantic Reformation: Religious Politics in English Literature, 1789–1824.* Cambridge: Cambridge University Press, 1998.

STC Poems   Samuel Taylor Coleridge, *The Complete Poems.* Ed. William Keach. Harmondsworth: Penguin, 1997.

TPP   William Wordsworth, *The Prelude, 1798–1799.* Ed. Stephen Parrish. The Cornell Wordsworth. Ithaca: Cornell University Press, 1977.

CHAPTER ONE

Wordsworth's Faith

Yet it is doubtful if on the basis of such declarations by its
champions and spokesmen we can consider the Enlightenment as an age basically irreligious and inimical to religion. . . . The strongest intellectual forces of the Enlightenment do not lie in its rejection of belief but rather in
the new form of faith which it proclaims, and in the new
form of religion which it embodies.

—Ernst Cassirer,
The Philosophy of the Enlightenment

WORDSWORTH AND SECULARIZATION

Toward the end of the eighteenth century, one of the leading imaginative writers of his day climbed in company to a summit in order
to watch the sunrise. Confronted with the magnificence of the
heavens, he rapturously professed his belief in God. This particular
scene did not occur on Mount Snowdon, however, nor did the profession of faith much resemble Wordsworth's affirmation in *The
Prelude* "of life endless, the one thought / By which we live, Infinity and God" (13.183–84). "I believe! I believe in you! Powerful
God, I believe," the aged Voltaire exclaimed, before adding archly,
"as for monsieur the Son, and madame His Mother, that's a differ-

1

ent story."[1] It is an amusing anecdote, but one which can disconcert the Romanticist who recalls Voltaire as Teufelsdrockh's nay-saying skeptic, an unqualified enemy of religion with "only a torch for burning, no hammer for building."[2] We usually identify the Enlightenment as the period which witnessed the ascendancy of secularization in European intellectual and cultural life. The eighteenth century in England was the era of Hume and Gibbon; of Latitudinarian moderation, with its prudential appeals to self-interest; of deism and other forms of rational theology, each reflecting the declining prestige of revealed religion; of a mood of satisfied worldliness; and of the incursions of empirical methodology into all areas of inquiry. Because the image of a thoroughly secularized eighteenth century looms so large in cultural and literary history, it is worth recalling that even the scoffing Voltaire consistently believed in a supernatural deity. In short, it is worth recalling the resilience of religious faith in the eighteenth century.

Eighteenth-century intellectual life largely revolved around religious questions. In England, where Christianity remained less contested than in the France of the *philosophes*, those questions were usually resolved in religion's favor. In the writings of Newton, Locke, Boyle, Bentley, and others, science vindicated the claims of Christianity, even as natural theology confirmed the truths of revelation. Despite his virtual deification by the French atheists, the great Newton remained a devout if unorthodox Christian whose legacy to the Enlightenment included his studies of the Apocalypse. The Locke of the *Enquiry* also wrote *The Reasonableness of Christianity*. Even at the end of the century, the most prominent scientific materialists of the era, men like Hartley and Priestley, ordinarily accepted some form of religious creed. As in all ages, guardians of the faith could discover its apparent decay. But Roland N. Stromberg justly remarks that

> despite lamentations to the contrary there was not, after all, much real disbelief. "An atheist or a deist is a monstrous kind of creature, which in the country we only know by report," Philip Doddridge wrote in 1726, when deism was at its peak. Perhaps, as Doddridge implied, they existed in the cities; but we need only read the fashionable literature of the day—*Spectator*, *Tatler*, or a Fielding novel—to sense the odium in which "free-thinking" was held.[3]

Leading English authors were almost all believers. In fact, when the term "enlightenment" is restricted in meaning to the liberation "of men's minds from the 'superstitions' fostered by institutional Christianity," it becomes difficult to speak of an English Enlightenment, for as Donald J. Greene comments, it is "absurd to suggest that Pope, Swift, Johnson, and the vast majority of eminent writers of eighteenth-century England held this fundamental position in common with their French contemporaries."[4] The poetry of sensibility featured contemplative speakers who so regularly discovered divinity immanent in the natural world that "the sacredness of nature," in Basil Willey's phrase, became "almost a first datum of consciousness" for eighteenth-century readers.[5] Sermons became an especially respected literary mode and, along with devotional tracts, sold in enormous numbers throughout the century.[6] Meanwhile, the literature of doctrinal dispute produced by eighteenth-century divines was truly prodigious, ranging from instructional pamphlets for the lower classes to such abstruse and difficult works as Butler's *Analogy*.

Social life in England was similarly immersed in religious habit and convention, particularly in the ceremonies underlying "the continuing life of the Church of England," within which, Gordon Rupp reminds us, "the greater part of the nation was baptized, married, and laid to rest."[7] The eighteenth century began with Tillotson's reconsolidation of Anglican ecclesiastical authority and social centrality. In ensuing decades, the great threats faced by the Anglican establishment—aside from those posed by its own fox-hunting clergymen—arose from recognizably Christian sources. They stemmed from denominational alternatives produced by the traditions of English nonconformity. These included rational theologies granting the compatibility of natural and revealed religion, dissenting sects ranging from Quakers and Baptists to Socinians and Unitarians, and the religion of the heart later championed by Whitefield and the Wesleys. The enduring vitality of eighteenth-century English religious life lies in great measure with the devotion, piety, and good works of Christians who dissented from the Thirty-Nine Articles. The "repeal campaign" waged in England by Dissenters chaffing at restrictions on their civil rights "dominated national politics for ten years, from 1787 to 1796," Robert Ryan observes, and the entanglement of religion and politics in the Romantic era ramified through every major social crisis.[8] Still, the last years of the eighteenth century witnessed not only the emergence of Romanticism in England but a resurgence of Anglican orthodoxy. The Methodist secession in 1795, four years after the death of Wesley, effectively ended the conflict of Arian and Calvinist forms of

Evangelicalism in the Church, allowing a unified Evangelical Anglicanism to pursue both ecclesiastical and social reform—as in the efforts of Wilberforce, whose widely read *Practical View of Christianity* appeared in 1797. The French Revolution controversy arose in England in these same years. The formal abolition of Christianity in France, the execution of countless priests, and the assaults on Christian "superstition" by the Revolution's more ferocious defenders combined with Anglican Evangelicalism to revitalize and deepen England's attachment to its own national Church.[9]

So the indisputable secularization of eighteenth-century intellectual life did not exhaust faith and enthrone skepticism.[10] As cultural historians have long observed, the impact of secular attitudes appears most decisively in the ways religion survived. "To speak of secularization" in characterizing eighteenth-century intellectual life, remarks Peter Gay, "is to speak of a subtle shift of attention: religious institutions and religious explanations of events were slowly being displaced from the center of life to its periphery" (Gay, 338). In offering this summary, Gay depends, as he acknowledges, on a definition "of 'secularization' as the demotion of the church-centered life rather than the death of religion."[11] That definition has long enjoyed considerable prestige among cultural and literary historians. Romanticists can testify that the same basic understanding of "secular" underlies M. H. Abrams' claim that the natural supernaturalism of Romantic poetry and philosophy involved not "the deletion and replacement of religious ideas but rather the assimilation and reinterpretation of religious ideas, as constitutive elements in a world view founded on secular premises" (*NS*, 13). Unfortunately, the application of this eminently sensible notion of secularization to English literary history, and to English Romanticism in particular, requires an evenhandedness of emphasis which can prove hard to sustain.

When by common agreement secularization manifests itself principally in the (peripheral) ways religion survives, the fact of religion's survival can be marginalized—and the continuing authenticity of religious experience and conviction slighted. Developments such as "the reduction of the supernatural to the natural, the mysterious to the rational, and the depreciation of faith in favour of the good works of charity"[12] were at once signs of religion's cultural displacement and, again, adaptive strategies by which religion maintained quite tenacious claims on belief. The faith of most eighteenth-century men and women remained a living faith: contradictory in the concessions and compromises underlying it perhaps, too occasional and worldly perhaps, but nonetheless faith and not *mauvaise foi*. Gay cautions wisely that "all styles of thinking are composite, but they appear congruent to those who live with them—that is why they live with them" (Gay, 124).

Understanding secularization as the mere displacement of religion, however, permits the claim that any composite faith, incorporating the secular and spiritual in mutually qualifying interaction, is ultimately secular in import simply by virtue of its composite aspect. We might recall in this connection that the concept of God serves unavoidably as a foundational postulate—the archetypal premise—and that a majority of Romantic writers considered themselves theists. Is then the defining enterprise of Romanticism, as Abrams suggests, the effort to adapt revaluated religious motifs to "a world view founded on secular premises?" Or did the Romantics more typically attempt to accommodate secular influences to a world view founded upon religious allegiances?

The latter, I think, but most Romanticists seem inclined to disagree, and no less so in the particular case of William Wordsworth. The prevailing view of Wordsworth's 1798–1805 religious attitudes derives from arguments which can sometimes be traced back to Ernest de Selincourt and Émile Legouis, but which received fullest formulation in *Natural Supernaturalism*. With this still enormously influential book, Abrams joined the visionary company of scholars who virtually reinvented Romanticism in the 1960s and 1970s by presenting it as a mythopoeic humanism. These critics portrayed Wordsworth as a bold internalizer of orthodoxies and literalisms. Geoffrey Hartman's Wordsworth ends up "the most isolated figure among the great English poets" in part because Hartman's Hegelian reading stages Wordsworth's encounters with Spirit as encounters with the apocalyptic potential of his own human consciousness.[13] Hartman's depiction of "the difficult humanizing of imagination . . . in Wordsworth" (Hartman, xi) concedes the poetry's sacramentalism, its invocations of divinity, and its affinities with the conventions of Protestant meditation, yet leaves us a Wordsworth whose viewpoint remained profoundly humanistic. The humanism of this Yale-and-Cornell Wordsworth, moreover, was what I will call "radically secular": a predominantly naturalistic outlook in which ostensibly religious claims figurally designate underlying human realities. In a justly admired book written within this same critical tradition, John Hodgson can even declare that his chief "concern is with Wordsworth as a religious poet" and yet assert that *"The Prelude* is a great triumph of humanistic thought; but, as events proved,

Wordsworth could not long persist in the skepticism which under-lies and sustains its human affirmation."[14]

More recent models of reading, often for vastly different rea-sons, have left Wordsworth's humanism thoroughly discredited. But they typically place his humanism in essentialist or political complicity with the idea of God, and dismiss the two together. Despite the "dazzling and varied revisionism in the Wordsworth criticism of the last thirty years," in Paul H. Fry's phrase, the most influential readings of Wordsworth continue to treat the poetry's transcendental affirmations as displacements of a materialist ground variously termed gender, culture, or history.[15] The undeni-able conceptual sophistication of this work has come at a cost. The liabilities of the notion of displacement in critical negotiations of Romantic supernaturalism are perhaps especially apparent in recent historical scholarship. In theory, the new historicism should have had little difficulty reconstructing the relations between poetry and nineteenth-century religious culture. In practice, the difficulties have often proven insurmountable. New historicist studies usually argue that "the poetry of Romanticism is every-where marked by extreme forms of displacement and poetic con-ceptualization whereby the actual human issues with which the poetry is concerned are resituated in a variety of idealized locali-ties."[16] This opposition of history to idealization has encouraged the attitude that the spiritual proclamations of a Romantic text are precisely what we are *not* interested in—that those affirmations are not historically authentic in their own right but, rather, the form taken by Romantic political mystification and evasion. The reli-gious investments of Wordsworth's poetry can be read responsibly, it almost seems, only by a displacement—reversing revisionism prepared to divest the poetry of its religious investments.

Wordsworth scholarship has never entirely lost its ability to take the poet's affirmations of the sacred at face value. Stephen Gill spoke for many readers, I realize, in stating with unabashed straightforwardness that "Wordsworth is clearly a profoundly reli-gious poet."[17] Because outright assertions of Wordsworth's natural-istic viewpoint remain comparatively rare—the position most com-monly operates as an unspoken assumption—a defense of the poetry's religious interests can appear all the more unnecessary. It has seemed worthwhile nonetheless to organize my study around the leading claim that Wordsworth's poetry articulates a spiritual vision of human experience—that it is secular in its alertly engaged modernity, of course, but not "radically secular" in the sense indicated above. If some readers think I belabor the self-evident at times in arguing simply that Wordsworth professed a religious faith and wrote a religious poetry, I can only answer that such an argument seemed pertinent in light of my reading of the secondary literature. In any event, even the few recent books concerned with religious aspects of Wordsworth's poetry leave ample room for my own interests. While Nancy Easterlin attempts to "hypothesize [Wordsworth's] unconscious motivations" and Robert Ryan contents himself with "examining the public articulation rather than speculating on the private content of the [poet's] creeds," I examine the poetry in light of Wordsworth's consciously held private convictions as they evolved from 1798 to 1805.[18]

For readers inclined to take demonstrations of Wordsworth's faith as rather unexceptional, my study also offers some further specifications. It argues not only that Wordsworth's religious development from 1798–1805 reveals a progressively emergent identification with Christian values but that his religious viewpoint even in 1798 at least verged on Christianity, a claim that will surely not be considered unexceptional. Ryan's recent *Romantic Reformation*, helpful in many respects, has proven especially helpful to me in its judicious rearticulation of the case against Wordsworth's early Christianity. Ryan argues that in 1793 "Wordsworth abandoned his affiliation with the national Church *and* the Christian faith in which he had been baptized" (italics mine), came to accept a "religion of nature as an alternative to Christianity," and renewed his "commitment to the Christian religion in his public and private life" by mid-1803.[19] This argument gains in force from Ryan's good-humored acknowledgment that "critics are never more likely to pursue their own hidden, even unconscious, agendas than when reading religion into their favorite poets," a likelihood illustrated by the fact, as he points out, that "one critic found no Evangelicalism in Wordsworth's religious background and another has found little else" (*RR*, 10). Yet the dangers of sectarian agendas are no greater, surely, than the obverse dangers posed by what Gay calls "the prevalent liberal cliché that sensible men [and women] must be irreligious" (Gay, 538). Seeking to strike a balance, I argue for Wordsworth's early Christian sympathies while emphasizing that his faith was consistently heterodox, stubbornly individualistic, and often casual, a secondary implication of other interests and commitments. The reasons for insisting on Wordsworth's Christianity—despite all that qualified it—rest first with the evidence provided by Coleridge's correspondence.

THE TESTIMONY OF COLERIDGE

Like all accounts of Wordsworth's religious attitudes, dismissals of his Christianity have relied mostly on the poetry itself. For the years 1796–1803, however, critics also enlist statements appearing in Coleridge's letters and notebooks in the case for an unreligious Wordsworth. One document supposedly buttressing that case is Coleridge's notebook entry about "a most unpleasant Dispute with W. and Hazlitt Wednesday Afternoon, Oct. 26. 1803":

> I spoke, I fear too contemptuously—but they spoke so irreverently so malignantly of the Divine Wisdom, that it overset me. Hazlitt how easily roused to Rage. . . . But *thou*, dearest Wordsworth—and what if Ray, Durham, Paley, have carried the observation of the aptitudes of Things too far, too habitually—into Pedantry?—O how many worse Pedantries! how few so harmless with so much efficient Good!—Dear William, pardon Pedantry in others & avoid it in yourself, instead of scoffing and reviling at Pedantry in good men in a good cause, & *becoming* a Pedant yourself in a bad cause—even by that act becoming one! But surely always to look at the superficies of Objects for the purpose of taking Delight in their Beauty, & sympathy with their real or imagined Life, is as deleterious to the Health & manhood of Intellect, as always to be peering & unravelling Contrivances may be to the simplicity of the affections, the grandeur & unity of the Imagination.—O dearest William! Would Ray, or Durham, have spoken of God as you spoke of Nature?[20]

This entry offers some highly characteristic Coleridgean criticism of Wordsworth's delight in natural beauty—"the superficies of Objects"—and his intuitions of a vaguely pantheistic spiritual presence—the "real or imagined Life" of natural objects. But Coleridge calls Wordsworth's religious values directly into question in referring to him speaking "so irreverently, so malignantly of the Divine Wisdom." Perhaps the definitive explanation of this statement can be found in Mary Moorman's biography, where the entry illustrates Wordsworth's impatience with the mechanistic contrivance of the argument from design.[21] Wordsworth seemingly believed that Christian apologists such as Ray, Derham, and Paley studiously pried into the structures of the natural world—unravelling nature's contrivances—in ways precluding an emotionally unified response to natural beauty. In the heat of conversation, Wordsworth sneered at what passed for evidence of "Divine Wisdom" with these scholars, all so busily murdering to dissect, and thereby seemed to refer dismissively to God too in Coleridge's eyes. The natural theologians themselves remained the real objects of Wordsworth's strictures. He objected not to their conclusions—their discovery of God in nature—but their pedantic methods.

Far more formidable is the earliest Coleridge statement, made in his 13 May 1796 letter to the atheist John Thelwall:

> Some for each—is my Motto.—That Poetry pleases which interests—my religious poetry interests the religious, who read it with rapture—why? because it awakes in them all the associations connected with a love of future existence &c—. A very dear friend of mine, who is in my opinion the best poet of the age (I will send you his Poem when published) thinks the lines from 364 to 375 & from 403 to 428 the best in the Volume—indeed worth all the rest—And this man is a Republican and at least a Semi-atheist.— (CLSTC 1.215–16)

This letter has been cited as evidence of Wordsworth's abandonment of religion from at least the time of Legouis.[22] Nonetheless, the rhetorical context in which Coleridge introduces his term "Semi-atheist" renders it enormously problematic as evidence. The letter belongs to an ongoing argument between Coleridge and Thelwall on poetic theory and the merits of Religious Musings, a poem extremely important to Coleridge, and one he strives to defend as resourcefully as possible. His defense begins by explaining away Thelwall's displeasure with Religious Musings on the grounds of ideological antipathy: the irreligious Thelwall could not be expected to admire a religious poem. The subsequent reference to Wordsworth then allows Coleridge, without retracting his disclaimer, to imply that Thelwall's atheism should not preclude appreciation of Coleridge's poem after all. So the description of Wordsworth is far from disinterested. The closer Coleridge could nudge Wordsworth to the atheistic Thelwall, the stronger his point that Thelwall too should take pleasure in Coleridge's most ambitious poem. The letter's rhetorical occasion is extremely important: it goes a long way toward explaining how the term "atheist," however qualified, should occur to Coleridge when recalling Wordsworth.

Coleridge's "Semi-atheist" epithet is frequently cited in the secondary literature because its apparent straightforwardness supports radically secularizing interpretations of Wordsworth. But the meaning of the term "atheist" was far from straightforward in the late eighteenth century. Commenting on Godwin's "atheism," Mark Philp notes that one account of atheism available in the eighteenth century equated it with materialism, another with a lack of the sense of divine justice, and it is a term used pejoratively to cover deists, materialists, free-thinkers, and unitarians. Paine, for example, was universally hailed as an atheist on the publication of the *Age of Reason*, but it is clear that he was far from what we would call an atheist.[23]

Presuming to doubt the soul's immortality, Joseph Priestley was similarly denounced as an atheist despite his Unitarianism. The great likelihood, when the matter is considered contextually, is that Wordsworth too was hardly an "atheist" in the contemporary sense of the word. The Coleridge capable of describing Wordsworth as a "*Semi*-atheist," let us recall, was a passionate Unitarian whose intellectual orientation on all questions was theistic, an ardent believer in the power of prayer, a daily reader of the Bible, an intimate friend of distinguished Unitarian ministers, and, as the young Hazlitt could avow, an inspired preacher—and his rigorous standards of doctrinal propriety could be both demanding and tendentious.

Clearly Coleridge's reference to Wordsworth as a "*Semi*-atheist" reflects the term's personal associations for him. In fact, to understand why Wordsworth's beliefs might have drifted halfway toward a Coleridgean "atheism," we can enlist another of Coleridge's letters. Writing to Thelwall seven months after the "*Semi*-atheist" letter, Coleridge reduced Christianity to two determining tenets:

> now the Religion, which Christ taught, is simply 1 that there is an Omnipresent Father of infinite power, wisdom, & Goodness, in whom all of us move, & have our being & 2. That when we appear to men to die, we do not utterly perish; but after this Life shall continue to enjoy or suffer the consequences & [natur]al effects of the Habits, we have formed here, whether good or evil.—This is the Christian *Religion* & all of the Christian *Religion*. (*CLSTC* 1.280)

Coleridge's 1795–1796 correspondence with Thelwall included a running debate on religion in which Coleridge continually opposed not simply theism but his own version of Christianity to the atheism of Godwin, Thomas Holcraft, Erasmus Darwin, and Thelwall himself. His reference to Wordsworth's "*Semi*-atheism" presupposes that polemical context. Only Coleridge's two-pillared definition of "the Religion, which Christ taught" explains how someone could qualify specifically as a "*Semi*-atheist." In truth, there are finally three ways rather than two because Coleridge's second requirement—while he presents it as the second of merely two principles—compounds the idea of the soul's postmortal survival and, though he mentions neither Heaven nor Hell, the idea of morally differentiated afterlives whereby the spirit would either "enjoy or suffer." Wordsworth's faith in an immortal soul was occasionally anxious. He most probably never formally renounced the belief, however, and if he did it was in response to metaphysical theories—Coleridge's notion of an assimilative One Life—to which he had not been introduced at the time of the "*Semi*-atheist" statement.[24]

Wordsworth *could* still qualify as a Coleridgean "*Semi*-atheist," however, simply by meeting requirement one (and believing in God) while failing to meet requirement two because of doubts about a punitive afterlife—a Hell. In 1843, interestingly, the High Church Wordsworth told Henry Crabb Robinson "in strong terms [of] his disbelief of eternal punishment" (*HCR* 2.628). These pronouncements come, I am aware, nearly half a century after Coleridge's "*Semi*-atheist" accusation. But in 1824 Wordsworth similarly told Crabb Robinson that "the great difficulty which had *always* pressed on his mind in religion [was his] inability to reconcile the divine [foreknowledge] with accountability in men"—a difficulty which calls into question the justification of eternal punishment for sin (*HCR* 1.304; italics mine). Many eighteenth- and early-nineteenth-century Christians—Southey, for instance—rejected the orthodox idea of Hell and Wordsworth could easily have belonged in their ranks as early as 1796.[25] His instinctive resistance to the idea of humanity's innate moral depravity would help explain an analogous resistance to the idea of Hell. But we need not adjudicate contending probabilities. The mere possibility of reading Coleridge's "*Semi*-atheist" phrase as a reference to disbelief in a punitive eternality—conceivably as a consequence of belief in a benevolent God—sufficiently emphasizes how unconventional a notion of "atheism" may underlie Coleridge's comment to Thelwall.

The one other possible explanation of Coleridge's "*Semi*-atheist" phrase emerges in his 19 March 1796 letter to the Reverend John Edwards. Here, just two months before the letter to Thelwall, Coleridge asked Edwards,

> How is it that Dr Priestley is not an atheist?—He asserts in three
> different Places, that God not only *does*, but *is*, every thing.—But
> if God *be* every Thing, every Thing is God—: which is all, the
> Atheists assert—. (*CLSTC* 1.192)

This indictment of Priestley again presupposes strict standards of doctrinal rectitude. The Priestley Coleridge censures for atheism preached sermons in Christian churches, interpreted the French Revolution as a sign of apocalypse, declared his faith in revelation repeatedly, and proved so tireless an apologist for the Unitarian creed that Coleridge later (and more justly) declared him "the author of the modern Unitarianism."[26] More important, in this letter Priestley's supposed atheism lies with his pantheistic identification of God and physical reality ("every Thing"), a position always objectionable to Coleridge as a materialistic reduction of God to nature. If Priestley appears an atheist in March 1796 for identifying the divine and natural, why cannot Wordsworth appear a "*Semi*-atheist" in May 1796 on similar grounds, or even for professing beliefs which, while less extreme than Priestley's, tended in the same direction? So construed, Coleridge's "*Semi*-atheist" phrase prefigures his later criticism of Wordsworth's "vague misty, rather than mystic, Confusion of God with the World & the accompanying Nature-worship" (*CLSTC* 5.95). The "*Semi*-atheist" description of Wordsworth may glance at nothing more than the poet's spiritual reverence for nature. If it does, Wordsworth becomes guilty of a moderate atheism in Coleridge's eyes precisely because he believed nature to be infused with the divine presence.

In any event, Coleridge knew Wordsworth only casually in 1796. To my mind, the more informed comments in subsequent letters—though Coleridge's prose remains elliptical and ambiguous—depict a more conventional poet. These letters actually permit the inference that Coleridge considered Wordsworth a Christian, even if his Christianity rested on unexamined temperamental inclinations and failed to meet Coleridge's standards for a philosophically responsible faith. Writing to his Unitarian friend the Reverend John Prior Estlin in May 1798, Coleridge reflected,

I have now known [Wordsworth] a year & some months, and my admiration, I might say, my awe of his intellectual powers has increased even to his hour—& (what is of more importance) he is a tried good man.—On one subject we are habitually silent—we found our data dissimilar, & never renewed the subject / It is his practice & almost his nature to convey all the truth he knows without any attack on what he supposes falsehood, if that falsehood be interwoven with virtues or happiness—he loves and venerates Christ & Christianity—I wish, he did more—but it were wrong indeed, if any incoincidence with one of our wishes altered our respect & affection to a man, whom we are as it were instructed by our great master to say that not being against us he is for us. (*CLSTC* 1.410)

In this passage Coleridge seemingly suggests, writes Alan Bewell, that "although Wordsworth was skeptical of the revelatory status of the Bible, he recognized its importance as a moral institution."[27] Bewell's sense of the implications of Coleridge's remarks typifies Wordsworth criticism, and I both understand and fully concede its apparent plausibility: Coleridge appears to express his preference that Wordsworth, in addition to venerating Christianity, would go further and actually believe in it. From this perspective, the Wordsworth of the letter to Estlin wanders between worlds in Arnoldian fashion, remaining emotionally attracted to creeds he considers intellectually discredited.

Yet that is not the only reading possible. It is not true that Coleridge's phrasing definitely contrasts veneration with belief. The statement "he loves and venerates Christ & Christianity—I wish he did more" could well express merely Coleridge's preference that Wordsworth's veneration of Christianity should become energetic enough to carry Wordsworth to commitments he currently declines. Moreover, readings of this letter as unproblematic proof that in 1796 Wordsworth considered "Christianity a falsehood, albeit a harmless one that inspires some good," as Richard E. Matlack writes,[28] lose force by failing to account for the "truth" which Coleridge says that Wordsworth "knows." If Wordsworth's attitude towards "Christ and Christianity" consists exclusively of moral veneration unallied to belief, if it does not involve an acceptance of truth claims, what are the truths Coleridge mentions? He mentions them only after the issue of religion has been broached, so they seem to have religion as their referent. The logical development of the letter to Estlin is far from explicit. But from my perspective, the letter seems to place the statement that Wordsworth conveys truth without attacking error in apposition with the clarifying statement that he venerates Christianity yet might well proceed further with his veneration. The letter, in short, associates Wordsworth's love and veneration of "Christ & Christianity" *with* "the truth he knows." Wordsworth's failure to act further on this veneration ("I wish he did more") would signify merely his unwillingness to criticize error. If Wordsworth's veneration of Christ included belief, how could the Unitarian Coleridge, unconvinced of Christ's divinity, wish his friend's veneration greater? By wishing it more systematically doctrinaire and critical, again, or simply by preferring that Wordsworth's Christianity were less casual, a creed he lived by in a properly Coleridgean manner.

In sum, the letter to Estlin becomes a revelation of Wordsworthian heterodoxy or skepticism only when its doctrinal references are interpreted more generally than they deserve. When Coleridge's remarks are given a denominationally specific context, they yield a nearly opposite meaning. Here too we must recall that Coleridge's philosophical Christianity was fiercely Unitarian in 1798. Writing to the Reverend John Prior Estlin, Unitarian minister and personal friend, Coleridge could presume upon a sympathetic response to distinctly Unitarian sentiments. Far from illustrating "the embarrassing awkwardness Coleridge felt in presenting Wordsworth to friends who shared his religious belief and values," as Matlack contends, Coleridge's account of Wordsworth's religious sentiments displays a thoroughly unembarrassed Coleridge not above patronizing the unelect in private correspondence.[29] Less defensive than condescending, the letter unfolds as a Unitarian tête-à-tête so complacent that one can almost hear the wistful sigh accompanying Coleridge's "I wish he did more." As Edith Batho suggested, the great shortcoming motivating such disappointment may have been nothing more than Wordsworth's resistance to Unitarian inculcation (Batho, 268).

The "one subject" Coleridge learned to avoid with Wordsworth, then, is not Christianity but Unitarianism. Their Unitarian subtext acknowledged, Coleridge's statements to Estlin censure Wordsworth for his instinctive conventionality. He remained unconventional enough to disagree with some orthodox dogmas; and given his highly individualistic temperament and the range of doctrinal dispute in the late eighteenth century, disagreement of that sort should surprise no one. Those Anglican dogmas—and not what either Coleridge or Wordsworth understood simply as Christianity—represent "what he [Wordsworth] supposes falsehood." Unable to accept certain orthodox theological positions, a more doctrinaire mind might have abandoned one sect for another. Wordsworth apparently preferred to think of himself as a conventional Christian despite selective reservations about particular creeds. He declines to "attack" the established faith because its errors remained "interwoven" with a religious orientation which he found predominately admirable, and which supported the moral conduct and spiritual fulfillment (the "virtues or happiness") of countless people. Indeed, if Coleridge's references to Wordsworth's spiritual limitations indict the poet for his divergence from Christianity, rather than for his divergence from Unitarianism, how could he conceivably seem a passive ally of the Unitarian cause ("not being against us he is for us") as surely no skeptic outside the pale of Christianity possibly could?

For these reasons, the greatest probability is that in this Estlin letter the "truth he [Wordsworth] knows" denotes the truth of Christianity. If that interpretation seems farfetched, consider Coleridge's "I wish he did more" letter in the broader context of his correspondence with Estlin. Writing on 10 June, 1797, Coleridge told his Unitarian friend that Wordsworth "admires your sermon against Payne much more than your last—I suppose because he is more inclined to Christianity than to Theism, simply considered" (CLSTC 1.327). In part, this revealing observation invokes Wordsworth's aversion to pedantic reformulations of the argument from design—the subject of Estlin's "last" sermon—of the sort which prompted the 1803 notebook entry discussed previously. But "Theism" cannot be restricted in meaning to that one association. The term expressly denotes belief in God, and Coleridge employs it with that meaning in mind. The Wordsworth of this letter accepts the existence of a supernatural divinity; from the spectrum of subsidiary theological options created by that acceptance, he proceeds beyond arguments for the sufficiency of natural religion and endorses the Christian revelation. Preferring Christianity to theism, Wordsworth preferred Jesus Christ and the Trinity to the impersonal deity of Unitarian rationalism. So Coleridge reports in 1797, and in a letter lacking the elliptical transitions and ambiguities of the later "I wish he did more" letter. We need only assume the consistency of Wordsworth's religious attitudes from 1797–1798 and Coleridge's second Estlin letter will vindicate my reading of the earlier one. In my view, the Estlin letters jointly suggest that Wordsworth was enough of an Anglican loyalist to convince his disappointed friend not to press the issue. By no means do Coleridge's letters to Estlin unambiguously support the case for an irreligiously humanistic Wordsworth.

What Coleridge's letters do demonstrate unmistakably is that the two men differed in their religious attitudes. The letters reveal Wordsworth's wariness of speculative analysis and doctrinal partisanship. For Wordsworth, the spiritual sublime evoked a "Hebraic" mysteriousness, with faith requiring in turn a Keatsian "Negative Capability," an acceptance of "uncertainties, Mysteries, doubts, without any irritable reaching after fact & reason."[30] Wordsworth

seems to have felt that way early on. Not until 1836 did Crabb
Robinson quote him advocating acceptance of "the mysteries of the
Gospel" and dismissing overly fussy doctrinal precision (*HCR*
2.482). Yet the poetry, of course, criticizes analysts who "murder to
dissect" as early as 1798 ("The Tables Turned," line 28). Coleridge
served Keats himself as a counter-example of someone "incapable
of remaining content with half knowledge." The depiction would
have given no offense to the Coleridge who told Estlin in May 1798,
"tho' Christianity is my *Passion*, it is too much my *intellectual*
Passion" (*CLSTC* 1.407). The religious divide separating the two
poets in March, 1798, when Wordsworth undertook his One Life
revisions of *The Ruined Cottage*, was hardly enormous or
Wordsworth would not have found Coleridge's One Life idea so
appealing and useful. A divide nonetheless existed, created in part
by Wordsworth's resistance to Coleridge's ceaseless intellectualiz-
ing of religious issues. Wordsworth's resistance to Coleridge's zealous Unitarianism completed the division.

Taken altogether, the evidence of Coleridge's letters to Thelwall and Estlin remains more suggestive than conclusive. But *what*
those letters suggest differs appreciably from what critics ordinarily
find. The testimony of Coleridge implies that Wordsworth believed
in a Deity and felt considerable loyalties to orthodox religion—
emotional loyalties accompanied most probably, given his preference for Christianity over theism, by intellectual acceptance of
some tenets of orthodox faith. If reasons exist to insist on
Wordsworth's dismissal of Christianity in 1798, they exist elsewhere than in Coleridge's correspondence.

ROMANTIC ANGLICANISM

Moving from the Thelwall to the Estlin letters, we moved from the
question of Wordsworth's skepticism to the question of his Christianity. With respect to this first issue, scholars should concede
that no real evidence exists beyond Coleridge's "*Semi*-atheist" epithet that Wordsworth at any point doubted the reality of God—and
the "*Semi*-atheist" claim is thoroughly dubious. Its evidential
unreliability was stressed years ago by de Selincourt, Edith Batho,
and Hoxie Neal Fairchild among others, and more recently by
Stephen Gill, who allows himself simply to remark, regarding the
poet's supposed disbelief in God, that "the testimony of
Wordsworth's poetry and letters of the period denies the possibil-

ity."[31] As late as 1794, Wordsworth was struggling with the issue of taking orders. While the struggle bespeaks his spiritual restiveness—even later in life Wordsworth considered himself unfit for the ministry—there would surely have been no struggle at all, no question of ordination, financial difficulties notwithstanding, if his views tended toward atheism.[32] In the one piece of historical evidence that expressly addresses the issue, Christopher Wordsworth claimed that his uncle never "lapsed into scepticism" and, despite the concern for family respectability in the *Memoir*, the claim deserves respect.[33] Wordsworth's brief period of Godwinian discipleship proves nothing. Godwin's atheism may have proven a sticking point for Coleridge, who constantly upbraided him for it, yet William Frend and other political reformers who considered themselves theists and Christians made common cause with Godwin for political reasons. The account of intellectual error in *The Prelude* makes no mention of a crisis of faith. We have no incentive, in short, for thinking that Wordsworth ever lost his faith in God.

The exact character of his attitude toward the Christian revelation is a vastly murkier issue. There exist accounts, variously troubling, of even the later Wordsworth making statements suggesting incomplete or heterodox belief. In one of the better known reports, Henry Crabb Robinson quotes the poet saying that

> he could not feel with the Unitarians in any way. Their religion allows no room for imagination, and satisfies none of the cravings of the soul. "I can feel more sympathy with the orthodox believer who needs a Redeemer and who, sensible of his own demerits, flies for refuge to Him (though perhaps I do not want one for myself) than with the cold and rational notions of the Unitarian." (*HCR* 1.87)

Contextual analysis can tone down the spiritual *hubris* of these words. In truth, Wordsworth's comments only show him dissociating himself from two contrary religious sensibilities. He turns not from faith but from particular modes of faith, his references to orthodoxy and Unitarianism allowing him to specify denominationally his preference for heart over head in matters of religion. It was a qualified preference, for Wordsworth's denigration of "a Redeemer"—the Evangelical Christ of the Atonement—betrays considerable impatience with Evangelical histrionics over personal guilt. Both the Methodists and Evangelical Anglicans of Wordsworth's day harped constantly on humanity's sinfulness and positive *need* for redemption through Christ. Wordsworth's disavowal of the need for a Redeemer, then, reveals his distaste for moralistic Evangelical rhetoric and emotionalism. Yet here Crabb Robinson clearly catches his opinionated friend, in Jane Austen parlance, "revealing" himself.[34] Crabb Robinson's journal entry shows Wordsworth launching into an attack on Unitarianism only to recollect, apparently, that he was addressing a Unitarian. With the dismissal of Christ the Redeemer, he backpedals into an overplayed concession to Unitarian demotions of the Atonement—which allows him, having bowed to the proprieties, to revert to his own opinions and censure Unitarian rationality in concluding.

So Wordsworth's remarks finally seem more socially awkward than theologically arrogant. Not the most determined special pleading, however, can entirely rid them of a spiritual self-sufficiency that sorts ill with conventional Christianity. Wordsworth's unguarded waving away of a Redeemer clearly marginalizes central orthodox tenets. For as R. D. Havens fairly observed, "one who felt no need of a Redeemer might well question the necessity of the Son's taking human form and suffering as a man"—the necessity of the Incarnation, Crucifixion, Resurrection, and, in brief, the entire Christian salvational scheme—and even "the divinity of Christ."[35] Yet Crabb Robinson's journal entry dates from 1812. Wordsworth's Christianity has satisfied his more stringent critics in neither his day nor ours. But most Wordsworthians would agree that by 1812 the poet's acceptance of Anglican orthodoxy was an accomplished fact. Those who wish to argue that the Crabb Robinson reminiscence demands a reassessment of the later Wordsworth's Christianity may proceed as they wish: that endeavor I resign to them. The commonest view of Wordsworth's spiritual development is that he was moved to an "acceptance of orthodox Christian thought," in Jonathan Wordsworth's words, when the pain of his brother's February 1805 drowning "made it necessary for him to accept the doctrine of an afterlife."[36] Most scholars at all uncomfortable with Jonathan Wordsworth's formulation of this position would nonetheless endorse a variation of it: Hodgson, for example, sees Wordsworth's Christian reorientation underway in 1805 but incomplete until 1809 (Hodgson, xvi). In the chapters which follow I date Wordsworth's identification with Christianity to 1804. For the moment, I simply point out that the statements reported by Crabb Robinson originate at a time when most Wordsworthians believe the poet's Christian allegiances to be self-evident.

The belief is entirely valid: by 1812 Wordsworth was well within the Christian fold. The testimony of Crabb Robinson's journal alters/nothing. Nor does the additional evidence of the poet's doubts and heterodoxies, and there exists an abundance of it: the inattentiveness to Christian doctrine throughout the poetry, the hesitancy about immortality confessed in "O dearer far," the anguished struggles Catherine's death occasioned him, the "incomplete and occasionally heterodox" faith of The Excursion,[37] and the various other equivocal statements included in the historical record. Given this body of evidence, Wordsworthians who routinely acknowledge the later Wordsworth's Christianity agree, perhaps implicitly but no less unavoidably, that it was doctrinally selective and unrigorous, that it was motivated in part by nostalgia (memories of his mother especially), that it waxed and waned with his personal tribulations, and that it was embroiled with such essentially non-theological issues as his support of the national Church as a social bulwark. In effect, most Wordsworthians concede all this and still insist on the older poet's Christianity. My concern is to see his earlier religious attitudes referred, simply for the sake of consistency, to the same evaluative criteria which move critics to grant his later Christianity. In both cases, we confront a faith which is Christian not by virtue of unfailing doctrinal fidelity but, rather, by virtue of the dominant sensibility suffusing it. If we begin by admitting Wordsworth's belief in God, we must place him, finally, either within or without the religious conventions of his time and culture. If religious individualism ever carried Wordsworth, as a prophet unto himself, beyond the pale of an undoctrinaire Christianity, it was surely during the height of his enthusiasm for the One Life—and my second chapter argues that residual Christian sympathies complicated and finally ended his flirtation with Coleridge's One Life idea.

In fact, I want to suggest further that there exists considerable continuity in Wordsworth's religious outlook. It is a commonplace of Wordsworth scholarship that the poet's orthodoxy increased as he aged, and I by no means deny the point. But in many cases the differences in question remain differences of emphasis involving the fuller emergence of deeply rooted predispositions and antipathies. To pursue this issue we need merely turn to the 1836 journal entry in which Crabb Robinson summarizes Wordsworth's leading opinions on religion by way of extended quotation:

> "The Atonement is a doctrine which has its foundation in that consciousness of unworthiness and guilt which arises from an upright self-examination—as all the orthodox doctrines are war-

ranted by a humble spirit and all that is best in our moral nature. There is internal evidence for all these doctrines, which are a source of happiness. And the difficulty of comprehending the mysteries of the Gospel is no sufficient reason for rejection. It is not necessary to define with precision the doctrines thus received, and the Church of England has encumbered itself by needless and mischievous attempts at explanation. The Athanasian Creed is one of these unhappy excrescences. Nor does the idea of the personality of the Spirit come with such authority, or claim so imperiously our adoption, as the doctrine of the divinity of Jesus Christ. The thought that an infinitely pure being can receive satisfaction from the sufferings of Jesus Christ and accept them as a satisfaction for the sins of the guilty is declared by Coleridge to be an outrage on common sense. It is a hard saying, nor can I explain it to my satisfaction. I leave this as an awful mystery I am not called to solve. Coleridge used to declare that the belief in miracles is not a necessary part of a Christian's creed; but this is contrary to the express and uniform declaration of the Scriptures, and I have no difficulty in believing in miracles since I consider as superstition the imagined knowledge and certainty which men suppose they have as to the laws of nature." (HCR 2.481–82)

Consider how many of the opinions Crabb Robinson notes here either corroborate or confirm at one remove, confirm by association, religious opinions Wordsworth held well before 1836.

His qualified assent to "the personality of the Spirit" accords, for example, with his description of God as an impersonal Spirit in conversation with his son John—to whom he compared God to the "thoughts in his mind" (LMY 2.189)—and throughout his poetry. Near the beginning of the 1805 Prelude Wordsworth characteristically addresses God, for example, as an impersonal "Wisdom and Spirit of the Universe! / Thou Soul that art the Eternity of Thought!" (1.429–30). His resistance to anthropomorphism was not so entrenched, however, as to preclude frequent pronominal humanization and masculinization of the Deity. He further implies a divine personality, a personal protectiveness, by depicting God as the origin of a providential moral order experienced as love, the Pedlar's "lesson deep of love" (Pedlar narrative, MH, line 89) and the spiritual love of Prelude 13 (13.160–70). So the poetry illustrates Wordsworth's willingness to countenance a personal Creator, but suggests that the idea's claims upon his spiritual imagination were only moderately powerful. For reasons discussed later in this chapter, Wordsworth's 1798–1805 poetry permits virtually no inferences concerning his feelings about Christ. Yet Coleridge's 1798 account of Wordsworth as someone who both "loves and venerates Christ & Christianity" *and* prefers Christianity to theism (*CLSTC* 1.410, 327) looks ahead to the Wordsworth who found the idea of Christ's divinity more arresting than the idea of God's personality.

The Crabb Robinson synopsis also touches on Wordsworth's deep aversion to the idea of humanity's innate sinfulness. This attitude has been condemned as a sign of personal arrogance, yet it underwrote Wordsworth's optimism about human nature and respect for human life in its humblest forms. The theological difficulties bequeathed him by this respect centered on the Atonement. In Crabb Robinson's 1836 transcription, Wordsworth starts by mentioning the Atonement respectfully, noting the "consciousness of unworthiness and guilt" induced by introspection, but ends up tacitly endorsing Coleridge's description of vicarious moral compensation for "the sins of the guilty" as an outrage to reason. For Wordsworth, the Atonement seems to have been entangled in conceptions of both crime and punishment which he deemed unjust. His previously mentioned confession of "disbelief of eternal punishment" to Crabb Robinson dates from 1843. But, again, skepticism about a punitive afterlife may explain Coleridge's 1796 reference to him as a "*Semi*-atheist" (*CLSTC* 1.216). Wordsworth's 1836 reservations about the Atonement closely correspond to a statement (cited above) which Crabb Robinson recorded in 1824: "Wordsworth stated that the great difficulty which had always pressed on his mind in religion is the inability to reconcile the divine [foreknowledge] with accountability in men" (*HCR* 1.304). The same reluctance to acknowledge human responsibility, to concede guilt and the necessity of deliverance, motivates his 1812 renunciation of a Redeemer. To all this evidence, one can add the testimony of the Immortality Ode. The Ode's Platonism lends its affirmation of innocence a mythic extravagance. The poem's representation of childhood's celestial "glory" nonetheless reflects a deeply felt denial of innate human corruption.

Perhaps the most deeply grounded religious attitude evident in the 1836 Crabb Robinson entry, however, emerges in Wordsworth's opinions on the relation of doctrinal subscription to Church membership, specifically his statements (worth repeating) that

> the difficulty of comprehending the mysteries of the Gospel is no sufficient reason for rejection. It is not necessary to define with precision the doctrines thus received, and the Church of England has encumbered itself by needless and mischievous attempts at explanation.

A version of his distrust of the meddling intellect, Wordsworth's distrust of precise doctrinal formulations derives from his sense of theological codification as secondary to authentic religious experience. The categorical demotion of doctrine implicit in this dismissal of doctrinal precision as "needless and mischievous" bespeaks what Batho calls the "Catholicism" of his spiritual outlook:

> There are two types of Christians, who may, for this purpose and without prejudice, be called Catholic and Protestant, though they do not necessarily belong by profession to the religious bodies which these titles suggest. The Protestant, when he finds himself in disagreement with the body to which he has hitherto belonged, protests and leaves it: religion is for him an entirely personal thing. The Catholic may also, though he does not always, protest: he may reason with his fellows, he may reluctantly conclude that they are not at present to be persuaded and so keep his private opinions to himself, he may even be induced to remain where he is by spiritual humility, a sense that he is but one and fallible, that the consensus of opinion may be right as against him, and that even if it is wrong on some points the Church of his allegiance holds more of the truth than he will find elsewhere, and that the loss of community and communion is greater than can be compensated for by yielding to what is as likely to be intellectual arrogance as honesty. (Batho, 262)

The "Catholic" temperament subordinates doctrinal systematization to vital experiences of faith, which can alone provide rules of conduct. Such "Catholicism" remains patiently respectful of religious mystery and, in the value it places on community, it is also tolerant of incidentally differing viewpoints. But as Batho argues, Wordsworth's wariness of doctrinal systematization is also implicated in the single most important continuity in his religious development: the residual Anglican sympathies which survived the vicissitudes of his early intellectual career.

Those sympathies, without question, waned tremendously during the period of the *Letter to the Bishop of Llandaff*. Even after their resurgence, they consistently proved incomplete. Wordsworth at his most orthodox cared little for High Church ceremonialism. His mature faith clearly incorporated various influences, including Protestant habits of self-examination and emotional response more typical of dissenting sects. No compelling evidence suggests, however, that the Evangelical revival ever influenced him deeply. The contrary view has been urged by Richard E. Brantley, who argues that "Wordsworth built his faith on the Evangelical Anglican middle ground staked out by Simeon at Cambridge."[38] The case for Evangelical influence on Wordsworth fares better, I believe, in shifting from Simeon to Wilberforce, even though Wordsworth and Wilberforce did not meet until 1815. A *Practical View* certainly abounds in sentiments Wordsworth would have approved—such as the claim, its holistic emphasis anticipating the Preface to *Lyrical Ballads*, that "it is [Christianity's] peculiar glory and her main office to bring all the faculties of our nature into their just subordination and dependence; that so the whole man, complete in all his functions, may be restored to the true ends of his being."[39] Yet the *Practical View* also abounds in sentiments Wordsworth could never have accepted, such as Wilberforce's insistence on doctrinal rigor and his claim that the majority of (merely nominal) Christians hold "a most inadequate idea of the guilt and evil of sin" (*Practical View*, 219). Wilberforce's personal geniality notwithstanding, Evangelicalism could seem morally earnest to the point that Ruskin could drape his Turners on Sundays. The moralistic solemnity of Anglican Evangelicalism resulted in strictures against reading novels and attending the theatre, promoting a depreciation of intellectual endeavor and literary culture.[40] Despite Wordsworth's support for certain Evangelical social reforms, it seems best to construe Wordsworthian spiritual intensity not as a Methodist or Evangelical legacy but as his reconciliation of Anglican traditionalism with what we can simply call "Romanticism." Wordsworth's "Romantic" sensibility explains his emphasis on the epiphanic, self-exploratory, and emotional in religious experience. Yet Anglicanism provided that spiritual individualism a welcome foundation in tradition.

So Wordsworth's religious viewpoint can best be understood as a form of Romantic Anglicanism. Never wholly losing contact with his Anglican origins, Wordsworth emerged from his radical period a casual Christian predisposed toward Anglican norms by his upbringing and personal temperament. His attitude toward human sinfulness draws on "the central Anglican tradition [which] emphasizes the Incarnation," and "which sees in the Incarnation rather than the Crucifixion the essence of the Atonement" (*HNF* 3.170; Batho, 283). Even his marginalizing of doctrinal questions reflects High Church institutional practice. Doctrinal accommodation had been an unofficial Anglican policy from the time of early Latitudinarian consolidations. In its conservatism, the Anglican Church resisted doctrinal reform, of course, cherishing its ideological differences from dissenting sects. But Anglican officials traditionally displayed considerable tolerance and flexibility regarding membership—including their own membership. Noting that "a deistic turn of thought was very common even within the Established Church," Willey adds that "most Anglican clergymen, indeed, managed to retain their Orders and benefices even if their views had veered, since ordination, towards Arianism, Socinianism or even pure deism" (Willey, "Coleridge and religion," 224). These common heterodoxies can be dismissed as the laxity of a superficial Anglicanism, all the more so since the amorphousness of the Anglican faith in Wordsworth's day, Church historians agree, was a sign of real complacency and corruption. The tolerant "Catholicity" of the Anglican Church nevertheless accommodated many people's sincere reservations about doctrinal conformity as a basis of spiritual community.[41] Wordsworth's own commitments to the Anglican community may not have rendered him devoutly orthodox. But they apparently immunized him against Coleridge's Unitarian proselytizing. They certainly fostered his attachment to his family traditions and childhood recollections: by publicly returning to the Church after moving to Grasmere, Wordsworth went home spiritually, reclaiming his religious past.

As a result, Wordsworth's religious development in 1798-1805 unfolded as a profoundly conservative process, conservative in its political import but in its emotional logic too. It is hard to think of a temperament more instinctively conservative than Wordsworth's. Fiercely protective of the attachments he formed, and absorbed by his own past, Wordsworth associated change with loss and longed for "a repose which ever is the same" well before the "Ode to Duty" admitted to that longing. He confessed in letters, "It is not in my Nature to neglect old Friends, I live too much in the past for anything of that kind," and "I am naturally slow to love and to cease loving" (*LEY*, 436; *LMY*, 1.245). Layered with revision, surviving manuscripts constitute a remarkable record in their own right, needless to say, of the Wordsworthian impulses to return and to continue. In the case of Wordsworth there surely exists special reason to recall Thomas McFarland's observation,

> We too often think of "development" as a kind of progress up a series of steps, the improvement of one's position by the abandonment of a previous position. Actually the word implies an unwrapping of something already there. . . . The textbooks exult in the proliferation of developmental stages; but such stages do not allow us to see clearly the unfolding of a single, constant orientation to life. (McFarland, 161–62)

The continuities evident in Wordsworth's attitudes toward God, human moral dignity, and the derivativeness of doctrinal superstructures reflect the presence of a single religious orientation. So does his persistent belief in God. But so does the submerged Anglicanism which consistently inflected his moral sensibility and his idea of communal worship.

Controlled by that consistency, Wordsworth's religious development from 1798–1805 was itself essentially continuous, an unbroken process of amplification in which latent Christian "sympathies" became overt Christian "commitments." Wordsworth began either as a theist ready to admire Christianity from afar or, more probably, as an indifferent Christian with Anglican loyalties he found dormant but intact when prodded by Coleridge's inquiries. Faith having its different moods, the distinction between these positions need not have been absolute. Certainly it is easy enough to imagine Wordsworth defending the creed of his family upbringing in some conversations and then, recalling the complicity of Tyranny with Superstition, denouncing the Anglican establishment in others. Not enough evidence of Wordsworth's early religious opinions has survived for anyone to locate an exact moment when his residual Christian sympathies grew from emotional affinity into intellectual agreement. We can envision a 1798 Wordsworth politically disenchanted with the clergy and preoccupied spiritually with his own experiences of the numinous in nature, and still envision him moved, at the very least, by the moral grandeur of Christian humanitarianism, the beauty of the Bible and Book of Common Prayer, and the Christian associations scattered everywhere throughout his childhood memories. From this beginning he advances to the intellectually self-conscious Christianity which I date to 1804, the year which saw the completion of the Immortality Ode, with its "internalization of Incarnation"[42] and corroborating references to God, Heaven, and the soul. By revealing the poet's death-anxieties relenting to a grandly reaffirmed assurance of personal immortality, the Ode marks an important juncture in the progress of Wordsworth's faith, but not a critical juncture. No crisis energized the poet's eventual assent to Christian truth claims. Nor do we find him jockeying back and forth between competing theologies. Wordsworth's commitment to Christianity in 1804 resulted from the slowly cumulative emergence of "a single, constant orientation to life."

"Until he was thirty-five of forty," Havens writes, the central tenets of Christianity made little visible impression on

Wordsworth: "He believed in them, he accepted then as a matter of course but apparently without thinking much about them" (Havens, 180). This description of a casual, tepid Christianity seems fair enough, but I would like to quarrel with Haven's dating. Really, his generalizations pertain only to the period preceding 1798, the year in which Wordsworth first came under the philosophical spell of Coleridge. The Coleridge of 1797–1798 "did not just refer everything to the judgement of faith," Gill reminds us, but "lived and breathed in the conviction that 'We see our God everywhere—the Universe in the most literal Sense is his written language.'"[43] Even if he quickly learned to dodge issues of dogma in conversations with his new friend, Coleridge by his mere presence offered a standing challenge to Wordsworth to explore and define his own religious convictions. The challenge proved all the less avoidable because poetic interests and motifs borrowed from Coleridge—the idea of the One Life above all—trailed highly specific theological implications in their wake. Wordsworth's response to that challenge thrust him increasingly toward the conventional and conservative while leaving revisionism a place. He ended, in 1804–1805, with a Romantic Anglicanism which married Christian tradition to his faith in the human mind as a spiritual power and his confidence in the spiritual joy available in nature.

THE RELIGION IN POETRY

Wordsworth's Christian reorientation, I mentioned above, is often attributed to his grief over his brother's drowning. While Wordsworth had to all appearances returned to the Anglican Church sometime before 1805, John's death certainly consolidated the poet's Christian inclinations. As a result, we can fairly expect Christian values to appear in the deeply personal reckoning worked out in "Elegiac Stanzas, Suggested by a Picture of Peele Castle, in a Storm" (PTV, 266–68). But any such expectation goes unmet. The poem's closing comment encapsulates its steady avoidance of conventional religious reflection: "Not without hope we suffer and we mourn" (line 60)—hope, not faith. From "Elegiac Stanzas" one could infer a Wordsworth on whom Christian consolations had no emotional purchase. The fact is, however, that "Elegiac Stanzas" chooses to contemplate John's death specifically with reference to the poet's previous naiveté about nature: the poem is an elegiac retrospect concerned more with the speaker's past than present beliefs. The same Wordsworth who wrote "Elegiac Stanzas" also wrote elegies for John which affirm the relief to be found in "God's unbounded love," mention his sense that Heaven "Had laid on such a Mariner / A consecrating hand," and ask "gracious God" to spare him from any renewal of such intense pain: "Grant this, and let me be resign'd / Beneath thy chast'ning rod."[44] To such conventional if doctrinally imprecise Christian sentiments one can add the comments of Wordsworth's 3 June 1805 letter to George Beaumont, where, in Gill's useful summary, "the traditional Christian answer to the tormenting question, 'Why was he taken away?' was accepted" (*William Wordsworth: A Life*, 214).

By 1805–1806 Wordsworth was clearly a Christian. Yet "Elegiac Stanzas" resists being labeled a Christian poem. What are we to make of this discrepancy? How should we understand the equally thoroughgoing avoidance of Christian doctrine in most of Wordsworth's work? We should recall first, I think, that Wordsworth's interests were secular, political, psychological, and above all diverse: many of his poems are simply not about God. Wordsworth in his earlier years especially was often lax about his faith, rarely taking his intellectual bearings from religious considerations. Then, even when writing about experiences with pronounced religious implications, he characteristically wrote a poetry which is inflected by his faith but which gives his private convictions complexly mediated (and usually oblique) expression. And selective expression as well: clearly Wordsworth felt no obligation to write poems providing a comprehensive account of his beliefs. Thus the pertinence of Gill's caution that "any attempt to codify or systematise Wordsworth's religious beliefs . . . runs exactly counter to what the poetry is and does" (Gill, *William Wordsworth: The Prelude*, 41). For me, Wordsworth's 1798–1804 progress from Christian sympathies to Christian commitments can be followed in the poetry of this period. But to reconstruct that progress we must allow for the ways in which Wordsworth's particular poetic purposes conditioned his creative recourse to Christian tradition.

Wordsworth's spiritual imagination was shaped profoundly by the conventions of eighteenth-century English landscape poetry. His familiarity with this tradition was by any measure extensive. Fairchild claims justly that Wordsworth "derived his most characteristic philosophical and religious ideas largely, though of course not entirely, from poetry" and that this intellectual fodder consisted "mainly of ideas which had been blended by the poets of the eighteenth century" (*HNF* 3.185). While we still cannot say that

Wordsworth certainly read Hartley—as opposed to assimilating Hartleyan ideas ambiently—the poet's conversancy with Akenside, Chatterton, Collins, Cowper, Goldsmith, Gray, Macpherson, Pope, Prior, Shenstone, Smith, Thomson, Young, and countless lesser figures remains beyond all doubt. Recent work on poetic influence in Wordsworth has usually concentrated either on Milton or the Coleridge connection. Wordsworth's contemporaries, conversely, stressed his engagement of eighteenth-century British loco-descriptive conventions. In a characteristic observation, one (anonymous) reviewer of *The Excursion* placed the poem in literary history by remarking

> the shackles were burst by Thomson and Collins and Akenside, and, since their day, the works of nature have not wanted observers able and willing to deduce from them lessons, which Providence . . . intended them to convey. But none have ever entered so profoundly into this theory of their art as those commonly known by the name of the Lake Poets, particularly Mr. Wordsworth.[45]

In its religious ruminations, moreover, the main line of the eighteenth-century tradition had from Pope on either marginalized or omitted Christian doctrine. Dedicated to nature as a common ground, this verse aspired to be natural theology in meter. It represented the poetic expression of a commitment, widely held from the time of Tillotson,[46] to nature as the inspiring foundation of faith—a natural faith which revelation alone could complete, but which independently comprehended the existence of God, the moral order of His cosmos, and the immortality of the human soul. Wordsworth occasionally alludes to the more doctrinally explicit poetry of writers such as the Anglican Young and the Evangelical Cowper. His most formative allegiances, however, were to poetry which turns from God's doctrinal revelation to ponder the spiritual import of God's natural creation.

So Wordsworth's earlier poetry generally ignores Christ not because he privately doubted Christian truth claims—although some he probably did doubt—but because of the kind of poetry he was trying to write. In an 1840 letter to Henry Alford, Wordsworth remarked,

> I was particularly pleased with your distinction between religion in Poetry and versified Religion. For my own part, I have been averse to frequent mention of the mysteries of Christian faith, not

from a want of a due sense of their momentous nature; but the contrary. I felt it far too deeply to venture on handling the subject as familiarly as many scruple not to do. I am far from blaming them, but let them not blame me, nor turn from my companionship on that account. Besides general reasons for diffidence in treating subjects of holy writ I have some especial ones. I might err in points of faith; and I should not deem my mistakes less to be deprecated because they were expressed in metre. (LLY 4.23–24)

In the same year R. P. Graves reports Wordsworth confessing a similar aversion to writing sacred poetry, and protesting that his poems "should not be considered as developing all of the influences which his own heart recognised, but rather those which he considered himself able as an artist to display to advantage" (C. Wordsworth, Memoirs 2.370). He repeated several of these points in telling Aubrey De Vere that

when in youth his imagination was shaping for itself the channel in which it was to flow, his religious convictions were less definite and less strong than they had become on more mature thought; and that, when his poetic mind and manner had once been formed, he feared lest he might, in attempting to modify them, become constrained.[47]

Wordsworth's later explanation of his development as a religious poet has sometimes been interpreted as defensiveness designed to obscure earlier heterodoxies (HNF 3.254–56). I grant that his later statements may, for whatever reason, misrepresent his earlier motives and beliefs in some ways. If by "mysteries of Christian faith" he means Anglican Church dogma, Wordsworth's expressions of reverence in the Alford letter paint too rosy a picture of his earlier disinterest. Yet his acknowledgment of heterodoxy to De Vere—of former "religious convictions . . . less definite and less strong"—reveals a straightforward frankness. His account of his career seems similarly accurate: he employed religious motifs in ways encouraged by his talent, following the "channel" formed by the current of his abilities and interests.

The demotion of dogma in Wordsworth's religious poetry reflects other influences too, including the unofficial policies of Anglicanism discussed in this chapter's preceding section. The Protestant appeal from institutional authority to individual conscience—supported by the venerable Pauline distinction of letter from spirit—lent Wordsworth's rejection of "versified Religion" important support. I will also speculate in the conclusion of this book that Wordsworth's awareness of historicist biblical scholarship confirmed his marginalizing of doctrine while providing him a model of revisionary traditionalism. What seems clearest, however, is that Wordsworth set his "religion in Poetry" priorities on his sense of his own talent above all, finding his way artistically, as Theodore Roethke wrote, by going where he must. He judged both his ability and his time correctly. By 1798, in fact, Wordsworth's undoctrinaire dedication to "the religion in Poetry" was merging with his aspiration to a Romantic "poetry of experience," in Robert Langbaum's phrase, a poetry subordinating intellectual codification to the subject's firsthand experience of the world.[48] Thus Wordsworthian religious poetry ordinarily stages religious *experience*: visionary intimations offered as one man's heartfelt testimony. Such poems left Wordsworth the task of persuading a broad readership that his truths were theirs. But the greater risk of projecting "a paradise for a sect" resided, he rightly appears to have believed, with the exclusionary force of doctrinal specification.

Moved by these influences and the evolution of his own faith, Wordsworth composed a poetry which simultaneously conjures and displaces values he considered Christian. The result is a religious humanism with Christian associations which imply the poet's selective endorsement of Christianity—a Romantic theology anticipated in certain 1798–1802 texts and realized in the major achievements of 1804–1805, the Immortality Ode and the Thirteen-Book *Prelude*. The vehicles of a Wordsworthian "religion in Poetry," these texts strategically incorporate Christian motifs while leaving Church doctrine and the life of Christ unmentioned. One interpretative problem they raise, consequently, is whether any such texts can properly be designated Christian—a question sufficiently knotty to have inspired pronounced critical disagreements. In what remains the most detailed assessment of Wordsworth's religious opinions, Fairchild hotly denied the poet's Christianity on doctrinal grounds. For Fairchild, the ostensible Christianity of a poetry which ignores the Incarnation, Crucifixion, and Resurrection of Christ is no Christianity at all, and this position continues to surface in Wordsworth studies. Robert Barth was thinking of the poetry, and so reconfirming Fairchild's basic argument, in observing, "Wordsworth was at no point in his life what I would call a traditional Christian, because he had no belief that is discernible to me—even in *The Excursion*—of central Christian doctrine."[49] Yet the importance of doctrine for a poetics of faith was directly challenged by Lionel Trilling in "Wordsworth and the Iron Time," in part a rejoinder to Fairchild. For Trilling, "when we speak of a poet as being of a particular religion, we do not imply in him completeness or orthodoxy, or even explicitness of doctrine, but only that his secular utterance has the decisive mark of the religion upon it"; and, noting such marks in Wordsworth's characteristic work, Trilling surmised that "for modern taste" Wordsworth may well be "too Christian a poet."[50]

So, again, the disagreements seem pronounced: Fairchild and Barth entirely deny the poetry's Christianity while Trilling worries that the same poetry may prove excessively Christian. These alternatives obviously constitute a false dichotomy and we must avoid their extremism by borrowing a little from both. Trilling's refusal of doctrinal rigidity has considerable appeal and, in a sense, has been frequently embraced in Wordsworth scholarship. References to the "orthodoxy" or "Christianity" of the 1850 Prelude—especially as compared with the earlier 1805 version—recur almost routinely, for example, in the secondary literature. They do so despite the fact, as Barth justly insists, that even the 1850 version lacks "any of the . . . traditional concomitants of Christian doctrine or Christian faith" (Barth, 21). That lack has not prevented Wordsworth's editors, in particular, from emphasizing the Christian qualities of the Fourteen-Book Prelude. Most readers assented when the introduction and notes in de Selincourt's great facing-page edition called attention to what he described as the Christianizing revisions of the later text (EdS, lxviii–lxxiv). No real protests resulted when Jonathan Wordsworth's annotations in the Norton Critical Prelude censured certain 1850 passages as obtrusively Christian (see NCP, 301n.8 and the notes to 1850, Book 14, passim). Most Wordsworth scholars appear to agree that the poems can avoid "explicitness of doctrine," in Trilling's words, and at moments still seem decidedly Christian in moral ambience and spiritual perspective.

Yet only at moments. When we shift from localized passages to Wordsworthian poems in their entirety, the case for a Christian poetics instantly becomes problematic. From the time that Abrams' Natural Supernaturalism consolidated the idea of Romanticism as a humanistic tradition, the consensus, of course, has been that the Christian inflections of Wordsworth's language emphatically do not Christianize the poetry's philosophical stance. It is certainly true that Wordsworth's cultural milieu made biblical and liturgical phrases, and to a lesser extent Miltonic imagery as well, an almost unavoidable imaginative idiom. We rightly expect to find religiously resonant language in such non-Christian writers as Byron, Shelley, Keats, and Hazlitt. The Christian diction found in Wordsworth can appear as incidental as it does in the typical work of these other Romantic figures. "Tintern Abbey" includes many terms with conventional Christian associations in Wordsworth's contemporary culture: terms as "cheerful faith," "blessings," "worshipper," "blessed mood," "living soul," "prayer," and so on. No criticism known to me argues that this language imposes a Christian discipline on the spiritual vision of Wordsworth's poem. The spiritual vision seems manifest: "Tintern Abbey" ponders the alternately consolatory and elegiac aspects of the One Life. Yet it seems equally manifest that the poem's use of Christian diction is culturally unexceptional, a stylistic practice which merely creates mood. For Christian meaning, mood is not enough.

Consequently, I sympathize with Jeffrey Baker's statement that "natural religion of the kind Wordsworth seems to be expressing [in *The Prelude*] can never be Christian according to the common implications of the word."[51] It would be highly impositional, I agree, simply to designate *The Prelude* a Christian poem and move on. In its main thrust, the faith of the Thirteen-Book *Prelude* unfolds as a form of religious humanism sacramentally grounded in the natural world. In my view, however, the crucial issue lies with the relationship of that faith to Christian orthodoxy as Wordsworth understood it. For the poems themselves raise that issue—and in ways distinguishing Wordsworth from Shelley, Byron, Keats, and Hazlitt—by combining a verbal *and* intellectual invocation of religious tradition. With Wordsworth, Christian diction and imagery ordinarily come in tandem with thematically pertinent reassertions of central Christian *truths*: the existence of God, the reality of the Fall, the possibility of spiritual redemption through love, and the fact of a spiritual afterlife. Consider in passing merely the rhetorical orchestrations of the 1805 *Prelude*, Book 13. After beginning with locutions redolent of Milton and the Bible, Wordsworth's Snowdon episode culminates in Gospel-like celebrations of redemptive love: his "behold the fields / In balmy spring-time," and subsequent injunction to "see that pair, the Lamb / And the Lamb's Mother" (13.152–55), recalling Christ's "behold the fowls of the air. . . . Consider the lilies of the field" from the sermon on the mount (Matthew 6:26, 28). In Book 13, these Miltonic and biblical allusions coexist with intellectually consonant celebrations of God, spiritual love, and the soul's immortality. The allusions help justify Wordsworth's Romantic theodicy, which his text presents as an extrapolation from biblical precedent. The virtual gauntlet of Christian associations run by readers of Book 13 fashions it as a visionary reconfirmation of a (Christian) God of love, rediscovered in the workings of the creative imagination. Any demands for doctrine go unmet. Still, the text's Christian allusions and analogues, all dogmas left unnoticed, remain integral to both its affective power and spiritual insight.

The reinscription of biblical motifs in Wordsworth's Snowdon meditation is typical of his conservative revisionism. The Christian inflections of the Ode and Thirteen-Book *Prelude* create a middle-ground between an overt, doctrinally elaborated Christianity and a Romantic natural theology. Those inflections insinuate the texts halfway towards formal Christianity, positioning them on its margins. As a result, it bears repeating, the poems cannot be taken as unequivocally Christian in final import. But I will argue only that the displacement of dogma in Wordsworth's great 1804–1805 accomplishments does not divest them of intellectually functional Christian implications. The fascination of these poems—along with the problems of reading they pose—resides in their deliberately metaphorical relation to Christian orthodoxy. Naturally supernaturalistic, they both resemble and differ from overtly Christian statements. Depending on whether we privilege difference or likeness, we can read the faith of such texts as a predominately individualistic position with residual Christian affinities, or we can read it as a predominately Christian position with important revisionary tendencies. Neither reading can decisively banish its supplemental alternative. But each rightly concedes the seriousness of the poet's evocations of Christianity. The Christian aspects of Wordsworth's poetry are not just cultural reflexes—unexceptional, cosmetic, and unrelated to his concern with truth. They are contributive elements of a religious design that cannot be gauged apart from their significant contribution.

The Christian qualities of Wordsworth's poetry become increasingly recognizable and important over the years from 1798–1805. But the poetry of this period reveals an interest in Christianity, and is certainly engaged with religious issues, from the start. Wordsworth initiates his poetic maturity by recasting *The Ruined Cottage* in the light of Coleridge's quasi-pantheistic idea of the One Life. Failing to make the One Life yield a compelling elegiac resolution for his story of Margaret, he encounters his own latent attachments to a Christian humanitarianism. It is therefore no surprise to find a revisionist Christianity underlying the epic ambitions of his *Recluse* project as the famous Prospectus (1800) unfolds them. An expression of his growing conservatism, the sacramental world portrayed in the 1802 lyrics is even more conventionally Christian, even when the poet's touch remains light. By 1804 Wordsworth's absorption in religious questions emerges decisively in the Immortality Ode and in the expansion of *The Prelude* from five to thirteen books as a result of possibilities glimpsed during his 1804 work on the climbing of Snowdon. My fourth and fifth chapters will reconstruct the place of Christianity in the Ode and the Thirteen-Book *Prelude*. My conclusion will then turn back to the poet himself by arguing that the Christian implications of the 1804–1805 poetry reflect Wordsworth's own Romantic Anglicanism. We begin with *The Ruined Cottage*, however, and with Wordsworth's gradual discovery of the spiritual insufficiency of natural religion.

CHAPTER TWO

Vain Belief:
Wordsworth and the One Life

And what if all of animated nature
Be but organic Harps diversly fram'd,
That tremble into thought, as o'er them sweeps,
Plastic and vast, one intellectual Breeze,
At once the Soul of each, and God of all?
But thy more serious eye a mild reproof
Darts, O beloved Woman! nor such thoughts
Dim and unhallow'd dost thou not reject,
And biddest me walk humbly with my God.

—Coleridge,
"Effusion XXXV" (lines 36–44)

One of the most respected accounts of Wordsworth's intellectual development in 1798 centers on his acceptance, revision, and eventual abandonment of Coleridge's idea of the One Life. The theory of the One Life is routinely identified as the philosophy of Wordsworth's *Recluse* project. It clearly inspired the Pedlar narrative which, looking ahead to the retrospective writing done at Goslar, ultimately looks ahead to *The Prelude*. But this important theory also initiated Wordsworth's reconsideration of his religious beliefs during the period spanning his revision of *The Ruined Cot-*

tage and completion of the Thirteen-Book *Prelude*. My study of Wordsworth's evolving faith begins with the One Life and therefore with the distinguished scholarship of Jonathan Wordsworth. Wordsworth scholars have long agreed that the poet's early religious viewpoint was pantheistic in mood, and that he turned increasingly from nature to humanity, and from immanent to transcendent conceptions of godhead, as his career proceeded. In 1969-1970, however, Jonathan Wordsworth reoriented the study of Wordsworth's natural supernaturalism by publishing the primary texts and critical arguments from which subsequent studies of the poet's pantheist sympathies unavoidably derive.[1] My own debts to Jonathan Wordsworth's work can hardly be overstated. This chapter nonetheless advocates several modifications in the received position on Wordsworth and the One Life.

That position unreservedly refers to the theory of the One Life as a form of pantheism. It declares further that Wordsworth temporarily accepted the One Life ardently and completely, his belief producing a phase reaching from late 1797 to mid-1798. Finally, it leaves unanswered the question of why Wordsworth's faith in an immanent mind lapsed so soon: "for some reason that we cannot know," Jonathan Wordsworth remarks, "the system lost its hold."[2] In my view, both the relationship of the One Life idea to pantheist doctrine and Wordsworth's commitment to the idea remained qualified and incomplete. With one exception— discussed below—Wordsworth's use of the idea never suggests his self-conscious assent to a conceptually rigorous pantheism, with its denial of divine transcendence and compounding of God and Nature. Yet the suggestive power of the One Life motif remained inherently pantheistic in important respects. Using the motif poetically, Wordsworth inherited pantheistic implications which did not require his assent, in short, and which he could not always effectively control. In some poems, lyrics in particular, the pantheistic resonance of the One Life served Wordsworth's purposes admirably. But the philosophical problem raised by *The Ruined Cottage* resulted from his recourse to the One Life for his new, March 1798 version of the poem. Consequently, the compositional history of *The Ruined Cottage* clarifies Wordsworth reception of the One Life idea. That compositional history also suggests, I will argue, that a certain residual Christianity, an affective Christianity ingrained in the poet's habitual moral responses, was centrally implicated in his changing attitudes toward the One Life.

THE ONE LIFE, NECESSITY, AND PANTHEISM

When Coleridge leapt over the fence at Racedown, making his first visit to William and Dorothy in June 1797, he brought with him the notion of the One Life. As invoked in his poetry, and as no doubt elaborated in his conversation, the theory of the One Life posited a single vital energy permeating and ontologically underlying all natural creation. Coleridge's version of the idea represented his reformulation of the radical Unitarianism of Joseph Priestley. The One Life doctrine had arisen in Enlightenment France as a form of pantheism predicated on scientific theories of animated matter. Priestley retained the materialist orientation of the idea while assimilating it to his own version of Unitarian Christianity. Coleridge then further spiritualized the concept, recasting the universal life force as "one Mind, one omnipresent Mind" (*Religious Musings*, line 105). So Wordsworth writes in the Alfoxden Notebook, "In all forms of things / There is a mind" (DC MS. 14, 21^r; *RC&P*, 123). So the Pedlar, intimating the One Life, traces "an ebbing and a flowing mind" in ostensibly inanimate objects, the "fixed lineaments" of rocks and stones and trees (Pedlar narrative, lines 56, 51). He intuits the living consciousness of natural objects as oscillating modulations of the universal mind. Both poets understood the One Life as a morally progressive energy gradually assimilating all mundane conditions to its own ultimate harmony. As a One Life convert, Wordsworth "not only believed that 'There [was] an active principle alive / In all things,'" Jonathan Wordsworth summarily remarks, but went further to affirm from that belief "a universe of blessedness and love, based on the assumption that the individual could perceive as well as share 'the life of things'" ("Wordsworth's Borderers," 176).

In fact, from the beginning Wordsworth seems to have construed the One Life as the ontological vehicle of Necessity. Coleridge had described himself as "a compleat Necessitarian" in 1796, and he retained important Necessitarian allegiances at least until 1799.[3] He claimed in an 1804 letter, moreover, that Wordsworth too was for a time "even to Extravagance a Necessitarian."[4] In this instance Coleridge appears a reliable narrator, for subscription to the doctrine of Necessity would have followed from Wordsworth's adoption of Godwinian theory. There was, then, a politics to the idea of Necessity, a favorite idea of the radical London circles Wordsworth had frequented in 1794–1795. There was unquestionably a psychology to Necessity, a psychology best known from the meliorist associationism of David Hartley. It was as a psychological theory that Necessity may have retained its most enduring influence on Wordsworth for, as James Chandler argues, the Preface to *Lyrical Ballads* appears occasionally Necessitarian in its presumption of an empirical psychology.[5] The more important point here, however, is simply that the idea of Necessity also implied a metaphysics. Necessity was commonly deemed the causal force behind events, a "Mother of the World" in Shelley's phrase. While rejecting the theological arguments of Hartley and Priestley, Godwin himself envisioned Necessity as a teleological process grounded in natural law and, as such, informing but also transcending the human will: "in the life of every human being," he wrote, "there is a chain of events, generated in the lapse of ages which preceded his birth, and going on in regular procession through the whole period of his existence."[6]

Due to these metaphysical implications, Mark Philp comments, "debates on necessity and materialism were also debates about the nature of God and His relation to the human and natural world."[7] The religious implications of Necessity, as Wordsworth came to understand them, seem ultimately to have soured him on the concept. Hartley and Priestley had managed, cumbersomely, to construct a Christianized Necessity. But the idea's incompatibility with orthodox Christianity emerges clearly enough in Coleridge's 1795–1796 plan to write "a dissection of Atheism—particularly the Godwinian System of Pride," which in his view rendered man an "outcast of blind Nature ruled by a fatal Necessity—Slave of an ideot Nature!"[8] Even Godwin confessed in a manuscript note, "While I was writing my *Enquiry Concerning Political Justice*, the reflections into which I was led by the arguments respecting the doctrine of necessity, made me an atheist, to which doctrine I had hitherto been a resolute adversary."[9] But in 1798, briefly, Wordsworth felt untroubled by the irreligiousness latent in a Necessitarian viewpoint, or by the tendency of evocations of a fatalistic Necessity to marginalize human agency and individuality. In 1798 Coleridge's concept of the One Life appears to have struck him as supremely answerable to his imaginative situation. He had unlearned his admiration of Godwinian philosophy and been left to revise *Salisbury Plain* and compose *The Borderers* without intellectual grounds for a compelling moral optimism. Coleridge's theory of the One Life met Wordsworth's poetic needs by allowing him to transfer the idea of Necessity from its now-objectionable Godwinian setting to a new context which preserved faith in progress while divesting it of arid rationalism.

So the One Life, for Wordsworth, was Necessity in action, directly observable at privileged moments. His one explicit reference to Necessitarian power manifesting itself in the natural world comes in the "Not useless do I deem" passage written for the expanded version of *The Ruined Cottage* which occupied him in March 1798. There the Pedlar summarily remarks,

> Thus deeply drinking in the soul of things
> We shall be wise perforce & we shall move
> From strict necessity along the path
> Of order & of good. What'er we see
> Whate'er we feel by agency direct
> Or indirect shall tend to feed & nurse
> Our faculties & raise to loftier heights
> Our intellectual soul.

> (*RC&P*, 271, 275)

Although Wordsworth's other representations of the One Life lack any reference to "strict necessity," the imagery of "Not useless" closely resembles certain lines from "The Old Cumberland Beggar":

> 'Tis Nature's law
> That none, the meanest of created things,
> Of forms created the most vile and brute,
> The dullest or most noxious, should exist
> Divorced from good, a spirit and pulse of good,
> A life and soul to every mode of being
> Inseparably link'd.

> (*LB*, 228–34; lines 73–79)

Positing a vitalizing soul operative in "every mode of being" as both a natural law and moral energy ("pulse of good"), these lines depict what seems to be a naturalized mode of Necessity. The poet had Necessity in mind, presumably, when he wrote in the Alfoxden Notebook that "Some men there are who like insects &c / dart and dart against the mighty / stream of tendency" (DC MS. 14, 15^v; *RC&P*, 113). Equally reminiscent of Necessity is Wordsworth's description of a universally impelling "presence" in "Tintern

Abbey"—or so Hazlitt tellingly claimed. He used Wordsworth's description of a "motion and a spirit" as the epigraph for his 1815 essay "On the Doctrine of Philosophical Necessity" and commented, "Perhaps, the doctrine of what has been called philosophical necessity was never more finely expressed than in these lines."[10]

Yet the idea of the One Life was associated not merely with Necessity but with pantheism as well. Wordsworth's most powerfully pantheistic statements occur in "Tintern Abbey" and in two verse fragments, the first the "There is an active principle" passage dating from early 1798:

> There is an active principle alive in all things:
> In all things, in all natures, in the flowers
> And in the trees, in every pebbly stone
> That paves the brooks, the stationary rocks
> The moving waters, and the invisible air.
> All beings have their properties which spread
> Beyond themselves, a power by which they make
> Some other being conscious of their life;
> Spirit that knows no insulated spot,
> No chasm, no solitude,—From link to link
> It circulates, the soul of all the worlds.
> This is the freedom of the universe;
> Unfolded still the more, more visible,
> The more we know; and yet is reverenced least,
> And least respected, in the human mind,
> Its most apparent home.[11]

The second passage, notable for its "extreme pantheistic viewpoint," in Jonathan Wordsworth's phrase (NCP, 495), is a DC MS. 33 entry written in approximately February 1799:

> I seemed to learn
> That what we see of individual images & forms
> Which float along our minds & and what we feel
> Of active or recognizable thought,
> Prospectiveness or intellect or will,
> Not only is not worthy to be deemed
> Our being, to be prized as what we are
> But is the very littleness of life
> Such consciousness I deem but accidents

Relapses from the one interior life
That lives in all things far beyond the touch
Of that false secondary power by which
In weakness we create distinctions, then
Believe that all our puny boundaries are things
Which we perceive and not which we have made
—In which all beings live with god themselves
Are god existing in one mighty whole
As undistinguishable as the cloudless east
At noon is from the cloudless west when all
The hemisphere is one cerulean blue.

(*TPP*, 165; DC MS. 33, 50ʳ)

Slightly revised, these lines were positioned briefly in MS. RV of the Two-Part *Prelude*, where they followed the climactic assertion, "I saw one life and felt that it was joy."

But just how pantheistic is the intellectual outlook of these three texts? The question arises because "the idea of the immanence of God in the universe is . . . perfectly consistent with orthodox Christian faith," R. D. Havens justly remarks, "so long as there is no denial of His transcendence."[12] The lines from DC MS. 33 emphatically deny spiritual transcendence. In its revised MS. RV version, Wordsworth speaks more conventionally of "one interior life" in which "all beings live with god, are lost / In god & nature in one mighty whole" (*TPP*, 207). So one can argue that the poet, in reconsidering the passage, took care to differentiate between godhead and the world. Intuiting God's presence in nature, the soul "lost / In god & nature in one mighty whole," in the revised language of MS. RV, surrenders its sense of individuation to a natural world which, while natural, appears at that moment so suffused with God's presence that the soul *experiences* God and nature indistinguishably. The visually undifferentiated skies of the passage cited above may suggest pantheistic monism. Yet in MS. RV these closing images immediately precede lines which, depicting the speaker "With God and Nature communing" (*TPP*, 209), again reinstate the distinction which pantheism categorically disallows. In the earlier DC MS. 33 version cited above the pantheism is harder to wish away. The passage identifies God with the sum total of natural processes. In these lines, the unity Wordsworth affirms is apparently ontological, and as such a form of all-inclusive pantheistic immanence.

Matters change, however, as soon as one turns to "There is an active principle" and "Tintern Abbey." "There is an active principle" obviously affirms an immanent spiritual energy, and can therefore seem manifestly pantheistic. But Duncan Wu's identification of Wordsworth's "soul of all the worlds" phrase as an allusion to "the Platonic world soul" sufficiently demonstrates how the passage can accommodate idealist or transcendentalist readings (Wu, 298n.4). The pantheism of "Tintern Abbey" is similarly ambiguous and qualified, however much the text may appear to invite pantheistic interpretation. Admittedly, Coleridge's 1820 castigation of Wordsworth's "vague, misty, rather than mystic, Confusion of God with the World & the accompanying Nature-worship" (*CLSTC* 5.95) implicitly indicts "Tintern Abbey" by echoing Wordsworth's reference to himself there as "A worshipper of Nature" (line 153). When the speaker of "Tintern Abbey" becomes "a living soul" as the harmonizing joy of "the life of things" invests his being, Wordsworth's allusion subtly deifies the One Life, arguably, by comparing it to the God of Genesis, who made Adam "a living soul" by breathing into him. Such pantheistic touches notwithstanding, here too Wordsworth's natural supernaturalism stops well short of a philosophically rigorous pantheism. As in MS. RV of the Two-Part *Prelude*, Wordsworth at times invokes a unity less ontological than experiential. He praises

> that serene and blessed mood,
> In which the affections gently lead us on,
> Until, the breath of this corporeal frame,
> And even the motion of our human blood
> Almost suspended, we are laid asleep
> In body, and become a living soul:
> While with an eye made quiet by the power
> Of harmony, and the deep power of joy,
> We see into the life of things.
>
> (*LB*, 116–20; lines 42–50)

Here seeing "into the life of things" occurs only as the observer becomes "a living soul"—only as spiritual insight, that is, verges on a mystical union of self and oversoul.

But even Wordsworth's characterization of the all-harmonizing "life of things" never becomes in itself explicitly pantheistic:

And I have felt
A presence that disturbs me with the joy
Of elevated thoughts; a sense sublime
Of something far more deeply interfused,
Whose dwelling is the light of setting suns,
And the round ocean, and the living air,
And the blue sky, and in the mind of man,
A motion and a spirit, that impels
All thinking things, all objects of all thought,
And rolls through all things.

(lines 94–103)

This immanent and universal presence, the images hint, exists beyond the world it informs, for it suffuses a light leaving the earth with the setting sun, disappearing visually beyond the horizon. Wordsworth's reference to setting *suns* suddenly places the Wye valley landscape in massively enlarged cosmic perspective. His doubled locution at the height of vision—"A motion and a spirit"— bows similarly to transcendent possibilities by keeping the natural and supernatural related but separate. What he felt registered like a "motion," a materialist term connoting the world of measurable properties, and yet like a "spirit" too: and so his feelings, requiring both terms, reconfirm the gap between them.

So are the affirmations of "Tintern Abbey" pantheistic? The poem's "sense sublime" surely refers to the One Life. The notion of a spirit impelling all things resembles the "spirit and pulse of good" in "The Old Cumberland Beggar," a universal "life and soul to every mode of being / Inseparably linked"—which itself recalls "There is an active principle," where Wordsworth avowed, "From link to link / It circulates, the soul of all the worlds." The recurrent phrases and images of Wordsworth's early 1798 philosophical poems show them drawing in common from a constellation of One Life motifs. What is less clear—despite the DC MS. 33 fragment— is that the poet himself means to present the One Life as a literally pantheistic energy. The spiritual intuitions of "Tintern Abbey" are for the most part compatible with pantheism; they do not restric- tively demand pantheist interpretation. "To assert that a 'spirit . . . rolls through all things,'" Paul Sheats sensibly remarks, "is, strictly speaking, no more or less pantheistic than to assert that 'the spirit of God moved upon the face of the waters.'"[13] Wordsworth's motion and spirit avoid systematic pantheism partly because Wordsworth's

poetry, as Sheats also comments, "is guided to its objects by feeling, and not by the methods of systematic exposition" (Sheats, 211).
At the same time, the avoidance of rigorously pantheistic formulations in "Tintern Abbey" seems to have been guided in part by
thought. It appears intellectually deliberate and self-conscious. For
Wordsworth's most characteristic representations of the One Life
envision a spirit both immanent and transcendent.[14]
   The chief exhibit for his conception of the One Life must
finally be deemed the Pedlar narrative from early 1798. Here is the
young Pedlar's first visionary experience of the One Life:

> The ocean and the earth beneath him lay
> In gladness and deep joy. The clouds were touched,
> And in their silent faces did he read
> Unutterable love. Sound needed none,
> Nor any voice of joy: his spirit drank
> The spectacle. Sensation, soul and form,
> All melted into him. They swallowed up
> His animal being. In them did he live,
> And by them did he live. They were his life.
> In such access of mind, in such high hour
> Of visitation from the living God,
> He did not feel the God, he felt his works.

> (lines 98–109)

These lines exemplify the joy the idea of the One Life inspired in
Wordsworth, and his conception of it as an agency of love. At the
same time, the Pedlar's vision avoids the conceptual specifications
of a rigorous pantheism. It is pantheistic in ambience, perhaps,
stressing the boy's personal experience of "the living God" as manifested in the natural scene before him. Yet here "God is invisible,"
Sheats notes, "but his love can be seen and felt in his works—a distinction that is quite impossible to a pantheist" (Sheats, 212). The
later passage recounting how the Pedlar "saw one life, and felt that
it was joy" (line 218) similarly displays the all-informing immanence of the One Life, and the joyfulness occasioned by experience
of it—and similarly fails to conflate God and Nature in a pantheistic monism.
   Scholarship content to characterize Wordsworth as a pantheist
defends the lapsing of systematic pantheism in his poetry as simply
unexceptional, a predictable consequence of the ambiguities of

poetic language and of the poet's aversion to systematic thinking. If it is wrong to expect conceptual specification from Wordsworth poems, however, reading those poems for their ostensible affirmations of the One Life becomes tendentious to begin with. I am not convinced, in any event, that the avoidance of a pantheistic representation of divinity in Wordsworth's One life poetry is either incidental or unimportant. The avoidance is impressively systematic in its own right, recurring quite clearly in every statement of One Life belief except the February 1799 lines from DC MS. 33. We can only speculate as to the compositional rationale of those lines. Working to construct a prophetic persona for the Two-Part *Prelude*, Wordsworth wrote a passage in which the pantheistic affinities of the One Life became strikingly overt. Still, the passage remains highly atypical, was conventionalized when revised for the Two-Part *Prelude*, and then was finally deleted—and not published even in revised form, unlike "Not useless do I deem" and "There is an active principle," in the poet's lifetime. These lines remain anomalous, let me add, even for critics who emphasize the pantheism of the One Life idea. For the received position on Wordsworth and the One Life reads "Tintern Abbey" as a valediction, and declares Wordsworth's pantheist commitments to have ended months before he wrote the lines preserved in DC MS. 33.

In his poetry Wordsworth used the One Life notion for visionary scenes which, in their experiential immediacies and natural settings, dramatize discoveries of spirit *in* nature. The emphasis of the Pedlar narrative certainly falls on natural forms joyfully vitalized by a spiritual energy pulsing through them. There can be little doubt that for Wordsworth the One Life idea had a pronounced pantheist resonance. That resonance was powerful enough that Wordsworth, employing the idea in *The Ruined Cottage*, inherited the traditional philosophical problems of pantheism. But simply declaring the Wordsworth of the One Life a pantheist seems unjustified. Familiar with Coleridge's conversation—familiar merely with "The Eolian Harp" in its 1795 version—Wordsworth could hardly have remained unaware of the distinction between radical pantheism and commonplace belief in the divinity of nature. The distinction was of paramount importance to Coleridge, an adversary of philosophical pantheism throughout his career. We do well to recall that Wordsworth was introduced to the One Life doctrine by a man who, from the beginning, would have propounded the doctrine's compatibility with the idea of a transcendent deity.[15] We should also recall just how unconventional and uncommon a literal pantheism would have been in the cultural milieu of Wordsworth's day: not even the notorious radical Priestley, for all his materialist leanings, actually professed pantheist beliefs.

What we see in the Pedlar narrative, "Tintern Abbey," and the One Life fragments associated with *The Ruined Cottage* is a form of intuitive natural supernaturalism. The outdoor settings of the poems encourage spiritual affirmations powerfully pantheistic in mood but not literally pantheistic in philosophical viewpoint. The Necessitarian power of the One Life attests to a providential design radiating through mundane affairs from its source in eternity. All told, Wordsworth's One Life poetry reveals a responsiveness to the numinous in nature on the part of a poet accustomed to thinking of a God who both informs and transcends his creation.

POETRY AND BELIEF

My presentation of the One Life philosophy draws it closer to the poet's personal beliefs by conventionalizing it, making it a variation on a conviction of nature's sacredness shared by many educated people in late eighteenth-century Britain. What I want to suggest now is that Wordsworth's belief in the One Life may nonetheless have remained provisional and incomplete. The poet's *interest* in the concept of the One Life seems entirely clear. My account of his revisions of *The Ruined Cottage* in the light of the One Life, later in this chapter, presupposes absolutely his emotional and intellectual investment in the ideas at stake. At the same time, the idea of the One Life seems to have prompted occasional doubts and anxieties in his mind. It seems fairer to the existing evidence to view Wordsworth's imaginative engagement of the One Life as enthusiastic but exploratory—a way of testing the implications of an idea which poetic appropriation alone could definitively clarify for him.

The scholarship on Wordsworth and the One Life posits a conversion and a consequent phase of conviction lasting from late 1797 to July 1798 when, as noted above, the "new hesitation" and "elegiac tone" discerned by Jonathan Wordsworth in "Tintern Abbey" indicates the lapsing of wholehearted assent (*MH*, 213). The problem with this notion of "phase" emerges when we scrutinize the texts falling within the phase. Leave aside "Tintern Abbey" temporarily for its terminal position, postpone discussion of the Pedlar materials, and we are left with a mere handful of poems. Worse, these poems, or so I have argued, give the One Life idea rather ambiguous expression. "The Old Cumberland Beggar" may fall within the orbit of the One Life by affirming an immanent Necessity in language reminiscent of "Tintern Abbey." But do the references to a universal "spirit and pulse of good" in "The Old Cumberland Beggar" help to establish Wordsworth's personal commitment to the idea of the One Life? They seemingly invoke a form of Necessity, but one could believe in Necessity without assenting to the One Life. Is the imagery of natural harmony in "The Old Cumberland Beggar" so powerfully dependent upon the One Life theory that, as in the case of the Pedlar narrative, we could hardly explain the poem without invoking the theory? Despite its comments on "Nature's law," the "the benigant law of heaven" in "The Old Cumberland Beggar" (line 160) wrests its moral vision toward what contemporary readers would have understood readily enough as Christian moral sentiment. As employed to defend the beggar's social usefulness and human dignity, Wordsworth's affirmation of "Nature's law," for all its pantheistic quality, neither affronts nor dramatically differs from orthodox belief that life down to the least sparrow's fall manifests an inclusive moral design.

Similar problems arise with the other One Life poems extrinsic to the Pedlar project. The gentleness toward nature counseled in "Nutting"—on the grounds that "there is a spirit in the woods" (line 54)—appears entirely commonplace in its natural piety. "Lines written in early spring" declares "that every flower / Enjoys the air it breathes" (lines 11–12). But the poetry of Wordsworth's day abounds in fictions of natural sentiment and sympathy: the Wordsworth of *Descriptive Sketches* had avowed, "Blows not a Zephyr but it whispers joy" four years before Coleridge acquainted him with the One Life notion (*DS*, line 18). Some of the other *Lyrical Ballads* poems ostensibly praise the One Life. In phrases reminiscent of "Tintern Abbey" and the Pedlar narrative, "Lines written at a small distance from my House" declares,

> And from the blessed power that rolls
> About, below, above;
> We'll frame the measure of our souls,
> They shall be tuned to love.

> (lines 33–36)

Even in this case, however, Wordsworth's conceptual dependence on One Life motifs remains imprecise. The "power" in question, after all, may be no more than the naturalistic "vertu" lauded by Chaucer, a force awakening the natural world and human feeling from winter dormancy. The Pedlar's intimation of "the power / Of nature" is a privileged metaphysical insight, earned through a development which only gradually prepares him to "receive / Deeply the lesson deep of love," and which makes him a prophetic figure whose wisdom sets him apart from ordinary people (lines 86–87, 88–89). In "Lines written at a small distance from my House" the speaker invites his sister to join an easily accessible community of feeling—invites her to experience nature's "blessed power" simply by enjoying springtime beauty.

With *Lyrical Ballads*, the editors of the Cornell edition leave the One Life unmentioned in their annotations, preferring to attribute Wordsworth's depictions of a living nature to his familiarity with Erasmus Darwin and botanical literature.[16] It is not my intention to escort these poems from the charmed circle of the One Life. I merely question the terms of their membership in that circle and, above all, their evidential value for the question of Wordsworth's personal philosophy. Stephen Parrish has observed that "the difficulties of defining a genre like the 'pastoral ballad' while at the same time using the definition to identify members of the genre are sufficiently sobering,"[17] and similar difficulties beset formulations of a Wordsworthian One Life canon. "The Old Cumberland Beggar," "Nutting," and the *Lyrical Ballads* poems cannot independently demonstrate Wordsworth's faith in any conceptually particularized natural theology. Establish that faith on surer foundations—ground it on evidence extrinsic to the poetry—and then texts incidentally recalling the One Life idea can be placed in (secondary) relation to it. By themselves, poems like "Lines written at a small distance from my House" may conceivably reflect a purely verbal enthusiasm. Citing the "motion and a spirit" passage from "Tintern Abbey," Coleridge once distinguished "the language" from "the sense or purpose of the great poet of our age."[18] The same distinction pertains to "Lines written at a small distance from my House." Its resemblance to passages in the Pedlar narrative may represent little more than stylistic overspill: Wordsworth falling back on the expressive resources of an exciting new poetic idiom for a text only casually concerned with the theories for which that idiom was originally developed.

With "Tintern Abbey," other considerations leave the question of Wordsworth's convictions equally unsettled. Mary Jacobus has called "Tintern Abbey" "Wordsworth's most successful statement

of his belief in the One Life," and certainly the text's representations of visionary intuition and a spiritual presence in nature
invoke the One Life.[19] But those representations also leave the
speaker doubting himself. Wordsworth quite self-consciously wrote
a poetry of experience, never more so than in his religious poetry,
which focuses from the beginning not on those theoretical problems which fascinated the doctrinaire Coleridge but, rather, on doctrinally revalidating religious *experience.* If the "business of
poetry . . . is to treat of things not as they *are,* but as they *appear;*
not as they exist in themselves, but as they *seem* to exist to the
senses and to the *passions"* ("Essay, Supplementary to the Preface,"
WPr 3.63), but if truth remains solemnly important in all matters
of religion, then a Wordsworthian poetry of religious experience
will tend to become self-questioning—and "Tintern Abbey" provides a case in point. For Wordsworth's elated description of how

> we are laid asleep
> In body, and become a living soul:
> While with an eye made quiet by the power
> Of harmony, and the deep power of joy,
> We see into the life of things

is immediately succeeded by the undercutting reflection,

> If this
> Be but a vain belief—yet how oft
> . . . .
> How oft, in spirit, have I turned to thee
> O sylvan Wye! Thou wanderer through the woods,
> How often has my spirit turned to thee!

> (lines 46–51, 56–58)

The vanity of belief may indict the One Life itself or just the
speaker's ability to achieve an unmediated encounter with it. In
either case, he acknowledges uncertainty, and gratefully embraces
the consolation afforded merely by his memories of a river freely
wandering. A self-contesting use of the conditional also follows
Wordsworth's climactic description of a motion and spirit rolling
through all creation. For the lines following that description begin
with the qualifying reflection, "Nor, perchance, / If I were not thus
taught, should I the more / Suffer my genial spirits to decay" (lines

112–14). In this comment the speaker denies the One Life in nature its tutelary role—"the nurse, / The guide, the guardian of my heart" (lines 110–11)—by turning to Dorothy as a substitute teacher. The turn mutes the affirmations which preceded it, making them ring a little hollow. The spiritual continuities which Wordsworth praises should preclude the need for secondary grounds of consolation, for surrogates who arguably remind the poet less of nature's eternality, finally, than of his own mortality.

It is easy to see why Jonathan Wordsworth stresses the darkened tentativeness of the One Life references in "Tintern Abbey." For the poem's undercutting reservations are not idle concessions themselves undercut by the intensity of the passages preceding them. They testify to a Wordsworth who shared his culture's wariness of religious enthusiasm. For all his emphasis on justification by faith, the great Wesley himself, G. R. Cragg points out,

> never allowed experience to stand alone. It was always checked by the evidence of Scripture and by the judgment of his reason. Experience confirms authority, it does not establish it. It verifies the truth we have discovered, but it is not the source of that truth. Consequently we cannot authenticate our faith by appealing to our feelings.[20]

For Wordsworth too, Gene Ruoff has shown, religious intuitions could be trusted only when reconfirmed by extrinsic standards.[21] So "Tintern Abbey" deliberately renders its spiritual revelations conditional. The poem presents a speaker subject to emotionally profound moods of unity which may, he thinks at moments, have unveiled an ontological power infusing the outer world. His claims remain tentative—or, at other moments, unconvincingly overstated. Responding to Wordsworth's portrait of the artist as a One Life pilgrim worshipping nature "With warmer love, oh! with far deeper zeal / Of holier love" (lines 155–56), Harold Bloom justly comments, "certainly he protests too much; we feel a desperation in his insistence, another presage of waning faith, or faith affirmed more vehemently even as it ebbs."[22] Mark Foster seems equally justified in claiming that "Wordsworth's access of natural piety in 'Tintern Abbey,' the apparent maturing of his passionate enthusiasm into quasi-religious adoration, seems to represent an intensification of his relationship with the natural world, but more truly reflects a kind of estrangement from it."[23]

With the Pedlar texts, the Pedlar narrative and the drafts associated with it, the difficulty of inferring Wordsworth's personal convictions takes another form. This material, needless to say, depends more specifically and systematically on the concept of the One Life. Consequently, the problem of belief posed by this poetry rests not with its representation of the protagonist's spiritual experiences. It rests, first, with the uncertain mix of personal identification and dramatic projection marking Wordsworth's imaginative relation to the Pedlar; and, second, with the implications of the fact the texts in question belong to a single poetic project.

No one denies that Wordsworth presents "his own development through the figure of the Pedlar."[24] The Pedlar obviously serves Wordsworth as an authorial surrogate, with the Pedlar texts prefiguring the autobiographical writing undertaken subsequently at Goslar. But surely Wordsworth and his protagonist, a dramatic fiction, cannot be categorically identified. In his Fenwick note to *The Excursion*, Wordsworth may have remarked of the Pedlar, "I am here called upon freely to acknowledge that the character I have represented in his person is chiefly an idea of what I fancied my own character might have become in his circumstances" (*PW* 5.373). Yet the need to disassociate the poet and the Pedlar emerges in this very statement. For if Wordsworth identifies the Pedlar as a self-projection, he also notes the Pedlar's lower social class and limited formal education. We must recognize the compounded qualifications of Wordsworth's comments: he says that the Pedlar is *chiefly* a dramatization of how he, Wordsworth, *might* have grown up *if* he had shared the Pedlar's background and prospects. We must then read further into the Fenwick note and notice Wordsworth's enlistment of James Patrick and the Hawkshead Packman as additional, and additionally complicating, Pedlar prototypes. Even with *The Excursion*, the text to which Wordsworth's Fenwick statements actually pertain, one cannot simply take the Wanderer as Wordsworth's personal spokesman. Hazlitt rightly maintained that all of the poem's main characters function as authorial personae.[25] Replying to the charge that he failed to discriminate "between nature as the work of God and God himself" in *The Excursion*, Wordsworth was similarly right to stress "the *dramatic* propriety" of one of the Wanderer's ostensibly pantheistic speeches (*LMY* 2.188)—for, dramatic situation aside, he was entirely justified in insisting on the Wanderer as a dramatic character.

Poetry, T. S. Eliot reminds us, "is not the expression of personality, but an escape from personality."[26] The displacements of Wordsworth's poetry typically combine expression and escape. Chandler conjectures perceptively that authorial detachment from the Pedlar "was no doubt helpful in allowing Wordsworth to draw on his own experience at this trial stage without risking the charge of self-aggrandizement" (Chandler, 96). But the opposite is surely true as well: the figure of the Pedlar no doubt freed Wordsworth's from "his own experience," permitting vicarious investigation without the obligations of belief. We must approach the Pedlar as a construct with a distanced, complexly mediated relation to the irrecoverable ground of the poet's "own" experience. *The Prelude* itself sanctions no other approach. Remarking that Wordsworth's struggles with *The Ruined Cottage* "produced a Pedlar sequence which is, in fact, the poet's first autobiographical work," James Butler declares it unsurprising "that feelings here attributed to the Pedlar were later transferred to *The Prelude*" (*RC&P*, 17)—to *The Prelude*, that is, conceived as personal revelation on an epic scale. Yet Wordsworth's relocation of Pedlar passages in *The Prelude*—and he was equally prepared to place them in *The Excursion*—cannot independently establish the status of the Pedlar poetry as a transcription of Wordsworth's own experiences and convictions. Relocations of that sort cut both ways as evidence. Like most autobiographies, *The Prelude* retrospectively restructures certain occurrences in its author's life. Noting that "many scholars have expressed great difficulty in locating in Wordsworth's mid-twenties a crisis of precisely the same description as the one we find in *The Prelude*," Chandler points out that the pivotal event of Wordsworth's crisis autobiography may be an after the fact Burkean reconstruction (Chandler, 57). That the Pedlar biography and *The Prelude* once shared lines in common can, depending on one's perspective, alternately nudge the Pedlar closer to fact or *The Prelude* closer to fiction.

We might notice in this connection that the Pedlar narrative differs significantly from the autobiographical writing done at Goslar in late 1798 even in passages which invite comparison. Consider this depiction of the young Pedlar walking home from school at twilight:

> He many an evening to his distant home
> In solitude returning saw the hills
> Grow larger in the darkness, all alone
> Beheld the stars come out above his head,
> And travelled through the wood, no comrade near.
> To whom he might confess the things he saw.
>
> So the foundations of his mind were laid.
> In such communion, not from terror free,

While yet a child and long before his time,
He had perceived the presence and the power
Of greatness, and deep feelings had impressed
Great objects on his mind with portraiture
And colour so distinct that on his mind
They lay like substances, and almost seemed
To haunt the bodily sense.

(Pedlar narrative, lines 20–34)

Here the boy confronts the haunting sublime in a scene reminiscent of the stolen boat scene in *The Prelude*, with its ominously
looming mountain growing "larger in the darkness." But the two
incidents differ enormously. If the Pedlar lines mention "terror,"
they fail to render it in any way palpable and gripping. Here no
"unknown modes of being" defamiliarize the natural world, or
move slowly through the boy's mind, like Yeats's beast, to become
"the trouble of [his] dreams" (*TPP* 1.122, 129). The stolen boat incident, and with it the other spots of time from the first part of the
1799 *Prelude*, convey a disquietude, an intimation of uncanny
threat, conspicuously absent from the Pedlar narrative. They arise
as projections of guilt, evoke the horror of death, are in some cases
sufficiently implicated in the dynamics of family romance to have
encouraged Freudian interpretation, and retain a psychological
ambivalence and mystery unlike anything in the young Pedlar's
encounters with the life of nature. That unlikeness also hinders
identifications of Wordsworth and the Pedlar.

But, leaving aside the issue of Wordsworth's imaginative relation to the Pedlar, the material written about the Pedlar poses an
additional problem for critics interested in Wordsworth's early-
1798 religious beliefs. For it is problematic in its own right that
Wordsworth's few unclouded affirmations of the One Life must be
restricted to the Pedlar narrative. "Tintern Abbey" equivocates in
its treatment of the One Life, leaving the poet's faith in the idea
thoroughly tentative. The other texts enlisted to illustrate
Wordsworth's One Life convictions develop motifs reminiscent of
the One Life—affirming necessary progress or discovering the spirituality of nature—but leave those motifs so generalized and conventional that they lack any power of specific conceptual reference.
Again, the received position postulates a phase in which the theory
of the One Life dominated Wordsworth's outlook and produced a
philosophical viewpoint which finds expression in several poems

written in early 1798. In truth, however, the poems in question either fail to invoke the One Life clearly, however, or, in the case of "Tintern Abbey," offer it as merely a possible explanation of visionary intimations which resist conceptualization—and these facts unsettle the whole notion of a Wordsworthian pantheist phase.

For if we limit the poet's assertions of the One Life basically to a single imaginative project, we need not hypothesize a phase to explain the assertions. We may not be dealing with a discrete chronological zone in which a controlling philosophical attitude produced a constellation of mutually similar texts. Instead we may be dealing with a discrete poetic enterprise—the characterization of the Pedlar—which secondarily confined Wordsworth's affirmations of the One Life to early 1798 because those months happened to encompass his revision of *The Ruined Cottage*. Wordsworth's commitment to the idea of the One Life seems to have been project-specific, in short. When he turned from *The Ruined Cottage* to *Peter Bell* in April-May 1798, he maintained his interest in religious issues. Amid its comic play, *Peter Bell* sustains an anthropological meditation on the psychological origins and cultural dissemination of Christianity, and implies a serious critique of the Enlightenment skepticism personified by Pierre Bayle—whose Wordsworthian surrogate, Peter Bell himself, undergoes a conversion demonstrating the inadequacy of his irreligious hardheartedness to the experiences which Wordsworth's plot provides him.[27] Yet no one ever called *Peter Bell* a One Life poem. Turning from *The Ruined Cottage* to *Peter Bell*, Wordsworth's interest in religion remains consistent; the One Life itself disappears.

Did Wordsworth ever unreservedly embrace the notion of the One Life? Possibly and, to speak personally, I have no great objection to critics preferring to think that he did. For me, the existing evidence weighs against the possibility. The pantheistic ambience of Wordsworth's earlier poetry remains clear enough, as does his enduring attraction to both an ontological and psychological ideal of unity: he was prepared to praise Coleridge even in the 1850 *Prelude*, after all, as a thinker to whom "The unity of all hath been revealed" (2.221). With significant but by no means extensive revision he could take passages of One Life doctrine composed for the Pedlar and locate them within the Christian framework of *The Excursion*—so the idea of the One Life, even in its systematic particularity, clearly verged on positions according with his mature theological allegiances. Still, none of these considerations bears directly on the issue of his 1798 commitment to the theory of the

One Life across the breath of its systematic implications. No remarks in Wordsworth's letters, records of his conversation, or statements made by acquaintances independently confirm even his passing assent to the One Life as a certain truth. Reconstructions of Wordsworth's attitude towards the One Life must fall back on the poems. The poetry reveals a Wordsworth convinced of nature's spiritual import, and initially enthusiastic about the idea of Necessity, a legacy of his Godwinian days, but uncertain about the notion of an immanent, naturalistic divinity—and troubled by that uncertainty despite his predisposition to regard the One Life as a power simultaneously immanent and transcendent. So I advocate viewing Wordsworth's poetic deployment of the One Life idea as intellectually exploratory. He wrote of the One Life not because he was certain it existed, but because for him writing alone could resolve the question of its existence.[28]

What he wrote in seeking resolution was *The Ruined Cottage* as revised in February-March 1798. Whatever Wordsworth's beliefs, *The Ruined Cottage* remains the primary vehicle of his reception of the One Life idea, a reception which was textually localized. Concerned to explain Wordsworth's abandonment of the notion of the One Life, we need not interrogate the months spanning Coleridge's first visit and the composition of "Tintern Abbey" for an obscure process of conversion and disillusionment. Instead we can simply concentrate on the movement of certain passages into and out of a particular text. For in my view the logic of those movements can be plausibly inferred. In introducing the One Life into The *Ruined Cottage*, Wordsworth attempted to use Coleridge's philosophy to circumvent his poem's moral problems, above all to solve the problem of elegiac closure. In later removing One Life lines previously added to the poem, Wordsworth reversed himself on the issue of the specific contextual usefulness of the One Life theory, of course, but on the issue of the theory's fundamental moral adequacy as well. The ebb and flow of the One Life into and out of *The Ruined Cottage* testifies to a failed experiment. Buried in the poem's compositional history lies the story of Wordsworth's changing evaluation of the One Life idea.

NECESSARY EVILS:
THE ONE LIFE AND *THE RUINED COTTAGE*

Critics of *The Ruined Cottage* detect in the poem's expansion beyond its MS. B state a newfound optimism based on faith in the

One Life. *The Ruined Cottage* read to Coleridge at Racedown in 1797 was apparently a severely tragic narrative without final consolation. In February-March 1798 Wordsworth rewrote this narrative—preserving its bleak conclusion—to produce *The Ruined Cottage* MS. B, a version showing signs of completion sufficient to allow for its presentation as a reading text in Butler's Cornell edition. Shortly after recasting the poem in this form, however, Wordsworth decided to enlarge it. He wrote an additional four hundred lines for it, which included a consolatory conclusion, the important Pedlar narrative, and the "Not useless do I deem" lines often called "the reconciling addendum" (*RC&P*, 17–20). These passages surrendered Margaret's loneliness and death to the healing embrace of the One Life. These were also the passages—the consolatory conclusion excepted—which Wordsworth later deleted to produce *The Ruined Cottage* MS. D, a version which scholars sometimes date to early 1798, but which exists in a transcription from late 1799. In any event, Wordsworth's deletion of the Pedlar biography and "Not useless" from *The Ruined Cottage* underlies the scholarly tendency to dissociate the One Life poetry of March 1798 from *The Ruined Cottage* MS. D.

That tendency deserves reconsideration for several reasons. For one thing, Wordsworth's deletions of One Life doctrine still left *The Ruined Cottage* an ambient pantheism. The poem remained palpably pantheistic in both mood and elegiac rationale, especially given the Pedlar's closing evocation of an encompassing natural harmony. So the ghost of the One Life clearly haunts *The Ruined Cottage* MS. D. But another disadvantage of dissociating the One Life from *The Ruined Cottage* MS. D is that doing so deflects critical attention from text to phase. It encourages critics interested in Wordsworth's growing unhappiness with the idea of the One Life to look ahead chronologically, to compare his early 1798 One Life texts to the late 1798 writing done at Goslar instead of focusing their analyses on two different stages of a single text. For the moment I want to ignore Goslar and compare Wordsworth's projected expansion of *The Ruined Cottage* MS. B in 1798 to *The Ruined Cottage* MS. D. Even in the event that this version of the poem did not achieve its final extant form until 1799, the two texts invite comparative analysis. For they embody the poet's changing attitudes toward the One Life philosophy.

Most explanations of Wordsworth's revisions of *The Ruined Cottage*, as he shaped its expanded MS. B form into the MS. D version, credit the poet with formal motivations. This Wordsworth revised out of considerations of narrative economy. By increasing the presence of the One Life in his poem in March 1798, Wordsworth also increased the presence of the Pedlar, who served as philosophical expositor. The poet thereby divided the poem between "the story told about the Pedlar," in Geoffrey Hartman's phrase, and "the story he himself tells," and so bequeathed the text problems of narrative unity over which he vacillated for years.[29] I entirely agree that Wordsworth's commitment to *The Ruined Cottage* MS. D in part reflects formal considerations, signifying his preference, then at least, for a narrative centered on Margaret's situation. And certainly no one can prove that Wordsworth's elimination of the One Life from *The Ruined Cottage* MS. D was anything other than a secondary consequence of his demotion of the Pedlar. But does it seem plausible that so momentous an alteration as Wordsworth's banishment of the One Life, a theology crucial for his reconception of the story's optimistic ending, followed coincidentally from exclusively formal considerations? During the period spanning *The Ruined Cottage* MS. B and "The Wanderer," Wordsworth alternately separated and recombined the stories of Margaret and the Pedlar. When he finally reunited them for Book 1 of *The Excursion*, he toned down the Pedlar's intimations of a disturbingly pantheistic presence in nature. While we would expect such conventionality from the later Wordsworth, the fact remains that of all the changes evident in *The Ruined Cottage* MS. D, it was not Wordsworth's marginalizing of the Pedlar but his eviction of the One Life idea which, instructively, proved most lasting.

It strains credibility, surely, to imagine Wordsworth deleting all explicit allusions to the One Life from *The Ruined Cottage* MS. D without realizing that he had done so. Yet it strains credibility equally to imagine a Wordsworth self-consciously making those deletions without the exercise of philosophical judgment. If he was prepared to sacrifice the One Life for a more tightly constructed story, even that willingness reflects the idea's weakening grasp on his convictions. I speculate that in transforming his nearly completed One Life version of *The Ruined Cottage* into the MS. D version, Wordsworth was indicating his disenchantment with One Life doctrines. Through the philosophical lacunae unobtrusively present in it, MS. D renders Wordsworth's unhappiness with the One Life textually localized—and readable in its absence. From Wordsworth's acts of revisionary erasure, contextually evaluated, we can extrapolate back to the intellectual dissatisfaction motivating them. Those erasures represent the traces of a critique of the

One Life born of Wordsworth's attempt to use it poetically. Wordsworth removed the theory of the One Life from *The Ruined Cottage* MS. D because the theory could not satisfactorily realize the purpose prompting its inclusion in the poem. His dissatisfaction seemingly centered on the issue of closing consolation and therefore on "Not useless do I deem." Helen Darbishire characterized "Not useless" as merely an "addendum to MS. B," which her notes to *The Excursion* print in a form including a version of the Pedlar narrative (*PW* 5.379–404). These editorial decisions tended to privilege the Pedlar biography as Wordsworth's chief One Life exhibit, demoting "Not useless" to ancillary status, a mere "addendum." By providing a reading text of only the shorter, earlier MS. B version of *The Ruined Cottage*, Butler insists on the distinction between the 528-line fair copy of *The Ruined Cottage* MS. B and later draft additions and insertions. Yet he also shows that "Not useless" was included in a coherent version of *The Ruined Cottage*—a discernible stage of revision whether or not it ever became a formally complete *poem*—which Wordsworth wrote in March 1798. Citing Dorothy's 5 March letter to Mary Hutchinson and the line tabulation evidence on MS. B 43ʳ, Butler describes a version of *The Ruined Cottage* which William envisioned as an elaboration of the 528-line MS. B version (*RC&P*, 17–20). This 905-line elaboration—I have been calling it Wordsworth's "projected expansion" of the poem—served as the forum for the poet's affirmative reconception of Margaret's death in the light of a Necessitarian spiritual presence in nature. In this version, the idea of the One Life supplies an ending in which the Pedlar, Butler writes, can "view Margaret's tragedy from a different background and in a wider context, since 'in all things / He saw one life, and felt that it was joy'" (*RC&P*, 16).

If Wordsworth "never wrote more important lines than these," as Stephen Gill claims of "Not useless," that reflects their importance for his reconceived resolution of Margaret's situation.[30] While Butler cautions that "the order of composition of the Pedlar expansion and the reconciling addendum . . . remains doubtful," he also contends that they must have been composed at approximately the same time—and understandably so, since they represent the complementary parts of a single reconception of the poem (*RC&P*, 21). The redemptive ending Wordsworth wrote for his expansion of *The Ruined Cottage* MS. B depended conceptually on "Not useless," which preceded the spear-grass passage and the actual closing lines, and which lent the concluding mood of serenity its doctrinal underpinning. Just so, the Pedlar narrative introduced into the text at roughly this same time sketched the genealogy of the wisdom summarized in "Not useless." Wordsworth's "Not useless" lines dilate upon the moral implications of those confrontations with the One Life recounted in the Pedlar biography. The passage thereby established a specific rationale for the transcendence of suffering dramatized as the Pedlar finishes describing Margaret's decline into death. What then is the argument of "Not useless"?

"Not useless do I deem" offers Wordsworth's most incisive explanation of how love of nature leads to love of man, which itself leads to triumphant social progress. The passage interconnects the ontological, psychological, and moral aspects of the notion of Necessity. By declaring progress to be grounded in the dynamics of human responsiveness to the world—declaring it latent in even those "quiet sympathies with things that hold / An inarticulate language" (RC&P, 261; lines 2–3)—"Not useless" affirms a meliorist optimism encompassing both Margaret and the men who ponder her fate. Here, in Gill's incisive overview, the Pedlar spells

> out the argument, not as an intuition but as a demonstrable truth, that love of Nature, which demands intense participation in the life of "this majestic imagery, the cloud, / The ocean, and the firmament of heaven," must lead both to a perception of the harmony of all things and to acceptance "of human suffering or of human joy." The Pedlar's exhortation to the poet, "no longer read / The forms of things with an unworthy eye," and his concluding words of reconciling wisdom do not diminish Margaret's tragedy. By absorbing it into a larger whole the Pedlar enables the poet to pass beyond impotent grief and thus justifies the telling of her story. (Gill, 135)

The metaphysics of the One Life afford consolation for Margaret's death by denying that death demands incessant mourning. "Why should a tear be in an old man's eye," or why, at least, should it linger there more than momentarily? As incorporated in *The Ruined Cottage*, Wordsworth's "Not useless" lines make awareness of an eternal spirit immanent in nature—symbolized by the peaceful stillness of organic processes, spear-grass studded with raindrops—the ground of belief in a final transcendence of human pain and mutability. The problem of time, the anguish occasioned "From ruin and from change," ends by seeming almost illusory, an "idle dream" fostered by the passing "shews" (semblances) of life (*The Ruined Cottage* MS. D, lines 521–23). The true reality is the

One Life, and to that all-healing power Margaret has been assimilated by death. In the mere fact of the One Life resides a naturalistic theodicy. The existence of the One Life also justifies the poet's
attentiveness to both the Pedlar's story and the story's setting. For
"Not useless" celebrates a moral evolution whereby empathy for
"inarticulate" objects—the remnants of a garden, the seemingly
saddened waters of a spring—promotes an inherently expansive
capacity for moral love.

The problems emergent in this consolatory argument follow
from its Necessitarian premises. At one point in "Not useless,"
Wordsworth summarily writes,

> Thus deeply drinking in the soul of things
> We shall be wise perforce & we shall move
> From strict necessity along the path
> Of order & of good.

> (RC&P, 271)

As the phrasing reminds us, Necessity mandated an improvement
"perforce." For all its attractions, the concept remained radically
deterministic. Moreover, its determinism inevitably marginalized
human agency—human effort, achievement, and failure equally—by
relegating causal power to an ontological imperative beyond the
individual will. The determinism hardly went unnoticed in
Wordsworth's day. Godwin attempted to differentiate his philosophical system from Hartley's, for example, precisely by substituting an
ideal of the rational will for what he considered the automatism of
Hartleyan empiricism. Insisting on the distinction of sensation and
understanding, Godwin portrays human action not as the mechani-
cal reflex of pleasure and pain but as a willed consequence of truth
and reason. He could nevertheless write in *Political Justice*:

> Though mind be a real and efficient antecedent, it is in no case a
> first cause, a thing indeed of which we have in no case any exper-
> imental knowledge. Thought is [merely] the medium through
> which operations are produced. Ideas succeed each other in our
> sensorium according to certain necessary laws.[31]

According to necessary laws, he comments elsewhere, which make
it "impossible for [a man] to act in any instance otherwise than he
has acted" (Godwin 1.384). Through such statements *Political Justice* underscores the intrinsic determinism of the concept of Neces-

sity, its tendency to reintroduce deterministic explanations even when Necessitarian thinkers attempt to leave room for human moral and intellectual freedom. The absence of such freedom renders ethical judgment and action illusory. Thus the critical problem which any Necessitarian system raises, H. W. Piper notes, "is that of the existence of evil" (Piper, 46), and with it the attendant question of moral responsibility. Strict Necessitarians acknowledged the reality of neither evil nor guilt: "*Guilt* is out of the question," the early Coleridge admonished Thelwall; "I am a Necessarian, and of course deny the possibility of it" (*CLSTC* 1.213).

Necessity and pantheism, moreover, were mutually supportive aspects of a single philosophical outlook. Their coincidence in the theory of the One Life—Coleridge's aversion to pantheism notwithstanding—was hardly gratuitous. For pantheistic identifications of God and the world unavoidably presupposed a world where everything that is, is right. Wordsworth's recasting of *The Ruined Cottage* from the perspective of the One Life consequently opened his poem to problems continually raised in eighteenth-century debates over Spinoza's pantheism. These debates centered on the competing claims of world-premised and self-premised philosophical systems. "As the hypothetically complete form of 'it is' thinking," Thomas McFarland remarks, pantheism "wages mortal war with the sense of 'I am.'"[32] In the eighteenth century that warfare was understood to threaten conventional notions of both God and human identity, as McFarland rightly emphasizes:

> Spinozism, with all its logical and emotional rightness . . . involved, as we have seen, a dreadful set of corollaries, that not only subverted orthodox religion but struck at the very roots of man's emotional sense of self. For if God is immanent (*causa immanens*) in the world, rather than transcendent (*causa transiens*) or essentially separate from the world, man will have no personal identity, but will only be a finite mode of the world substance that Spinoza calls God. . . . the corollary of pantheism would be the destruction of man's freedom and man's responsibility; for if everything is God all responsibility is God's; there can be no right or wrong, for both right and wrong would be equally aspects of God. (McFarland, 87–88)

As with Necessitarian systems, the ethical implications of pantheism reduce human action to virtual meaninglessness. Worse, the allness of pantheism fundamentally devalues human individuality. No single person can count for much when construed as the transitory derivation of a holistic ontological energy.

I believe that when Wordsworth retracted "Not useless do I deem" from his projected expansion of MS. B, he was specifically rejecting the idea of Necessity as an elegiac rationale. Clearly the affirmation of Necessitarian progress stands as the central statement of the "Not useless" lines. Clearly the abiding problem of the One Life theory, given Wordsworth's recourse to it for a moral optimism, was concentrated in the role of Necessity as an ontological determinant. Wordsworth may have developed reservations about the Pedlar narrative as well. No doubt the Pedlar biography and "Not useless," interdependent arcs of a single revisionary curve, were removed from *The Ruined Cottage* at basically the same time. But Wordsworth's banishment of the One Life from *The Ruined Cottage* seems far more likely to have been motivated by emergent dissatisfaction with "Not useless." For "Not useless," positioned just before the reconciling ending, bears directly on the poem's conclusion. If the point of the One Life insertions was to offer consolation for Margaret's death, the definitive test of the material's effectiveness would have remained the final verse paragraphs. I suggest that it was at the conclusion, with what came to seem its Necessitarian complacency, that Wordsworth's dissatisfaction with the One Life reached its flash point. He appears to have abandoned the One Life idea because it could not bring Margaret's misery and dignity together in tragic perspective. In the end Wordsworth could apparently not acquiesce to a totalizing spirit which assimilated human restlessness to its own harmony only by assimilating and nullifying human identity. Wedded to the affirmative ending he had planned, he jettisoned all explicit references to One Life doctrine and relied on the Pedlar's infectious buoyancy and peaceful twilight images to carry the poem's optimism. He attempted to preserve the emotional resolution projected for the expanded version of the MS. B text while excising the philosophy originally presupposed by that resolution.

He also diminished the moral authority of the Pedlar. In Wordsworth's first two 1798 efforts to move his conclusion beyond the stark statement of Margaret's death, he made the Pedlar an inspiring teacher: the poet figure listening to the Pedlar comments, "I lookd and looked again [at the scene], & to myself / I seemed a better and a wiser man," and, secondly, "And for the tale which you have told I think / I am a better and a wiser man" (*RC&P*, 257, 259). In the version which follows the "Not useless" meditation, Wordsworth validates the philosophy of the One Life by again stressing the Pedlar's authority as preceptor and storyteller:

The old man ceased
The words he uttered shall not pass away
They had sunk into me, but not as sounds
To be expressed by visible characters
For while he spake my spirit had obeyed
The presence of his eye, my ear had drunk
The meanings of his voice. He had discoursed
Like one who in the slow & silent works
The manifold conclusions of his thought
Had brooded till Imagination's power
Condensed them to a passion whence she drew
Herself, new energies, resistless force.

(*RC&P*, 275)

Here the Pedlar's language mediates the very pulse of the One Life. His words do not register as "sounds / To be expressed by visible characters" because they invite a sympathy "With things that hold / An inarticulate language" ("Not useless"; *RC&P*, 261). The poet drinks in the Pedlar's meaning much as the Pedlar's "spirit drank / the spectacle" of the sunrise experienced as a theophany (lines 102–103). The proponent of a Necessitarian resignation, the Pedlar could hardly wield greater moral authority or rhetorical power. For his speech displays "new energies, resistless force" because, a self-fulfilling prophecy in its own right, it verbally incarnates the resistless betterment ordained by "strict necessity."

In *The Ruined Cottage* MS. D, however, the Pedlar's prophetic authority declines notably. In the reconciling conclusion which succeeded "Not useless" in Wordsworth's 1798 expansion of the MS. B version of the poem, the Pedlar's celebration of a healing spirit in nature had drastically curtailed all mourning gestures. The lesson he imparted disallowed grief, permitting the listening poet only a "nearer interest" surviving in the scene amid Nature's "plants, her weeds & flowers, / And silent overgrowings" (*RC&P*, 275, 277). After this concession to human empathy and fondness, the Pedlar immediately resumes his commentary, absolving the narrative of any touch of elegiac nostalgia. In *The Ruined Cottage* MS. D, conversely, the Pedlar's narrational skills go wholly unpraised, there is no mention of easy moral improvement (of becoming "a better and a wiser man"), and the poet-figure's "interest" becomes only the "milder" form of a movingly evoked "grief":

The old Man ceased: he saw that I was mov'd;
From that low Bench, rising instinctively,
I turned aside in weakness, nor had the power
To thank him for the tale which he had told.
I stood, and leaning o'er the garden gate
Reviewed that Woman's suffr'ings, and it seemed
To comfort me while with a brother's love
I blessed her in the impotence of grief.
At length [   ] the [   ]
Fondly, and traced with milder interest
That secret spirit of humanity
Which, 'mid the calm oblivious tendencies
Of nature, 'mid her plants, her weeds, and flowers,
And silent overgrowings, still survived.

(lines 493–506)

Despite all injunctions to detachment, the poet here mourns fraternally by relenting to a grief all the more potent, in its hold on him, for his realization that it is utterly unavailing. The changes consist merely of adjustments of emphasis, yet adjustments capable of altering the poem both intellectually and affectively. Here Margaret commands a dignity which justifies grief. It is that justification which readers sense in insisting, with Reeve Parker, that in Wordsworth's story "the pathos of Margaret's blind but heroic self-destruction, recorded in the narrator's own voice, persists to argue the limitations of [the Pedlar's] wisdom."[33]

Responses of this sort to *The Ruined Cottage* have proven common. As James H. Averill remarks, "readers have often thought that the ending of *The Ruined Cottage* evades the poem's emotional and philosophical consequences" (Averill, 55). One form of evasion involves the breaking down of transition. "Not useless do I deem" had acted as an explanatory bridge connecting Wordsworth's account of Margaret's death to the cheerful faith advocated by the Pedlar in the final verse paragraph. That bridge removed, the transition from Margaret's enervation to the Pedlar's resiliency can seem disconcertingly abrupt: "at one moment Wordsworth offers intolerable suffering," Jonathan Wordsworth remarks, "at the next dispassionate wisdom" (*MH*, 98). For other readers, the poem betrays the moral consequences of its narrative in surrendering Margaret to the comprehensive natural harmonies conjured up by the closing lines. In considering *The Ruined Cottage* without the "Not useless" addendum, Cleanth Brooks found the Pedlar's closing cheerfulness baffling, a riddle to be solved. He discovered a prospective solution in the suggestion that "Margaret with her sorrows is simply one detail of an all-encompassing and harmonious pattern"—but then added, "one shrinks from concluding that such an interpretation as this is Wordsworth's own."[34] Similar critical unhappiness occasionally focuses on "Not useless" itself. Edward Bostetter argued that Wordsworth, by resorting to "Not useless" to contextualize his reflections on Margaret's death, "in effect repudiated the story as he . . . told it."[35]

Such reactions signify a rejection of pantheistic consolation: they implicitly expose the moral dilemma posed by pantheism in Wordsworth's day as well as our own. Actually, Brooks identifies the poem's holistic naturalism with pantheism. After glancing at the Christianity of *The Excursion*, he refers the religious vision of *The Ruined Cottage* to the poet's "earlier, more pantheistic notions" (Brooks, 385). In other cases critics do not associate the objectionable perspective with pantheism. Nevertheless, it remains the pantheistic affinities of the One Life idea to which these critics object. By removing the Pedlar narrative and "Not useless," Wordsworth freed *The Ruined Cottage* from any hint of a rigorous philosophical pantheism. He did not free it from an implicit pantheism—a sacramental naturalism sketched by the Pedlar's surmise about the water sharing his sadness; by his comments on "natural wisdom" and "natural comfort"; and by his depiction of a becalmed natural order marred only by human unrest, an order preserving "the secret spirit of humanity" but beautiful especially in its impersonality (line 503). Just before passing on to the image of the spear-grass "By mist and silent rain-drops silvered o'er," the Pedlar tells the poet, "She sleeps in the calm earth, and peace is here"—not "there" but, as Averill points out, "here" (lines 515, 512). The diction makes the healing serenity of *The Ruined Cottage* seem like a palpable presence in the immediate natural scene, and deepens the pantheistic resonance of the closing harmonies. It is this pantheism of mood, a pantheistic suggestiveness, which readers stumble over in finding the elegiac conclusion of *The Ruined Cottage* morally dissatisfying.

My conjecture is simply that these readings restage Wordsworth's own response to the expanded *The Ruined Cottage* MS. B—that he too found the text's Necessitarian consolation dehumanizing in the end. Lewis Patton and Peter Mann conclude that Coleridge's disenchantment with the "dry and abstract complacencies of Priestley on the themes of evil and suffering" was what terminated *his* faith in Necessitarian progress (Patton and Mann, lxvi), and Wordsworth may have known of Coleridge's early reservations about "fatal Necessity"in 1798. Certainly the changes introduced into the "Not useless" passage in its *Excursion* form center on the question of moral agency:

> Thus deeply drinking-in the soul of things,
> We shall be wise perforce; and, while inspired
> By choice, and conscious that the Will is free,
> Shall move unswerving, even *as if* impelled
> By strict necessity, along the path
> Of order and of good.
>
> (4.1265–70, italics mine)[36]

In their denial of moral automatism, these lines circumvent the Necessitarian meliorism capable of declaring human pain an existential illusion, a passing "shew." Closer to the time when Wordsworth retracted the Pedlar narrative and "Not useless" from *The Ruined Cottage* there is the disturbingly insensate Lucy "Roll'd round in earth's diurnal course / With rocks and stones and trees!" ("A slumber did my spirit seal"; *LB*, lines 7–8). The pantheistic objectification which Lucy undergoes here at least shows a Wordsworth troubled by the metaphysics of the One Life during his Goslar residence.

But the critical reception of *The Ruined Cottage* and the poet's lifelong reverence of individual human life—even in its humblest, most socially marginalized forms—encourage the inference that Wordsworth, perhaps months before Goslar, found Margaret's death and the Pedlar's detachment troubling. The results of his experiment with the possibilities of One Life consolation may well have contented him only briefly. In exploring the further implications of the One Life idea in *The Ruined Cottage*, the poet finally deemed it useless for elegiac consolation, unacceptable both for its Necessitarian imperative and its promotion of holistic Being over human individuation. The One Life philosophy seems to have lost its hold on Wordsworth because of its exemplary inadequacy to Margaret's prolonged anguish. Human pain disappeared too easily, and death counted for too little, against the cosmic backdrop of the One Life.

THE ONE LIFE AND CHRISTIANITY

Alert to the imaginative possibilities of the theory of the One Life, the Wordsworth of early 1798 eagerly initiated revision of *The Ruined Cottage*. He nearly completed those revisions, developing for them a complex of One Life images and phrases which spilled over into other poems written during that period—especially poems concerned with social progress, such as "The Old Cumberland Beggar" and poems of emotionally heightened responsiveness to nature, such as "Lines written at a distance" and "Tintern Abbey." By the time of "Tintern Abbey," however, he seems hesitant to invoke the One Life in explaining his own spiritual intimations: the usefulness of the One Life idiom for describing visionary rapture is clear enough, but no clearer than Wordsworth's sense that the One Life philosophy may be "a vain belief." So Wordsworth may have outgrown his first enthusiasm for the theory by July 1798. Or his doubts about the One Life may date to March of that year if, as I have speculated, he abandoned his projected revision of *The Ruined Cottage* MS. D due to his sense of the inhumanity, the unwise passiveness, of Necessitarian detachment toward Margaret's suffering. It is true that the completion of *The Ruined Cottage* MS. D—and thus Wordsworth's removal of the Pedlar narrative and "Not useless" from the poem—cannot with certainty be dated earlier than late 1799. It is also true that the powerfully pantheistic statement in DC MS. 33 dates from early 1799. At Sockburn later in 1799, I noted previously, Wordsworth briefly placed a revised form of that passage in the Two-Part *Prelude*, and he permanently retained Pedlar lines transferred to the poem. But in his continual reinvention of himself, Wordsworth habitually re-used verse. His 1799 return to the Pedlar biography for the Two-Part *Prelude* testifies to a compositional habit more than veering of conviction back to an earlier position. Based on the testimony of "Tintern Abbey," as well as the absence of One Life references in *Peter Bell* and the Goslar poetry, I am inclined to agree with Jonathan Wordsworth that by July 1798, if not March, Wordsworth's commitments to the One Life had waned appreciably.

What I want to suggest in closing is that the lapsing of the One Life clarified Wordsworth's instinctive allegiances to Christianity, that it may even have been prompted in part by them. The received position on Wordsworth and the One Life posits a pantheist who divested the idea of its Christian affinities in appropriating it. This Wordsworth, it is said, discarded not merely the theory's conceptual infrastructure, and not merely its Unitarian dogma, but its entire relationship to orthodox Christianity. Here Wordsworth is sometimes seen as dismissing Christianity with a mildly patronizing forbearance: the poet of 1798 "considers Christianity a falsehood," Matlack writes in an influential article, "albeit a harmless one that inspires some good" (Matlack, "Classical Argument and Romantic Persuasion," 107). Alternately, he is seen as simply (and completely) uninterested in Christian thought, so that in his hands, Jonathan Wordsworth writes, "the One Life lost any connection with formal Christianity" (MH, 202). In my view, conversely, the idea retained important ulterior connections to Christianity for Wordsworth as it did (to a far greater degree) for Coleridge. The residual Christianity of Wordsworth's One Life poetry is not a matter of dogma. In 1798 Wordsworth's interest in doctrinal questions was indisputably casual at best. His Christian sympathies did not clearly include intellectual assent to many High Church dogmas. Yet Wordsworth's faith in God, his insistence upon a God of love—a Deity whose intuited presence imparts "the lesson deep of love"—and his compassion for society's victims were all profoundly Christian in both their personal and cultural associations. Christian attitudes, imparted by his upbringing and reinforced by his society, were deeply ingrained in the poet's habitual moral responses. They explain his distinction between God and Nature in the Pedlar's theophanic visions. For the distinction reflects a religiously conventional tendency to think of a God who both inhabits and transcends the natural world.

The representation of deity in the Pedlar narrative, then, would not have unduly troubled the Christian readers of Wordsworth's day. But Wordsworth also insists on the integration of traditional faith and personal experience in the Pedlar's religious outlook. For Wordsworth's genealogy of faith derives the Pedlar's prophetic powers from certain preparatory experiences, among them a formative early acquaintance with the Bible. When the young Pedlar's work as a shepherd brought him into daily communion with nature,

> Oh then how beautiful, how bright, appeared
> The written promise. He had early learned
> To reverence the volume which displays
> The mystery, the life which cannot die
> But in the mountains did he FEEL his faith,

There did he see the writing. All things there
Breathed immortality, revolving life,
And greatness still revolving, infinite.

(Pedlar narrative, lines 119–26)

"Perhaps the culmination of the Pedlar's education at the hands of nature," Albert O. Wlecke writes, "occurs in the way nature *corroborates* the Christian doctrine of immortality."[37] In the lines above, "the written promise" signifies the Gospel promise of deliverance from death. The Bible proclaims spiritual truth, the immortality of the soul in particular. Here the Pedlar's ability to "see the writing" does not impart a faith. Rather, it emotionally intensifies—"in the mountains did he FEEL"—a faith already held. His boyhood introduction to that faith readies him for his later encounters with the universal mind mysteriously emanating through the natural world.

The Pedlar's faith consequently straddles nature and revelation, marrying mystical intimation to biblical authority. This marriage vindicates vision, but the vindications work reciprocally in the prophetic economy Wordsworth dramatizes. Certainly the Pedlar's prior faith in spiritual reality encourages his receptivity to the One Mind. But then the Pedlar's prophetic experiences reflexively reauthenticate Christianity's "written promise," inscribing nature with the Word made visible: there "did he see the writing." The reconfirmed authority of the Bible can then further legitimate the Pedlar's visions, tempering their enthusiasm or, more accurately, showing that they are not mere projections of enthusiasm at all. It remains the Pedlar's spiritual visions which Wordsworth, far and away, prefers to concentrate on. But like Wesley and other advocates of a religion of the heart, the poet refers visionary insight to traditional canons of truth. He vindicates the Pedlar's religious intuitions by declaring them continuous and consistent with Christian tradition. It is hardly accidental that, as David G. Riede writes, "like Moses or, more aptly, like Jesus, the Pedlar receives his prophetic vocation on the summit of a mountain."[38] Just so, the echoes of Genesis, the Psalms, and St. Paul which Wordsworth incorporates in the Pedlar narrative, allusively restage the reconciliation of scriptural truth and personal insight informing the Pedlar's religious experiences and outlook.

Initially, in fact, Wordsworth seems to have understood the One Life idea as a reconciliation of pantheism and with religious ideas most familiar to him from Christianity. The example of Coleridge foregrounded the theory's congruence with the Christian faith. Wordsworth could avoid a conceptually systematic pantheism, consequently, while still drawing on the ambient "pantheism" of the One Life notion so as to write a poetry dramatizing spiritual discovery amid nature. Having avoided literal pantheist commitments, he could also retain the Christian affinities of the One Life idea, in that way conventionalizing the spiritual affirmations of his poems. As a reconciliation of pantheism and Christianity, however, the theory of the One Life was a contradiction waiting to unravel. For "the great Romantic philosophical controversy over pantheism," McFarland summarily remarks, took shape, "in its ethical and eschatological implications, [as] a struggle between Spinoza and Christianity" (McFarland, 53). Entangled in that struggle, the notion of the One Life was a volatile construct incapable of maintaining the mediations for which Wordsworth employed it. He discovered its limitations, I suggest again, in attempting to base the elegiac rationale of *The Ruined Cottage* upon it. I suggest further that the discovery threw Wordsworth, by dialectical reflex, back upon his own deeply rooted but largely undeveloped Christian moral sympathies.

There is textual evidence hinting at Wordsworth's recognition of the Christian affiliations of his dissatisfaction with the One Life philosophy. As he revised *The Ruined Cottage* to minimize its pantheistic implications, he also gave the poem, at one point, an additional Christian inflection. In its transition from the projected expansion of the MS. B version to the completed MS. D version, *The Ruined Cottage* came to include these beautiful lines:

> my spirit clings
> To that poor woman: so familiarly
> Do I perceive her manner, and her look
> And presence, and so deeply do I feel
> Her goodness, that not seldom in my walks
> A momentary trance comes over me;
> And to myself I seem to muse on one
> By sorrow laid asleep or borne away,
> A human being destined to awake
> To human life, or something very near
> To human life, when he shall come again
> For whom she suffered.

> (lines 364–75)

Susan Wolfson correctly claims that here Wordsworth's "phrasing glimmers with a Christian promise," even as Averill correctly credits the Pedlar's language with "calling up a version of Christian immortality."[39] The Pedlar's vision of Margaret's redemption, Wolfson adds, "scarcely contains [his] recognition of its illusory nature," and Jonathan Wordsworth has commented similarly that "the associations of suffering and a second coming might seem to be Christian, but a tone nearer to romance or fairy-story has been evoked in 'By sorrow laid asleep or borne away'" (Wolfson, 108; *MH*, 138). It would be overly severe, however, to read Wordsworth's passage for an irony conjuring Christian hopes only to subvert them. The displaced Christianity of the Pedlar's trance no doubt reflects Wordsworth's own distance from a fully confident Christian faith in 1798. But the Christian palimpsest encoded in Wordsworth's beautiful lines—both in its pertinence to Margaret and its rendering of a Pedlar moved to transcendent surmise—eloquently captures Christianity's appeal to human suffering, and to William Wordsworth.[40]

The addition of this passage to *The Ruined Cottage* MS. D complemented Wordsworth's deletion of "Not useless do I deem" and the Pedlar narrative and helped pry the text away from the philosophy of the One Life. This turn from the One Life shows Wordsworth turning, slightly, toward Christianity. His evocation of Christian values remains muted, with the poem displacing all of the doctrines it (merely) glances at, and may have been neither self-conscious not intentional. It would prove prophetic nonetheless. Critics commonly agree that Wordsworth's early years disclose him celebrating a spirit seemingly immanent in nature, while his later years increasingly reveal him looking beyond nature for spiritual meaning and fulfillment. I object neither to this view nor its implication of the early Wordsworth's pantheistic sympathies. But the sympathies appear to have been self-interrogating and provisional from the beginning. If the Wordsworth of 1798 was unprepared to write an explicitly Christian poetry, he was unequally prepared to endorse a conceptually rigorous pantheism. Wordsworth's struggles with the ending of *The Ruined Cottage* display his awareness, perhaps as early as March 1798, that oneness with nature was no unequivocal good.

CHAPTER THREE

Faith's Progress, 1799–1804

'Twere long to tell
What spring and autumn, what the winter snows,
And what the summer shade, what day and night,
The evening and the morning, what my dreams
And what my waking thoughts, supplied to nurse
That spirit of religious love in which
I walked with Nature.

—Wordsworth,
The Two-Part *Prelude*, 2.401–7

The period from Wordsworth's initial reception of the One Life to his completion of the Immortality Ode—roughly, late 1798 to early 1804—witnessed no dramatic revolutions in his religious thinking. The poetry of these years often subordinates religion to other issues. While a reflection of his varied interests, this subordination follows in part from Wordsworth's merely fitful attention to *The Recluse*. Because Wordsworth projected *The Recluse* as the main vehicle of his religious thought—or so I will argue—he reserved major issues of faith for the sustained treatment that an epic compass would permit. But these years do reveal the gradual consolidation of two tendencies. The first involves increasing conventionality. Well before John Wordsworth's death in February

1805, William Wordsworth's religious outlook was becoming more obviously Christian. The Christian aspects of his 1799–1804 poems remain largely implicit, the poetry's orthodox sympathies emerging in its moral attitudes and use of diction and imagery with familiar Christian associations. Still, the differences between the personally intuited "motion and spirit" of "Tintern Abbey" and the traditionally designated "God," "Heaven," and "soul" of the Immortality Ode are revealing and important. As I have argued previously, these differences were delayed consequences of the self-examination which followed from Wordsworth's unhappiness with his One Life version of *The Ruined Cottage*. Another legacy of that restiveness was a certain preoccupation with death. In its theological implications, Wordsworth's interest in death and mourning came to rest on the notion of the soul. Culminating in the reaffirmations of the Immortality Ode, his broodings over mortality independently encouraged his return to the Anglican Church. So, finally, did his changing domestic situation and personal life. Taken altogether, the years 1799–1804 reveal the poet moving decisively closer to the individualistic, doctrinally selective Christian faith of his later years.

THE ONE LIFE AND THE BLESSED BABE

After his March 1798 revision of *The Ruined Cottage*, Wordsworth's first significant reconsideration of his religious outlook came with his efforts, in late 1799, to complete the Two-Part *Prelude*. In Part 1, written in late 1798, he had basically ignored religious questions. The conceptual framework surrounding the spots of time derives from aesthetic theory: the ideas of the beautiful and sublime, primarily as analyzed by Edmund Burke and deployed poetically by Mark Akenside.[1] When Wordsworth pauses in the Two-Part *Prelude* to refer nature's moral influence to an operative teleology, he postulates the actions of nature spirits, guardian genii loci:

> The mind of man is fashioned and built up
> Even as a strain of music. I believe
> That there are spirits which, when they would form
> A favored being, from his very dawn
> Of infancy do open out the clouds
> As at the touch of lightning, seeking him

With gentle visitation—quiet powers,
Retired, and seldom recognized, yet kind,
And to the very meanest not unknown—
With me, though rarely, in my boyish days
They communed. Others too there are, who use,
Yet haply aiming at the self-same end,
Severer interventions, ministry
More palpable—and of their school was I

(1.67–80)

These spirits Part 1 successively addresses as "ye beings of the
hills! / And ye that walk the woods and open heaths"; "Ye powers
of earth! ye genii of the springs! / And ye that have your voices in
the clouds," and so on (1.130–31, 186–87). There was a time in
Wordsworth studies when such lines provoked analysis of the
poet's animism. More recently, Jonathan Wordsworth has swept the
field in remarking that

> The "Godkins and Goddesslings" are unfortunate, but they fade
> out very early in the poem, and one could argue that they convey
> Wordsworth's sense of having had a divinely favored childhood
> with an acceptable *lack* of credibility (we should not, after all, be
> happier if he said that God had led him to steal boats). In fact I
> think we read past them easily enough, aware at once of their
> clumsiness and their usefulness to the poet.[2]

Scattered amid the powerfully authenticated scenes recounted by
Part 1 of the Two-Part *Prelude*, these eighteenth-century stage
props appear almost garishly misplaced. They are no more believ-
able than cartoon characters. The poet's invocation of them, however, shows the lengths he would go to *avoid* invoking the One
Life: for by giving nature's benevolent influence a spiritual explanation, Wordsworth's genii loci replace the "spirit and pulse of
good" which Wordsworth could praise in "The Old Cumberland
Beggar" (line 77), but which, by late 1798, he determinedly bars
from his autobiographical poem.
    What Wordsworth's "genii of the springs" finally suggest is a
poet somewhat adrift in his religious thinking, in the aftermath of
losing his One Life enthusiasm, and unwilling to let intellectual
irresolution call a halt to composition. We might even understand
the occasionally overt, almost self-regarding allusiveness of the
poem's initial part—its conjuring of *The Tempest*, "Frost at Mid-

night," and *The Pleasures of Imagination* (*NCP* notes)—as signs of its origin in artifice, in literary convention, with Wordsworth making his way imaginatively by falling back on poetic precedent. With the guardian spirits of Part 1, Wordsworth, depending on the dustiest neoclassicisms, could insist that nature guided him spiritually and still avoid specific philosophical rationales. But that strategy could not carry the second section of the poem. Part 1 had attempted to "make [the poet's] infancy a visible scene / On which the sun is shining" (1.463–64). Part 2 carried the story to the period of early adulthood, and needed more specific (and convincing) philosophical foundations. Part 2 consequently evolved into a religious poem in its closing passages, as Wordsworth, needing a theory of moral and imaginative development, returned to poetry of the One Life written the previous year. That return allowed him to construct a compelling prophetic persona for himself. But it also required him to intellectually alter the One Life motifs he borrowed—to tone down their pantheistic qualities, to present them as hypothetical surmises, and to juxtapose them with passages of a very different spiritual import.[3]

Wordsworth transferred two Pedlar passages to the Two-Part *Prelude*. The first, concerning the "possible sublimity" suggested by aural experience (2.351–71), both fit with Part 1 of the poem and avoided explicit reference to the One Life. The second consists of these lines:

> From Nature and her overflowing soul
> I had received so much that all my thoughts
> Were steeped in feeling. I was only then
> Contented when with bliss ineffable
> I felt the sentiment of being spread
> O'er all that moves, and all that seemeth still,
> O'er all that, lost beyond the reach of thought
> And human knowledge, to the human eye
> Invisible, yet liveth to the heart
> O'er all that leaps, and runs, and shouts, and sings,
> Or beats the gladsome air, o'er all that glides
> Beneath the wave, yea, in the wave itself
> And mighty depth of waters. Wonder not
> If such my transports were, for in all things
> I saw one life, and felt that it was joy.

(2.446–60)

The lines describe Nature as the domain of a soul, which over-
flows as a "sentiment of being" universally present in the world,
its creatures, and even the waters, interrelating them as variant
but harmonious modes of the "one life." To put the matter that
way, however, is to ignore the generalizing thrust of Wordsworth's
lyricism. The real unity affirmed here is a unity of sensibility
which leaves thought steeped in feeling. Wordsworth's opening reference to Nature's "overflowing soul" remains conventional, his
use of the -eth suffix giving his catalogue a biblical resonance.
Through the heightened tone he maintains, Wordsworth stages the
passage as an expression of the speaker's joy rather than an exposition of a philosophical system.

But this lyrical burst, revealingly, is also nearly surrounded by
qualifications. In "Tintern Abbey" a year earlier, Wordsworth at
one point wrote, "If this / be but a vain belief," allowing himself
roughly half-a-line of hedging (lines 50–51). Consider the Two-Part
Prelude transition to his relocated Pedlar passage:

> I mean to speak
> Of that interminable building reared
> By observation of affinities
> In objects where no brotherhood exists
> To common minds. My seventeenth year was come,
> And, whether from this habit rooted now
> So deeply in my mind, or from excess
> Of the great social principle of life
> Coercing all things into sympathy,
> To unorganic natures I transferred
> My own enjoyments, or, the power of truth
> Coming in revelation, I conversed
> With things that really are, I at this time
> Saw blessings spread around me like a sea.

> (2.431–44)

Wordsworth introduces his account of "the one life" as a mere possibility: "or, the power of truth / Coming in revelation." At the
same time, he expressly admits that his habit of teasing out fanci-
ful similarities "In objects where no brotherhood exists" or, alternately, that the "social principle" manifesting itself perceptually,
may account for his recognition of an omnipresent spirit in nature.
The One Life, in short, may be a projection, "To unorganic

natures . . . transferred" from the poet's mind. The lines which succeed Wordsworth's One Life affirmation similarly disallow certainty:

> If this be error, and another faith
> Find easier access to the pious mind,
> Yet were I grossly destitute of all
> Those human sentiments which make this earth
> So dear if I should fail with grateful voice
> To speak of you, ye mountains, and ye lakes
> And sounding cataracts, ye mists and winds
> That dwell among the hills where I was born.
>
>   (2.465–72)

The poet acknowledges the possibility of intellectual mistake, concedes the prospective advantages of "another faith," and then lets spiritual universality dissolve away before local attachment. Other lines near the end of Part 2 help undermine Wordsworth celebration of a pantheistic presence by touching upon the mind's "auxiliar light," and by showing Wordsworth characterizing himself as one who has lived "With God and Nature communing" (2.417, 476). In these ways the *Prelude* of 1799 massively compounds the equivocating doubts of "Tintern Abbey."

Wordsworth displaces his One Life affirmations further, however, by his portrait of the infant babe. This famous passage is of central importance for the argument of Part 2 of the 1799 *Prelude* and, although it refers to "the one great mind," it announces a religious vision notably unlike the Pedlar's intimations of the universal mind. In the Blessed Babe lines Wordsworth humanizes and internalizes a divinity which his One Life poetry had located in nature. In images prefiguring the mutual fittedness praised in the later Prospectus to *The Recluse*, Wordsworth insists on the infant boy's—"blest the Babe / Nursed in *his* Mother's arms" (2.269–70)—redemptive connection to nature. Unlike the celestial visitant of the Immortality Ode, this child hardly appears an alienated exile:

> No outcast he, bewildered and depressed;
> Along his infant veins are interfused
> The gravitation and the filial bond
> Of Nature that connect him with the world.
> Emphatically such a being lives

An inmate of this *active* universe.
From Nature largely he receives, nor so
Is satisfied, but largely gives again.

(2.291–98)

Wordsworth's use of the word "active" recalls "There is an active principle," but the overtly pantheistic quality of the early fragment gives way here to those reciprocal exchanges by which the human mind constructs meaning from experience. The humanizing orientation of the Two-Part *Prelude* emerges clearly if we simply dwell on a certain connection drawn by F. R. Leavis. Leavis compared "A motion and a spirit, that impels / All thinking things, all objects of all thought, / And rolls through all things" from "Tintern Abbey" (lines 101–3) to "A virtue which irradiates and exalts / All objects through all intercourse of sense" from the Two-Part *Prelude* (2.289–90): the motif employed to describe an ontological presence in "Tintern Abbey" in the 1799 *Prelude* describes the quality of the mother's emotional presence to the child.[4] The natural relents to the human as the locus of meaning.

And as the locus of the divine. Wordsworth's humanizing of the One Life in the Blessed Babe lines makes the child's mind a reduplicative agent of the mind of God. He posits an essential similarity between the creative power of the Deity and the child's imagination:

And—powerful in all sentiments of grief,
Of exultation, fear and joy—his mind,
Even as an agent of the one great mind,
Creates, creator and receiver both,
Working but in alliance with the works
Which it beholds. Such, verily, is the first
Poetic spirit of our human life—
By uniform control of after years
In most abated and suppressed, in some
Through every change of growth or of decay
Preeminent till death.

(2.300–310)

In Wordsworth's projected expansion of *The Ruined Cottage* MS B., the One Life was to assimilate Margaret's identity to its totalizing self-aggrandizement. The Blessed Babe, conversely, is ennobled by his relationship with "the one great mind." The divine sanctifies human individuality. Pantheistic unity vanishes before Wordsworth's emphasis on the orchestrations of human consciousness, the infant mind's eagerness "to combine / In one appearance all the elements" of his experience (2.277–78). So if the Two-Part *Prelude* recycles Pedlar material to avow the divinity of nature, the poem's greatest emphases fall nonetheless on the creativity of the human soul. Wordsworth's analysis of infant sensibility, its implications mythically elaborated, would culminate in the visionary claims of the Immortality Ode. Even his admission that most people lose their original creativity looks ahead to the Ode.

Wordsworth's earliest drafts towards the Two-Part *Prelude* in MS. JJ include lines prefiguring his portrait of the Blessed Babe. Here the poet hopes that his appreciation of nature's gifts will not make him

> Forget what might demand a loftier song
> How oft the eternal spirit, he that has
> His life in unminaginable things
> And he who painting what he is in all
> The visible imagery of all the worlds
> Is yet apparent chiefly as the soul
> Of our first sympathies—Oh bounteous power
> In childhood, in rememberable days
> How often did thy love renew for me
> Those naked feelings which when thou wouldst form
> A living thing thou sendest like a breeze
> Into its infant being.

> > (*TPP*, 95; MS. JJ Uʳ)

Given this passage's demotion of nature, and Wordsworth's concentration on nature's beneficent influences in the Two-Part *Prelude*, one can readily understand why these lines finally found no place in the completed poem. They nevertheless afford a revealing perspective on the conventionality of the poet's underlying religious attitudes in late 1798. In lines written not for a dramatic character but about himself, Wordsworth invokes a God who is a loving person, whose being remains unimaginable in its transcendence, and who images himself "in all / The visible imagery of all the worlds" just as the God of "Frost at Midnight" "from eternity doth teach / Himself in all, and all things in himself" (lines 66–67).

Equally revealing, however, is Wordsworth's passing reference to "a loftier song." Coleridge's advocacy of this more ambitious under- taking helps explain why Coleridge, as Jonathan Wordsworth points out (*NCP* 26n.2), looms so large in Wordsworth's mind at the ending of Part 2 of the Two-Part *Prelude*. But Part 1 had itself ended with the apologetic explanation, again addressed to Coleridge,

> Meanwhile my hope has been that I might fetch
> Reproaches from my former years, whose power
> May spur me on, in manhood now mature,
> To honorable toil.

> (1.450–53)

The "honorable toil" is of course "the loftier song": Wordsworth in both cases differentiates his autobiographical poetry from the weightier philosophic poem he plans to write. The Two-Part *Pre- lude* had been Nature's poem; the loftier poem dedicated to "the eternal spirit" was to be *The Recluse*.

THE IDEA OF *THE RECLUSE*

The secondary literature on Wordsworth has featured frequent dis- cussion of *The Recluse* in recent years. *The Recluse* was an ambi- tious philosophical epic which Wordsworth labored unsuccessfully to finish. It was to consist of three main sections—*The Excursion*, finished in nine books, represents the second part—and to include *The Prelude* as what the Preface to *The Excursion* calls the "ante- chapel . . . of a gothic church" (*PW* 5.2). The idea of *The Recluse* originated in Wordsworth and Coleridge's early conversations and, more specifically, from the notion of the One Life, the moral and social implications of which *The Recluse* would have propounded at epic length. Apparently, the project did not depend categorically on the One Life per se: to the extent that Wordsworth ever had the poem's philosophical premises firmly in mind—and his later corre- spondence suggests he never did (*LEY*, 452, 464)—they seem to have involved a conceptually imprecise ideal of unity. But clearly *The Recluse* emerged against a backdrop of religious speculation which Coleridge had mastered, reshaped, and in 1797–1798 passed on to an initially enthusiastic Wordsworth. This perspective on the genealogy of *The Recluse* has decided advantages. Waving off coincidence, it posits an integral relationship between Wordsworth's spiritual self-examination, as he mulled over the One Life, and his projection of *The Recluse*, events of momentous importance both of which occurred in early 1798. It also helps explain why Wordsworth found the poem so impossible to finish: it presumed a religious position he continued to find congenial in some respects, but which in other ways he had outgrown.

Yet not all critics agree that *The Recluse* was rooted in religious questions. Kenneth Johnston has preferred to describe the philosophy of *The Recluse* as a blend of German idealism and British empiricism oriented toward the question of the relationship of consciousness to the world, and of the individual person to society at large.[5] As unobjectionable as this description might seem, it serves Johnston's case for a radically secularized *Recluse*. In Johnston's reconstruction of Wordsworth's plans for *The Recluse*, the poem

> was to have displaced outmoded religious epics (and perhaps religious scriptures themselves) with persuasive representations of a humanistic philosophy integrating psychological, scientific, and sociopolitical truths into epistemological—or at least imaginative—coherence. (Johnston, xii)

Johnston recurrently allows the poetry's religious interests, but stresses its foundational secularism. In a discussion of the panoramic scope of Wordsworth's poem, for example, he at one point remarks,

> Only God is left out. Many epic dreams of the day were religious, but the *topoi* of projects like . . . Wordsworth's were not supernatural or mythological, but secular and modern, reflecting the enlightened advances their age was heir to. Their framework of justification would not be that of *Paradise Lost*: this is the significance of Coleridge's claiming *The Recluse*, some years later, as "the first and finest philosophical poem" in English—it would not be religious. (Johnston, 11)

Johnston's book on *The Recluse* has been called "the most comprehensive and valuable study of Wordsworth" since Hartman's by no less a Wordsworthian than Peter Manning[6]—and certainly one could find an adversary less formidable than Kenneth Johnston with whom to pick fights. Yet Johnston's account of *The Recluse* strikes me as seriously misleading. The secularization informing *The Recluse* does not replace Biblical scripture outright with radically humanistic truths, or leave out God and religion. The secularizing imperative of *The Recluse* seeks to revise and preserve religious tradition instead of casting it away.

We do well to recall, regarding Coleridge's characterization of *The Recluse* as a "philosophical poem" (*CLSTC* 2.1034), that in Wordsworth's day "philosophical" was not considered the antonym of "religious." The word "philosophy," Robert Ryan notes, was employed "to signify what is commonly called 'natural theology'— an area of investigation dealing with those truths about God and human destiny which may be discovered by reason or instinct without recourse to revelation."[7] As to how Coleridge himself intended the term in referring to *The Recluse*, we can only speculate, but later statements at least provide speculation a basis. Coleridge reminisced about the compass of *The Recluse* as he had understood it in an 1815 letter to Wordsworth: *The Recluse* was

> to have affirmed a Fall in some sense, as a fact, the possibility of which cannot be understood from the nature of the Will, but the reality of which is attested by Experience & Conscience— . . . to [have then pointed] out however a manifest Scheme of Redemption from this Slavery, of Reconciliation from this Enmity with Nature—what are the Obstacles, the *Antichrist* that must be & already is—and to conclude by a grand didactic swell on the necessary identity of a true Philosophy with true Religion, agreeing in the results and differing only as the analytic and synthetic process. (*CLSTC* 4.574–75)

Here the conservative Trinitarian of 1815 imposes himself pretty obviously. We may prefer to doubt that Wordsworth and Coleridge discussed (let alone agreed about) the inherent corruption of the "Will" in 1798. But throughout his life the fervently religious Coleridge insisted on the "identity of a true Philosophy with True Religion," and I cannot think him wrong in recalling the epic's central preoccupation with "a Fall in some sense" and a reconciling deliverance from it. Moreover, these memories agree with a second Coleridgean description of the scheme of *The Recluse*, this one from *Table Talk*. Here Coleridge remembers that Wordsworth's plan

> was to treat man as man—a subject of eye, ear, touch, taste, in contact with external nature, informing the senses from the mind and not compounding a mind out of the senses; then the pastoral and other states, assuming a satiric or Juvenalian spirit

as he approached the high civilization of cities and towns; and then opening a melancholy picture of the present state of degeneracy and vice; thence revealing the necessity for and proof of the whole state of man and society being subject to and illustrative of a redemptive process in operation, showing how this idea reconciled all the anomalies, and how it promised future glory and restoration.[8]

Once more *The Recluse* as Coleridge recalls it was to have dramatized moral error, spiritual redemption, and "future glory."

Beyond the testimony of Coleridge, there remains the manifest evidence of Wordsworth's own writings. His comparison of *The Recluse* to a Gothic cathedral in the Preface to *The Excursion* has not always been taken as seriously as it deserves. It hardly seems fair to dwell on the architectural implications of Wordsworth's metaphor and ignore the fact that he speaks specifically of a *church*. The metaphor allowed for certain evasive rationalizations, permitting Wordsworth to defend time denied *The Recluse* for work on shorter poems by systematically incorporating those poems, figured as "little cells, oratories, and sepulchral recesses," within the cathedral of *The Recluse* (Preface to *The Excursion, PW* 5.2). That point notwithstanding, Wordsworth's prefatory comments introduced the general public to the work on which he believed his reputation would finally depend: surely his central metaphor was carefully considered. It seems an appropriate metaphor for the sections of *The Recluse* which survive. The One Life work of early 1798 rests upon theories of an immanent divinity. Although its complexity can accommodate multiple readings, obviously enough, *The Prelude* recurrently invokes God: it is hardly for no reason that Stephen Gill can summarily declare, "*The Prelude* is a religious poem."[9] Leaving aside *The Prelude* and the One Life texts of early 1798, the surviving work intended for *The Recluse* consists most prominently of *The Excursion* and *The Tuft of Primroses*. The orthodoxy of *The Excursion* has been questioned in both Wordsworth's day and our own.[10] No one, however, can fairly question the poem's preoccupation with theological issues, or its faith in a superintending deity. *The Tuft of Primroses* moves from the problem of mutability and the ruined cottage of the Sympsons to the fate of the Grande Chartreuse and the monastic ideal of Saints Basil and Gregory. All extant *Recluse* materials, in short, disclose an organizing interest in religious questions, and affirm some form of religious faith.

What they disclose more specifically is Wordsworth's persistent efforts to adapt his religious heritage to the needs of an enlightened modern age. No text displays this revisionary struggle, or demonstrates the religious commitments of *The Recluse*, more clearly than the Prospectus to *The Recluse* itself—although for most Romanticists that claim may almost seem unaccountable. The quarter century which has elapsed since the publication of M. H. Abrams' *Natural Supernaturalism* has not seen his reading of the Prospectus powerfully called into question; and the Prospectus serves Abrams as a secular touchstone par excellence, the exemplary text in his presentation of Romanticism as a modern humanism. For Abrams, in the Prospectus "the heights and depths of the mind are to replace heaven and hell," and not merely as poetic *topoi* but as the site of truth (*NS*, 25). For Harold Bloom, similarly, the Prospectus affirms "a more naturalistic humanism than Blake could endure": the "most defiant humanism in Wordsworth salutes the immediate possibility of this earthly paradise naturalizing itself in the here and now."[11] Wordsworth scholars can attest that these two statements epitomize an influential consensus. From this perspective, the secular elements of the Prospectus do not locate it transitionally between traditional faith and modern denial. Rather, they control Wordsworth's text, rendering its intellectual vision fully and confidently naturalistic.

Arguments that Wordsworth disavows Christian supernaturalism in the Prospectus rest principally on the address to Urania. Here is its earliest version, MS. 1 from DC MS. 45, the version which should theoretically prove least Christian, composed between 1799 and 1802:

> Urania, I shall need
> Thy guidance, or a greater Muse, if such
> Descend to earth, or dwell in highest heaven.
> For I must tread on Shadowy ground, must sink
> Deep, and ascend aloft, and   worlds
> To which the Heaven of heavens is but a veil.
> All strength, all terror, single or in bands
> That ever was out forth by personal Form
> Jehovah, with his thunder, and the choir
> Of shouting Angels, and Th' empyreal Thrones
> I pass them unalarm'd. The darkest pit
> Of the profoundest hell, night, chaos, death
> Nor aught of blinder vacancy scoop'd out
> By help of dreams, can breed such fear and awe

As fall upon me often when I look
Into my soul, into the soul of man
My haunt, and the main region of my song[12]

Radically secularizing interpretations of this passage begin unob-
jectionably by construing the depictions of "Jehovah" and his
"shouting angels" as personifications, tropical "puttings[s] forth,"
of certain ideas of power and the emotions those ideas have typically elicited. These interpretations then mistakenly credit
Wordsworth with believing that the existence of figural representations of God means that all Gods are merely figures. From this failure of discrimination Wordsworth emerges as a kind of Lake District Nietzsche boldly declaring that man created God. Or at the
least as another Blake stipulating that "All deities reside in the
human breast" (*The Marriage of Heaven and Hell*, plate 11).
Declaring "Jehovah" a mere "veil" for certain potentials in human
consciousness, this Wordsworth rejects mystified externalizations
in favor of their sources in human thought and feeling, the real
ground of God's purely fictive existence.

In truth, nothing in the Prospectus supports so naturalistic an
interpretation. The Enlightenment traditions of comparative
mythography in the background of the Prospectus were occasionally skeptical, treating the gods as superstitions born of fear, and
occasionally theistic, charting the evolution of human apprehensions of God from cruder to more humane forms—as Wordsworth
would do in *The Excursion*. In fact, the issue of Jehovah's figurality
can best be approached through *The Excursion*. The Prospectus
affords not merely an overview of *The Recluse*, after all, but a preface to *The Excursion*, with which it was first published in 1814.
And *The Excursion* gravitates towards a Christian perspective on
human misanthropy and mutability. Wordsworth organized the
poem around a natural faith articulated by the Pedlar, but then
accommodated to orthodox Christianity through the presence and
discourse of the Pastor. This was hardly a poem to be introduced by
lines celebrating humanistic liberation from Christian delusions.
The Prospectus introduces *The Excursion* quite aptly by looking
ahead to what would prove one of its most influential sections:
Book 4, with its cultural history of the religious sensibility.

In Book 4 the Wanderer states that, after an age when God and
Angels appeared directly to man, came a time when "Jehovah—
shapeless Power above all Powers, / Single and one, the
omnipresent God"—manifested himself only through such mediat-

ing forms as "vocal utterance, or blaze of light, / Or cloud of darkness, localised in heaven" (4.651–654). So begins a history of humankind's efforts to infer the character of "the One, ineffable of name, / Of nature indivisible" from his natural creation and to embody those inferences in material substance (4.663–664). We hear successively of the Persian, Babylonian, Chaldean, and Greek images of divinity. These representations of spiritual reality remain crude, the Wanderer agrees, but nevertheless incorporate valid intimations "Of life continuous, Being unimpaired; / That hath been, is, and where it was and is / There shall endure" (4.755–757). For the Solitary, these cultural forms cannot be trusted as means of knowledge. In the Wanderer's contrary view, the imagination can envision, even if it cannot fully incarnate, "A spiritual presence, ofttimes misconceived, / But still a high dependence, a divine / Bounty and government" (4.927–929). When "the imaginative faculty [reigns as] lord / Of observations natural," then the universe itself serves as a shell "to the ear of Faith," imparting "Authentic tidings of invisible things" (4.707–708, 1142–1144). The Prospectus presupposes this dissociation of the idea of God from its various manifestations in cultural history. Wordsworth by no means embraced the fundamentalist literalism which would equate "God" and "Jehovah." That explains how he could tell his son Johnny that "God was a spirit, that he was not like his flesh which he could touch; but more like his thoughts in his mind which he could *not* touch" (LMY 2.189).

The Jehovah dismissed by the Prospectus is a flawed, naturalized representation of a transcendent being. Images of God are human constructs invested with human emotions—such as "fear and awe"—but that hardly means that God does not exist.[13] Just so, Wordsworth's ambition to surpass Jehovah does not reveal a religious skepticism or bespeak a campaign to topple Christianity. It reveals rather Wordsworth's determination to train his prophetic imagination on new objects, and to discover a rationale for faith in the fittedness of mind and nature. Romantic scholarship has taken too seriously Blake's indictment of the Prospectus for irreligious arrogance. The Prospectus merely refuses "to bow before idols manufactured by the human imagination," Paul Sheats counsels, with Wordsworth rejecting "an anthropocentric image of God on the grounds that justified Blake's own rejection of 'Nobodaddy.'"[14] Wordsworth's concentration on "the soul of man," moreover, can be referred to priorities articulated in his poetry at least as early as late 1798—when, in the lines from MS. JJ cited above, he declared that "the eternal spirit," while evident in nature "Is yet apparent chiefly in the soul / Of our first sympathies" (*TPP*, 95). Wordsworth's own religious development clearly shows a progressive transference of value from nature to the human mind and soul. Just so, the humanizing relocations of the Prospectus are entirely clear: I suggest merely that they provide faith a new site, with new spiritual mysteries to explore, rather than banishing faith from an enlightened modernity.

Only for these reasons can *The Recluse* appropriately take its visionary framework and point of departure from *Paradise Lost*. Wordsworth's daring evocation of Milton in the Prospectus is revaluative rather than subversive, with Wordsworth attempting to continue rather than debunk Milton's prophetic ambitions. At the same time, Milton serves only as chief exhibit in the prophetic lineage which the Prospectus invokes as a validating context for its speaker's claims. Wordsworth, for instance, avows that "Beauty . . . / waits upon my steps, / Pitches her tents before me as I move" (lines 30, 33–34) because in the Old Testament the Lord God, "went in the way before you, to search you out a place to pitch your tents in, in fire by night, to shew you the way that ye should go, and in a cloud by day" (Deut. 1:33). In like manner, Wordsworth hopes that his prophetically inspired soul "may live, & be / Even as a light hung up in heaven to chear / The world in times to come" (lines 61–63) because in the New Testament the Blessed, "the light of the world," are told, "Let your light so shine before men, that they may see your good works, and glorify your Father which is in heaven" (Matt. 5:16). Wordsworth's echoes of the Bible complement his echoes of Milton to place *The Recluse* within a prophetic tradition. The allusions cooperatively present *The Recluse* as the heir and continuation of England's great Protestant epic. The humanistic transferences are entirely clear: Wordsworth grandly internalizes all of the supernatural machinery. What God had accomplished through fire and cloud, "Beauty" will do for the poet, as the light-like moral influence accorded the redeemed in Christ's gospel becomes a power of illumination located in the poet's song.

But the unalarmed poet who passes Jehovah by can do so only because he traverses the same terrain. Because his self-conscious traditionalism is revaluative rather than skeptical, Wordsworth can appropriately invoke God and affirm his own faith in the Prospectus. So, anticipating the sounds of human anguish, he at one point asks, "Let me find meaning more akin to that / Which to Gods ear they carry" (lines 51–52). So, similarly, he concludes the Prospectus with a prayerful request:

O great God
To less than thee I can not make this prayer
Innocent mighty spirit let my life
Express the image of a better time
Desires more wise & simpler manners, nurse
My heart in genuine freedom, all pure thoughts
Be with me & uphold me to the end.

(lines 71–77)

Such references to God should prove an embarrassment to readings of the Prospectus as the vehicle of a radically secular humanism. One could argue, of course, that Wordsworth's secularizing revisionism dominates the Prospectus and remains its most historically impressive feature. Or, remembering Thomas McFarland's comments on the discontinuous, conflicted aspects of the Prospectus—its "hesitations, reluctances, and turbulence"—one could enlist a conflict of naturalism and supernaturalism among the unresolved aporias of the text.[15] It is less clear how one would explain away the closing apostrophe to God. In any event, qualified claims for the comparative unimportance of the religious statements of the Prospectus would differ notably from interpretations of Wordsworth's lines as the manifesto of a forthrightly naturalistic Romanticism.

The Recluse was intended as the first "philosophical" poem in English because it was projected as the first modern religious poem, a poem which would have accommodated its various interests to a revisionary religious traditionalism. Wordsworth ordinarily felt averse to engaging theological doctrines in his poems. Taking up the "distinction between religion in Poetry and versified Religion" in the 1840 letter discussed in my first chapter, he told Henry Alford,

For my own part, I have been averse to frequent mention the mysteries of Christian faith, not from a want of a due sense of their momentous nature; but the contrary. I felt it far too deeply to venture on handling the subject as familiarly as many scruple not to do. . . . Besides general reasons for diffidence in treating subjects of holy writ I have some especial ones. I might err in points of faith; and I should not deem my mistakes less to be deprecated because they were expressed in metre. Even Milton, in my humble judgement, has erred and grievously; and what Poet could hope to atone for his apprehensions in the way in which that mighty mind has done? (*LLY* 4.23–24)

What poet would not be frightened off, the later Wordsworth asks, by the example of Milton's spiritual errors? For one, the earlier Wordsworth of the Prospectus, emboldened to correct the spiritual errors of his visionary precursor. The other important point here, however, is simply Wordsworth's acknowledgment of hesitancy in treating issues of faith poetically. Such instinctive hesitancy accounts in some measure for the avoidance of religious subjects in the poetry of 1799–1804. But in part that avoidance suggests a poet declining localized commentary on the spiritual crises of his age in favor of the sustained treatment reserved for them within the design of *The Recluse*.

SACRED GROUND: CHRISTIANITY IN GRASMERE

Regardless of how we measure and date Wordsworth's conservative reorientation, it was clearly well underway by his first years at Dove Cottage. His 1802 visit to Annette and Caroline produced the patriotic sonnets published in the *Morning Post*, even as his homecoming produced a renewed appreciation of all things English. In 1803 the threat of French invasion further invigorated Wordsworth's national loyalties: in October Dorothy reports her brother's enlistment in the Grasmere militia, adding that "surely there never was a more determined hater of the French nor one more determined to destroy them if they really do come" (*LEY*, 403). Wordsworth's newfound conservatism can be overstated. Both his opposition to numerous government policies and his commitment to an ideal of liberty had remained consistent. It was less Wordsworth who changed, arguably, than the political situation in imperialist, Napoleonic France. Still, if the reactionary figure who opposed the Reform Bill and Catholic Emancipation remains below the horizon at this time, the image of Wordsworth among the Grasmere Volunteers itself carries us a considerable distance from the incendiary author of the *Letter to the Bishop of Llandeff*. Wordsworth's radical sympathies had declined appreciably, his social and political allegiances had become more conservative in 1800–1804. Unsurprisingly, these political changes came accompanied by a greater conventionality in religious matters as well.

The years following Wordsworth's return to Grasmere witnessed the spiritual development described in my first chapter: a slowly cumulative transformation of Christian sympathies into

Christian commitments. This transformation reveals "a single, constant orientation to life," in McFarland's phrase, reasserting itself after a temporary banishment.[16] Hardly a "*Semi*-atheist" in any ordinary sense of the term (*CLSTC* 1.216), Wordsworth appears never to have renounced his belief in God. Despite his political estrangement from the Anglican Church during the radical years, in all likelihood his theism never entirely lost a Christian coloring based, at the very least, on emotional affinities originating in his childhood. It is difficult to envision Wordsworth retaining his faith in God in 1798 and yet professing a faith systematically dissociated, in his mind, from the Christianity which dominated his cultural milieu and personal upbringing, and which he would shortly re-embrace—or so I have argued previously. From 1800–1804, in any event, Wordsworth grew progressively closer to Anglican orthodoxy. Several factors facilitated the convergence, including the poet's changing domestic situation and sense of social identity. Wordsworth's growing identification with Christianity required no renunciation of former creeds. Although entangled in his anxieties about death, it did not begin with his sufferings over John Wordsworth's drowning. But for all their power, the forces reshaping Wordsworth's religious disposition at first revealed themselves only in subtle ways.

Religious statements presuming Christian understanding began to recur more frequently, for instance, in his Grasmere correspondence. In so far as they capture the speaking voice, these letters show Christianity informing Wordsworth's personal habits of reflection and expression. The closings of his letters to friends sometimes included a form of "God bless you" from 1798 on.[17] After his relocation to Grasmere, the letters themselves advert to God more frequently. Wordsworth tells Thomas Poole in 1801 that Coleridge "is a great man, and if God grant him life will do great things"; in 1802 he remarks in passing to Sara Hutchinson, "I believe God has given me a strong imagination"; also in 1802 he tells Walter Scott, "God prosper you and all that belongs to you"; declaring himself "very anxious to have your notes for the Recluse" in an 1804 letter to Coleridge, he adds, "if it should please God that I survive you, I should reproach myself for ever in writing the work if I had neglected to procure this help"; he responds to De Quincey's testimony as to the moral influence of *Lyrical Ballads* with the wish, "May God grant that you may persevere in all good habits, desires, and resolutions"; finally, he informs Richard Sharp in 1804, "with Gods blessing I shall have finish'd it [*The Prelude*] long before next summer" (*LEY*, 324, 366, 413, 452, 458, 513). These conjurings of God are intellectual reflexes as well as habits of expression. They interject Wordsworth's faith in miniature, as it were, in both his instinctive sense of himself ("God has given me a strong imagination") and his typical responses to others ("God prosper you").

Like his letters, Wordsworth's Grasmere poems often invoke God as a rhetorical coordinate, a point of reference for a poet increasingly thinking and feeling in conventionally religious terms. These texts certainly mention God more often than do the 1798 *Lyrical Ballads*. In "To a Sky-Lark" (1802), for example, the bird is described as "Pouring out praise to the Almighty Giver" (line 24); "Resolution and Independence" (1802) concludes with the thought, "'God,' said I, 'be my help and stay secure; / I'll think of the Leech-gatherer on the lonely moor'"; "Composed Upon Westminster Bridge, Sept. 3 1803" includes the straightforward apostrophe, "Dear God!" (line 13); "October, 1803" ("When, looking on the present face of things") similarly calls upon "Great God!"; in "Inland, within a hollow Vale, I stood" the poet reflects, "Even so doth God protect us if we be / Virtuous and wise" (lines 9–10); "There is a trickling water, neither rill" (1802), an early version of "There is a little unpretending rill," recounts how "thanks burst / Out of our hearts to God for that good hour"; and in the eighth stanza of the "Ode to Duty," a stanza probably dating from early 1804, Duty wears "The Godhead's most benignant grace."[18] Such examples could easily be multiplied. The supernatural intimations of "Tintern Abbey prompted Wordsworth to think of "a motion and a spirit" (line 101). His Grasmere poems, tellingly, refer more conventionally to "God," and in poetic contexts implying the Christian God his projected audience believed in.

Some Grasmere lyrics leave God unmentioned and yet display Wordsworth's comfort with Christianity in the way they too presuppose and confirm readers' tendencies to infer Christian meaning. These poems employ a Christian cultural idiom in which certain images and acts are mutually *understood* to designate Christianity. In "To the Daisy" (1802), for example, Wordsworth relies on the recognizable gestures of Christian piety to glorify the simple. Exemplifying a spiritually admirable humility, his daisy can even serve as a devotional model: the flower not only seems to pray but also inspires prayerful reflection:

At dusk, I've seldom mark'd thee press
The ground, as if in thankfulness,
Without some feeling, more or less,
Of true devotion.

(lines 61–64)

No such devotion arises with the self-effacing violet of "She dwelt among the untrodden ways." In the 1802 lyric, we encounter nothing more than religiously inflected diction ("true devotion") at one point in Wordsworth's description of the flower. But the poet's touch can remain light because his discovery of spiritual import in the common flowers of the field would, for most of his readership, appear so utterly familiar. "To the Small Celandine" (1802) similarly evokes conventional religious sentiment. The flower is portrayed as a

Prophet of delight and mirth,
Scorn'd and slighted upon earth!
Herald of a mighty band,
Of a joyous train ensuing,

(lines 57–60)

Wordsworth's subject in these lines is the celandine as a harbinger of spring. Yet "Hymns in praise" of the flower (line 64) oppose its earthly lowliness to its impending glorification in ways recalling both the resurrection of Christ, that scorned prophet, and the individual soul's reunion with the heavenly host. The natural world of the 1802 Grasmere lyrics recurrently becomes, through adroit suggestion, a sacramental world implicitly Christian in diction, motif, and mood.

So, through such spiritually familiarizing touches, many of Wordsworth's Grasmere nature lyrics solicit Christian habits of moral response for new objects and situations. The displacement of Christianity which results is especially important because it is so typically Wordsworthian. Initially, Wordsworth's efforts to spiritually dignify the commonplace were often ridiculed as incongruous by his reviewers. Ultimately, they helped create the taste by which his poetry was to be enjoyed (*Essay, Supplementary to the Preface, WPr* 3.80) by encouraging his reception as a Christian sage by later nineteenth-century readers. For his Victorian disciples would discover "the insistent transvaluations of

Scripture," in Abrams' phrase, "in Wordsworth's characteristic oxymorons: the glory of the commonplace, the loftiness of the lowly and mean, the supreme import of the trivial, and the heroic grandeur of the meek and the oppressed" (NS, 395). Abrams emphasizes that Wordsworth's transvaluations derive "from the religious tradition, and ultimately from the Bible" (NS, 392), but, again, they derive mediately from the devotional rituals, values, and conventions of the life of faith as the Anglican Church had institutionalized it in the England of Wordsworth's day. By invoking those mediations, Wordsworth's 1800–1804 poetry incorporates motifs with widely recognized Christian associations. The endurance of this social context for reading allowed Lionel Trilling in 1951—while finding neither "completeness or orthodoxy, or even explicitness of doctrine" in the poetry—to deem Wordsworth a profoundly Christian poet.[19]

So the Christian suggestiveness of nature lyrics such as "To the Daisy" and "The Small Celandine" reflects Wordsworth's turn to Christianity in 1800–1804. But other poems from this period give his Christian allegiances more direct expression. On occasion, in fact, the poetry's presupposition of Christianity even verges on explicitness. Certainly the "mighty Being" whose "eternal motions" surge through the tides in "It is a beauteous Evening, calm and free" is no pantheistic life-force. Wordsworth surrounds the God of this poem with Christian associations. In its encouragement to religious reflection, its holiness, the serene evening of Wordsworth's sonnet is as "quiet as a Nun / Breathless with adoration." If the child whom Wordsworth addresses,

> appear'st untouch'd by solemn thought,
> Thy nature is not therefore less divine:
> Thou liest in Abraham's bosom all the year;
> And worshipp'st at the Temple's inner shrine,
> God being with thee when we know it not.
>
> (lines 10–14)

Wordsworth transfers the heavenly redemption celebrated in Luke—"and it came to pass that the beggar died, and was carried by the angels into Abraham's bosom" (Luke 16:22)—to a child in her natural innocence, finding in that innocence, however, not merely a sign of God but a reconfirmation of Christian spiritual deliverance.[20] While "It is a beauteous Evening" ignores Church doctrine, it establishes a resonantly Christian religious perspective for the scene it describes.

Even more explicitly Christian is the religious epiphany recounted in *Home at Grasmere* (1800):

> And when the trance
> Came to us, as we stood by Hart-leap Well—
> The intimation of the milder day
> Which is to come, the fairer world than this—
> And raised us up, dejected as we were
> Among the records of that doleful place
> By sorrow for the hunted beast who there
> Had yielded up his breath, the awful trance—
> The Vision of humanity and of God
> The Mourner, God the Sufferer, when the heart
> Of his poor Creatures suffers wrongfully.
>
> (lines 236–46)

Like Veronica's napkin, these lines are imprinted with an after-image of Jesus. The passage conveys a vision "of humanity, and of God" as one, a vision of the suffering and pity of the incarnated Christ. As he mourns the hart, Wordsworth both glimpses a "sacrificial image of Christ's crucifixion," Raimonda Modiano rightly observes, and earns "the blessing of a traditional Christian God."[21] The trance provides the most specifically Christian moment in Wordsworth's poem. Still, even before the grand swell of the Prospectus, *Home at Grasmere* makes its Christian visionary meditation part of a pattern—through reference to "yon gracious Church" as the "benignant Mother of the Vale," and through implicitly Christian phrasing ranging from Wordsworth's account of Grasmere society as "One Household, under God," to the expression "thanks to God / For what hath been bestowed," to the celebration of Grasmere unity as "an image for the soul, / A habit of Eternity and God" (lines 524–26, 822, 102–3, 214–15).

The tenderly Christian sorrow Wordsworth feels at Hart-leap Well appears consistent with the religious vision of *Home at Grasmere*. It appears consistent also with the Wordsworth depicted in the Coleridge letters my first chapter discusses—a Wordsworth who "loves and venerates Christ & Christianity" and is "more inclined to Christianity than to Theism, simply considered" (*CLSTC* 1.410, 327). By portraying a human God moved by suffering, the *Home at*

Grasmere passage probably explains Wordsworth's veneration of Christ, and the motivation of his Christian loyalties, better than any other surviving evidence. One can understand the inclusion of this vision in *Home at Grasmere*, given the poem's profoundly personal character. But similar religious sympathy suffuses Wordsworth's other treatment of the stricken deer of local legend, "Hart-Leap Well." Here Wordsworth's meditation on the deer's death modulates into moral reflection:

> The Being, that is in the clouds and air,
> That is in the green leaves among the groves,
> Maintains a deep and reverential care
> For them the quiet creatures whom he loves.
>
> (lines 165–68)

If these lines briefly seem pantheistic, in them the "active principle alive / In all things" of 1798 has changed, two years later, into a personified deity deeply moved by the anguish of the creatures *he* loves. Like *Home at Grasmere*, "Hart-Leap Well" associates the motifs of sacrificial death, a loving God, "sympathy divine" for creaturely pain (line 164), and, in the closing lines, the need to respect the dignity of even the humblest living things. Yet the poem interrelates these motifs while commemorating the death of an animal famously employed as a symbol of Christ in the Church Fathers, Malory, Marvell, and numerous other Medieval and Renaissance texts—as the author of *The White Doe of Rylstone* at least realized by 1806.[22] The death of the deer in "Hart-Leap Well" acts as a naturalistic analogue, faintly suggested, of the sacrifice of Christ.

But the special interest of these two Grasmere poems lies not in their evocation of Christ's self-sacrificing love. Rather, it lies in the light they cast on the complex motivations of Wordsworth's Christianity. "Hart-Leap Well" speculates that the deer was returning to its birthplace in seeking the spring near which it died (lines 155–56)—so the poem, glancing tacitly at the poet's own situation, honors the impulse to return home. Wordsworth's vision of "God / the Mourner, God the Sufferer" in *Home at Grasmere* occurs as he and Dorothy literally return to their origins. Through his journey to Grasmere Wordsworth was returning to his birthplace and childhood, to a vividly remembered familial past.[23] Rededication to Christianity would have fit easily within such an emotionally encompassing gesture of return. Two of Wordsworth's earliest memories of his mother were connected with attending Church.[24] First with Dorothy, then with Dorothy and Mary, William would share Dove Cottage with women whose conventional piety made Christian belief and feeling part of the solace their presence afforded, and part of the household. In 1800, moreover, ten years after the publication of Burke's *Reflections*, loyalty to the Anglican Church was still associated powerfully with the cause of England. "We know," Burke had proclaimed, "and it is our pride to know, that man is by his constitution a religious animal; that atheism is against, not only our reason, but our instincts; and that it cannot prevail long."[25] Burke portrayed the Anglican establishment not only as a bulwark of traditional social order but order conceived as an expansion of the domestic sphere. For the *Reflections* refigured the nation as an extended family, with Burke describing the British constitution as "a sort of family settlement," a "choice of inheritance" by which citizens give to their "frame of polity the image of a relation in blood, binding up the constitution of [their] country with [their] dearest domestic ties" (Burke, 29–30). For an increasingly conservative poet acquainted with such claims, patriotism signified another return home, and returning home again meant reaffirming the faith of one's family, the creeds of the Church of England.[26]

"Many people, perhaps most," Ryan remarks, "go to church for reasons that are more social than theological, more related to family life and community values than to credal formulations" (*RR*, 96). In a paragraph meriting quotation at length, he adroitly notes the force of such familial and communal considerations for the William Wordsworth of these years:

> If one were forced to name a single date that marked Wordsworth's renewed commitment to the Christian religion in his public and private life, one might be justified in selecting July 15, 1803, the day when his first child was baptized and his wife "churched"— brought before a clergyman to give thanks publically "for safe Delivery from Childhood's perilous throes," as Wordsworth put later it in sonnet celebrating the ritual. The fact that John Wordsworth was baptized less than a month after his birth becomes more significant when one recalls that Coleridge, with his supposedly stronger commitment to orthodoxy at this time, had not yet gotten around to baptizing any of his own children, the eldest of whom was then approaching his eighth birthday. I am not suggesting that Wordsworth's participation in these rites was

itself a crucial event in his own intellectual history, but it served
to announce publically his reintegration into the religious life of
his community as it was centered in Grasmere church. In a sense,
Wordsworth and all his family were "churched" on that day.[27]

The commitments mandating Wordsworth's re-acceptance of Anglican ritual would not preserve him unfailingly from doubt in future
years. Yet they were commitments he maintained throughout the
remainder of his days. The social and family reasons behind
Wordsworth's return to the Anglican Church do not render it an
insincere keeping up of appearances. Instead, they indicate his determination to include Christian faith in the daily life of his household,
and to include his household in the spiritual life of his country.

Wordsworth's return to the Church was prompted by the most
powerful experiences of love he had known. His relocation to Grasmere allowed for recovery of place, for recovery of childhood as
well, with William and Dorothy, and the frequently visiting John,
remaking the family home tragically lost to them in earlier years.
If crowded Dove Cottage could have qualified only on the most
wishful terms as "a house / Where all's accustomed, ceremonious,"
in Yeats's phrase, it became nonetheless the place in which
Wordsworth as husband and father could reestablish family traditions. He soon found himself leading a more settled, conventional
life than he had known for some time, and part of the conventionality, unsurprisingly, involved the reconsolidation of his ties to
Anglican orthodoxy. Even if Wordsworth's specific participation in
Johnny's baptism was hardly "a crucial event in his own intellectual history," in Ryan's phrase, the poet's return to the creeds and
rituals of Anglicanism qualified as a genuine act of intellectual self-
expression. It arose from demands for justice and consolation, from
a need to understand tragic suffering, which had preoccupied him
from his first explorations of the One Life. These moral and religious preoccupations centered on the problem of death.
Wordsworth's turn to Christianity in Grasmere was accompanied,
part cause and part consequence, by his emergent ability to affirm
the existence of an immortal personal soul.

DEATH AND THE SOUL

Considering the stolen boat incident of *The Prelude* in light of the
political reorientation he believes central to Wordsworth's career,

James Chandler suggests that the poet's self-representation in *The Prelude* "is haunted throughout by that early eerie image of a child's rowboat abruptly reversing its course on a moonlit lake."[28] A different spot of time provides perhaps an equally appropriate archetype for Wordsworth career: the one in which the corpse rising "bolt upright" on Esthwaite Water forces a confrontation with death upon a child surrounded by an idyllic landscape. One cannot interpret the Drowned Man episode merely as a prolepsis. Peter Bell's conversion had been motivated in part by his discovering another drowning victim, and other poems in *Lyrical Ballads* touch on death and dying. But "the work of the fall of 1798 and later years," Sheats rightly notes, testifies recurrently to the poet's suddenly sharpened consciousness of mortality."[29] As a genealogy of imagination, the spots of time in the first section of the Two-Part *Prelude* trace imaginative power back to initially implicit, finally quite stark encounters with death—forming a sequence ending with the gibbet scene and the poet's account of the death of his father. Goslar also witnessed the composition of the elegiac Lucy and Matthew poems. The following years saw Wordsworth write "A Poet's Epitaph," "The Brothers," "Michael," and other poems which explore mutability and mortality. This body of work makes Wordsworth one of the great death poets in English literature.

Where did this imaginative preoccupation with death come from? It came principally, I have suggested, from his experiment with the One Life as an elegiac rationale. Before *The Ruined Cottage*, Wordsworth's poetry tended to treat death as evidence of social injustice. *The Ruined Cottage* treats death as an existential and religious problem. Allied to a Necessitarian pantheism, the One Life threatens the very ideas of human individuality and moral agency. Latent in those threats, however, was the more harrowing threat of death itself. Were the premises of pantheism proven valid, McFarland writes, "there would be no Christian eschatology of a personal life after death, for at death man would merely be reabsorbed by the world-substance."[30] It is this distressing possibility which "A slumber did my spirit seal" renders with such gruesome subtlety:

> A slumber did my spirit seal,
> I had no human fears:
> She seem'd a thing that could not feel
> The touch of earthly years.

No motion has she now, no force;
She neither hears not sees;
Roll'd round in earth's diurnal course
With rocks and stones and trees!

Lucy becomes one more item in the naturalistic litany of the closing line, a line realizing the estranging force latent in the previous
description of her as "a thing." She undergoes her estranging earth-
change, moreover, in a lyric where Wordsworth's "Roll'd round"
clearly glances back at the One Life "roll[ing] through all things" in
"Tintern Abbey" (line 103). The idea of the One Life seems to have
created a nagging problem for Wordsworth by envisioning death as
the extinction of the human personality.

The integral connection between the One Life and the problem
of death attains clearest illustration in "Tintern Abbey." The poem
arguably takes the prospect of dying as its motivating occasion. Diction and phrasing leave Wordsworth's first verse paragraph massively
inflected by an awareness of death. The poet begins by compounding
a seclusion termed not greater but, funereally, "more deep"; he positions himself "Here, *under* this dark sycamore" and then accentuates
the suggestion of a gravesite by mentioning "*plots* of cottage-
ground"; he similarly introduces both the motifs of fading out, as the
orchard tufts "lose themselves," and movement upwards, with
"wreaths" (wraiths?) of smoke trailing upwards and away to the odd
"quiet" of the sky. Due to the collective weight of its deathly con-
notations, the opening paragraph of "Tintern Abbey," for all its realistic particularity, almost unfolds less as visual panorama than the
elaboration of a figural logic, a dramatization of prosopopoeia.

Only because the earlier passages hint at death so persistently
can Harold Bloom claim that in the lines,

Nor, perchance,
If I should be where I no more can hear
Thy voice, nor catch from thy wild eyes these gleams
Of past existence, wilt thou then forget
That on the banks of this delightful stream
We stood together . . .

(lines 147–52),

"the fear of mortality, which has been haunting the poem, finally
becomes overt."[31] Wordsworth's subsequent address to Dorothy—

"for thou art with me"—alludes fittingly to the Twenty-third Psalm, for "Tintern Abbey" envisions the Wye valley as one more "valley of the shadow of death." What makes it so shadowed is the totalizing spirit immanent in it, for that spirit may reduce human beings to oblivious nothingness. Surely the presence of the One Life and mortal disquietude *together* in "Tintern Abbey"—especially when the One Life idea explains the disquietude—should hardly appear coincidental. If "Tintern Abbey" ostensibly celebrates "the life of things," the fact remains that Wordsworth's great pantheistic affirmation closely precedes his turn to Dorothy, and thus the passage, cited above, where he seems to anticipate his own death. A legacy of the One Life, Wordsworth's anxieties about death shaped his religious development in 1800–1803 even though he had outgrown the One Life philosophy. Those anxieties interacted with his growing conventionality to produce the specifically theological problem of the existence of the soul.

Despite their use of religious imagery in depicting a sacramental natural world, Wordsworth's 1800–1803 poems typically avoid any reference to an eternal soul in their reflections on death. With respect to the ideas of immortality and heaven, Alan Grob contends,

> the poems on death prior to the *Ode*, though never openly repudiating these concepts, surely convey a deep disquietude about them. In neither the "Matthew" poems nor the "Lucy" poems is the irreducible fact of death in any way assuaged by the profession of Christian faith and the consolation of belief in the hereafter that Wordsworth characteristically appended to his elegiac verse after 1804. . . . Confronted by death, Wordsworth's consolations in 1798 and 1800 are wholly secular, remembrance and resignation. . . . Other works prior to 1804 also touch upon death, but in none of them does Wordsworth imply any conviction of hopes beyond the grave.[32]

Grob calls into question Thomas M. Raysor's denial that Wordsworth "at any time gave up completely the concept of a finite personal soul after death, or accepted the idea of the annihilation of personal identity and self-consciousness."[33] I want to negotiate these contrary positions by suggesting, with Grob, that the Immortality Ode marks a dramatic turn in Wordsworth's religious outlook, but that, as Raysor argues, Wordsworth probably never "gave up completely" his belief in an immortal soul.

The difficulty of reconstructing Wordsworth's attitudes towards the soul lies chiefly with the ambiguities of his poetic references to it. In the poems of 1800–1803, "soul" can refer to human identity and simply designate a person; or to consciousness, serving as a synonym for mind, reason, or imagination; or to moral heroism, principled courage conceived of as greatness of spirit (as in "Are souls then nothing?"). Perhaps, as Jonathan Wordsworth ruefully remarks, "it *is* disconcerting . . . to discover [the poet's] willingness in the manuscripts to cross out 'heart' and write 'soul,' 'soul' and write 'mind,' simply to avoid repetition" (italics mine).[34] But such casually variable wording seems significant in its own right. "Soul is an orthodox word in all our poets," Coleridge once remarked (*CLSTC* 1.278). Just so, the various inflections Wordsworth assigns "soul" from poem to poem, or in amending "soul" to "mind" within a single text, demonstrate his willingness to use "soul" as an orthodox poeticism. Wordsworth's poetic practice suggests that he was comfortable with the term's conventional range of implication: in short, his poetic practice suggests conventionality. Through 1803, at least, Wordsworth was clearly not invested in any particular, or philosophically rigorous, definition of the word. For him, "soul" had apparently not demanded the conceptual specification necessary to distinguish his use of the word from the cultural norms of his day.

We might reflect in this connection that in Wordsworth's day denials of the soul's immortality required a profound intellectual unconventionality—as the example of Joseph Priestley demonstrates. By 1775 Priestley had replaced Hume as England's most notorious denier of the soul, and the ferocity of society's resistance to such skepticism emerges in Priestley's *Memoirs*. There he remarks at one point that doubts about "the immateriality of the sentient principle in man," doubts expressed merely in passing in his edition of Hartley, occasioned a full-blown public "outcry": "In all of the newspapers, and most of the periodical publications, I was represented as an unbeliever in revelation, and no better than an Atheist."[35] Only a few bold freethinkers denied the soul's existence in early nineteenth-century England. Furthermore, if Wordsworth's 1800–1803 death poems ordinarily withhold religious consolation, as Grob rightly points out, the fact remains that they were never expressly conceived as religious poems to begin with. Geoffrey Hartman has written that in Wordsworth a "secondary consciousness of death and change associates itself with the very act of writing."[36] Just so, Wordsworth's meditations on death from *The Ruined Cottage* on were tied up with explorations of poetic representation—with issues of morally cathartic narration, of the commemorative power of language, and of revising traditional poetic forms for new artistic purposes. Wordsworth was also interested in the social construction of death, in mourning practices as a foundation of community.[37] The Matthew and Lucy poems, "Michael," and "The Brothers" locate the problem of death within the limited compass of their specific poetic interests, secular interests to which the afterlife remained irrelevant.

Still, from the time of *The Ruined Cottage*, the possibility that death meant finitude and oblivion seems to have preyed recurrently on Wordsworth's mind. "O dearer far" (1824) shows that even during his orthodox period his belief could turn anxious where his hopes were most insistent. There nonetheless exists no real evidence of outright denial on Wordsworth's part. The poet's belief in God strongly implies a correlative belief in the soul, and the poems and letters of these years mention God repeatedly. It is difficult to see Wordsworth embracing so radical a naturalism as to fully dismiss the notion of a spiritual afterlife: consider merely how powerfully the possibility tends against his refusal, on a related philosophical front, to sanction reductive approaches to human consciousness as the mere reflex of sensation. Wordsworth never embraced materialism. In addition, his poetry frequently invokes the "soul" in contexts which, while intellectually imprecise, to all appearances presume upon the word's religious resonance. Actually, the poetry even refers explicitly to an immortal soul at moments. "These words were uttered in a pensive mood" (1802) declares that "The immortal Mind craves objects that endure" (line 12), and similar assertions can be found in other 1800–1803 poems and draft passages. Early on, before Wordsworth fully assessed the elegiac implications of One Life consolation, he implied in passing that the universal life-force itself provided for personal immortality: so the Pedlar's belief that all things in nature "Breathed immortality, revolving life, / And greatness still revolving, infinite" briefly accords with his reverence for the Bible's revelation of "The mystery, the life which cannot die" (Pedlar narrative, *MH*, lines 124–25, 121).

Wordsworth's "skepticism" about the soul produced anxious moods and passing doubts, then, but probably never express denial. Clearly the anxieties and doubts were powerful enough to make death a pivotal issue for his poetic development. One can argue plausibly both that Wordsworth lost his faith in immortality following *The Ruined Cottage* and that he by no means clearly regained it during the first years of his Grasmere residency. So Ryan contends that "as late as 1805 [Wordsworth] still seems to have been struggling toward a confident assurance of an afterlife" (RR, 98). I make no great objection to a criticism which prefers to emphasize these struggles, or to a criticism which attributes the unquestionable importance of death in the 1798–1804 poetry to Wordsworth's belief that dying obliterates the human personality. My own sense of the preponderant evidence, however, is that the poet's attitudes toward the soul fluctuated within the compass of a prevailing assent. Wordsworth's faith in immortality could grow hesitant both before and after John's drowning. The affirmations of the "Ode: Intimations of Immortality" reflect not a shift from disbelief to conviction, however, but a process of reauthentication in which belief acquired emotional depth. The sublime declarations of the Ode break no new ground. They stage a climactic reconfirmation, celebrating a faith in immortality that Wordsworth seems likeliest never to have formally renounced.

CHAPTER FOUR

Wordsworth and the Immortal Soul

Children are blest, and powerful; their world
    lies
More justly balanced; partly at their feet,
And part far from them.

> —Wordsworth,
> "I am not One who much or oft delight"

Modern scholarship on Wordsworth's Immortality Ode proceeds from Lionel Trilling's claim that "despite its dominating theistical metaphor, the Ode is largely naturalistic in its intention."[1] The clearest exception to this critical orientation is Anya Taylor's essay on religious interpretations of the Ode, which views the poem as a Wordsworthian version of the argument from discontent.[2] Although my reconstruction of the religious design of the Ode differs from Taylor's account, I depend on her demonstration of the Ode's theological background. I depend also on Trilling's essay, including his restriction of the text's famous Platonism to a merely "suggestive validity": "we may regard pre-existence as being for Wordsworth a very serious conceit," Trilling wrote, a conceit "vested with relative belief, intended to give a high value to the natural experience of the 'vanishings'" (Trilling, 160). For me, the principal religious import of the Ode lies not in its preexistence metaphor but simply in its assertion that an immortal soul exists. Allied to this assertion, of course, is the poem's representation of the natural innocence of childhood, an innocence often celebrated in Romantic literature but powerfully contested in Wordsworth's day by Evangelical lectures on the inherent sinfulness of humankind, including newborn children. In the Ode Wordsworth shapes these contributory motifs into a response to the problem of mortality bequeathed him by the One Life. That response authenticates the notion of soul, making it personally and culturally pertinent, by finding proof for it in the visionary propensity of the poetic imagination. The Christian motifs and images accompanying this defense of immortality repeatedly associate the religious vision of the Ode with Christianity. Those associations alone do not cede Wordsworth's undoctrinaire poem to orthodoxy: in a manner typical of Wordsworth, the text's relationship to Christianity rests on resemblance rather than identification. But the Ode's self-conscious invocations of Christian precedents and analogues render it Wordsworth's mythopoeic variation on the Christian theme of life everlasting.

IMAGINATION AND THE SOUL

The secularization of Western civilization in the modern era resulted in a progressive decline in the philosophical prestige of the soul. An important aspect of this decline, Thomas McFarland shows, was the rise to prominence of the idea of imagination as a substitute for the increasingly attacked and discredited idea of soul.[3] As with Arnold's notion of the relationship of culture and religion, imagination often assumed the prerogatives of soul, with the two terms construed as opposites and placed in inverse relation to each other. McFarland also shows, however, that in certain transitional thinkers the notions of soul and imagination attained a mutually supportive coincidence. At times the two concepts were intimately connected, with the imagination deployed not to replace the soul but to shore up its importance. Over the centuries "soul" and "imagination" had often been associated in philosophical discourse; they occasionally appear as synonymous terms in eighteenth-century aesthetics. Nevertheless, the higher function accorded the imagination in Romantic criticism and poetry could place these two terms in unprecedented conceptual proximity. Taking Coleridge's discussions of the imagination and the poet in the

Biographia Literaria ("The poet, described in *ideal* perfection, brings the whole soul of man into activity") and the apostrophe to Imagination from Book 6 of *The Prelude* ("to my Soul I say / I recognize thy glory") as his touchstones, McFarland remarks that

> In such and similar examples, where imagination, subsiding from its glimpse of Godhead, hovers in tantalizing proximity to soul, we see that it begins not only to participate in but actually to take over the aura of soul.
> Romantic imagination, in short, not only moves in the sphere of soul, but it reciprocates and draws to itself the very meaning of soul. (McFarland, 150)

McFarland could easily have chosen the Immortality Ode to illustrate this reciprocation. In the Ode, Wordsworth vindicates the soul's existence by identifying soul with imagination.

Making a virtue of necessity, this identification marries two terms already related in the Enlightenment philosophical context which the Ode depends most upon. Needless to say, Wordsworth's poem richly incorporates various intellectual traditions. In celebrating the redemptive innocence of its child figure, Wordsworth reconsiders issues prominent in the evolution of Christian doctrine and rejects the orthodox Augustinian position on original sin.[4] With the Platonic myth of his fifth verse paragraph, he touches on the heretical idea of preexistence, an idea trailing its own complex history with it. Yet the truly formative philosophical matrices of Wordsworth's poem were less arcane: the Ode stages its affirmation of an immortal soul in relation to its immediate philosophical legacy, the traditions of Enlightenment rationalism and, more specifically, British empiricism. Scholarship on Romantic dissatisfaction with empirical models of perception and cognition rightly describes a Romantic revisionism concerned principally to defend the imagination. Yet these epistemological arguments unavoidably raised religious issues as well. Blake, Coleridge, and Wordsworth rejected the materialization not merely of perception but of identity. In its breadth of association, the Romantic critique of empiricism demanded a defense not just of "imagination" but of "soul": an immaterial site of personal identity which, though enclosed in the body, transcended the most formative mundane experiences, and which harbored our link to God. Defenses of the soul were all the more necessary, of course, for the frequency of attacks on it. In Enlightenment France the notorious polemics of materialists such as Diderot, Holbach, and Helvétius let no one forget that in the

French reception of empiricism, as R. R. Palmer comments, "the soul itself was at stake."[5]

In England it was Hume who waged the most culturally visible campaign against the soul. *The Treatise of Human Nature* takes the belief in a self-present identity as its primary target, but Hume's skepticism associated the ideas of identity and soul, with *The Treatise* declaring that men fabricate "the notion of a *soul*, and *self* " to deny the random flux of their actual mental experience.[6] Although commonly dismissed as an irreligious materialist, Locke himself never abandoned the notion of soul. But from the beginning of the eighteenth century, Deists inspired by Locke often disallowed the soul's existence. In *Second Thoughts concerning the human soul*, William Coward argued that the proposition of the soul's immateriality was a classical superstition offensive to true Christianity, a claim reiterated by John Toland, whose *Letters to Sirena* provides a critical history of belief in an eternal soul.[7] From the time of Bentley's inaugural Boyle lecture, orthodox counterattacks on Deism and Atheism continually derided thinkers who, as Samuel Clarke wrote, "having a prejudice against the Notion of the *Immortality of Human Souls*, . . . believe that Men perish intirely at Death."[8] The issue of the soul's immortality occasionally not only served apologists as a dominant theme—as in Francis Gastrell's *Moral Proofs of the Certainty of a Future State* and William Kenrick's poem *On the Immortality of the Soul*—but also played a contributory role in countless eighteenth-century orthodox treatises, sermons, reviews, pamphlets, and poems.[9] The great poetic defense of the soul's existence was Young's immensely popular *Night Thoughts*, which bore the full title *The Complaint: or Night-Thoughts on Life, Death & Immortality*, and which devoted Night 7 to proofs of immortality. While Wordsworth knew Young and the English poetry of religious meditation on nature, he would have had little direct knowledge of (or interest in) the religious controversies of earlier decades. But the ideas fueling those debates had been assimilated into influences readier to hand. Coleridge's familiarity with Andrew Baxter's 1745 *Enquiry into the Immateriality of the Soul*, for example, seems to have been mediated by a reference in Priestley.[10]

The case of Priestley demonstrates both the persistence of debates over the soul in the late eighteenth century and their particular importance for Coleridge, who adopted Priestley as one of his philosophical heroes. My previous chapter mentioned the widespread public outcry occasioned by Priestley's arguments against the soul.[11] In his *Disquisitions Relating to Matter and Spirit* (1777),

Priestley had argued that matter is not inert, because it possesses properties of attraction and repulsion. He could thereby collapse the distinction between the material and spiritual in favor of a materialistic monism which, in his opinion, avoided "all the embarrassment attending the doctrine of the soul."[12] Man is "*one being* composed of *one kind of substance*, made of the *dust of the earth*," in Priestley's view, and "when he dies, he, of course, ceases to think" (*Disquisitions* 3.286). Such disturbing claims would have assumed additional importance for the Unitarian Coleridge, demanding the most careful consideration, due to their bearing on Priestley's Unitarian conception of Christ. "That man is wholly material is eminently subservient to the doctrine of the *proper*, or *mere humanity* of Christ," Priestley asserted; "for if no man has a soul distinct from his body, Christ, who in all other respects, appeared as a man, could not have had a soul which existed before his body" (*Disquisitions* 3.220). So the soul was a living issue for the Coleridge who leapt the fence at Racedown in 1797. Piously proclaimed by Hartley, cheerfully denied by Priestley, the existence of an immortal soul remained one of the coordinates by which Coleridge positioned himself in relation to the thinkers he most admired.[13]

That fact brings the issue of spiritual immortality within the compass of Wordsworth's interests. Coleridge's philosophically engaged religious faith, on display both in his writings and conversation, clearly remained the medium by which eighteenth-century controversies over the soul reached Wordsworth. The insistence of Coleridge's interests underscored both the necessity of defending the soul and the cultural pertinence of such defenses: Coleridge made the soul a living issue for Wordsworth too in 1802–1804. More specifically, the interrelation of religious and epistemological interests in Coleridge's thinking would have also confirmed the irreligious implications of empiricism—the entanglement of "soul" in empirical efforts to redefine the mind, and imagination, as mere registers of sensation. The religious argument of Wordsworth's Ode—consisting essentially of the claim that "the mind has in it something innate, something not given in sense experience, an independent power which guarantees that the soul's origin is divine" (Hirsch, 170)—depends crucially on the Coleridgean case against empiricism. Coleridge's example showed Wordsworth that defenses of the mind's creative independence, of the imagination, implied and required a defense of the soul.

In this connection we should note that Coleridge's religious faith never lapsed from orthodoxy on the issue of soul. References to the soul recur throughout both his 1795 Bristol lectures on revealed religion and early correspondence. My first chapter alluded to his 1796 statement to Thelwall "that when we appear to men to die, we do not utterly perish," instead surviving spiritually to undergo judgment (*CLSTC* 1.280), but other examples could easily be adduced. It is true that Coleridge boasted to Southey in 1794, "I go farther than Hartley and believe in the corporeality of *thought*— namely, that it is motion" (*CLSTC* 1.137). Yet Jerome Christensen and J. A. Appleyard both caution that even Coleridge's early religious writings contain no indications of any real belief in the corporeality of thought, even in the immediate aftermath of Coleridge's progress beyond Hartley to Priestley.[14] Moreover, the statement to Southey represents the only significant evidence of materialist leanings in Coleridge. Latent in Coleridge's thought as early as 1796, his reservations about empiricism had evolved by 1801 into explicit denial that human perception remains the mere reflex of sensory experience. In a 23 March 1801 letter to Thomas Poole, to offer only one example, Coleridge observed that

> Newton was a mere materialist—*Mind* in his system is always passive—a lazy Looker on on an external World. If the mind be not *passive*, if it be indeed made in God's Image, & that too in the sublimest sense—the Image of the *Creator*—there is ground for suspicion, that any system built on the passiveness of the mind must be false, as a system. (*CLSTC* 2.709)

By 1802 Coleridge's reading in Kant had enhanced this transcendentalist orientation enormously. More to the point, Coleridge's description of the mind as "the Image of the *Creator*" resembles the Blessed Babe passage, anticipates Wordsworth's vision on Snowdon, and hints at a complex of beliefs held in common. In the 16 March 1801 letter in which he boasted of having "overthrown the doctrine of Association, as taught by Hartley," Coleridge also claimed to have constructed a rejoinder to Locke, Hobbes, and Hume "entirely to Wordsworth's satisfaction" (*CLSTC* 2.706, 707)—and Wordsworth's familiarity with Coleridge's case against empiricism cannot well be doubted.

In his role as philosophical mediator, then, Coleridge encouraged Wordsworth's interest in the soul's immortality as a poetic subject and shaped his sense of the subject's ramifications. He further encouraged Wordsworth's celebration of spiritual transcendence, evidence suggests, by calling his friend's attention to the enormously useful preexistence motif. Coleridge's early sonnet "Composed on a Journey Homeward" had speculated that "We lived, ere yet this robe of flesh we wore" (line 6). John Rea plausibly identified this poem as the "verses to Hartley" mentioned in Dorothy's 6 May 1802 journal entry, and suggested that Coleridge's poem occasioned lively discussion of Proclus and Neoplatonic theories of prenatal existence at Dove Cottage.[15] The subsidiary ideas of preexistence and innate spiritual power not only confirmed the idea of a soul but dramatically freed that soul from any ground in physical sensation. Yet Coleridge made his greatest contribution to the Ode, if only to the development of its latter stanzas, through his own Verse Letter to Sara Hutchinson, composed on April 1802, of course, as a revisionary meditation on Wordsworth's first four verse paragraphs. Coleridge's poem could influence the Immortality Ode so profoundly only because the Verse Letter confirmed tendencies independently adumbrated in Wordsworth's opening stanzas. In no way did it confirm those tendencies to greater purpose, I will argue, than in its representation of the "Soul." For, by specifically naming the "Soul" the source of human creative power, the Verse Letter provided a memorable precedent for Wordsworth's identification of soul and imagination in the Immortality Ode.

VISIONARY GLORY AND BLANK MISGIVINGS

The imagery of the Immortality Ode serves as the chief vehicle of its religious argument. Wordsworth's spiritual affirmation rests on the visionary glory of his opening stanzas, the "Blank misgivings" of stanza nine, and the connection between his experiences of an alternately irradiated and darkened natural world. The radiance described in Wordsworth first four stanzas—it is called a "light," a "glory," and a "gleam"—has been variously defined in the critical literature. It may prove simplest, consequently, to begin by saying what the radiance is not. To my mind, it is patently not the light of spiritual preexistence. While we must turn to the poem to pursue this point, it is worth noting that both Coleridge and Wordsworth credited the Ode's Platonism with a merely metaphorical function. Coleridge himself had expressly denied his belief "in this descending, & and incarcerated Soul"—the preexistent soul surmised in "Composed on a Journey Homeward"—in an early letter to Thelwall (*CLSTC* 1.278). Discussing the Immortality Ode in the *Biographia*, Coleridge confidently declared that attentive readers of the poem "will be as little disposed to charge Mr. Wordsworth with believing the platonic pre-existence in the ordinary interpretation of the words, as I am to believe, that Plato himself ever meant or taught it."[16] For Coleridge, Plato himself could never have assented seriously to this doctrine. Wordsworth, in any event, followed Coleridge in relegating the idea to an analogical role in his Fenwick commentary. He allowed it a shadowy place among "our instincts of immortality," emphasized the metaphorical leverage it generated as an Archimedean point, and further dignified it by likening it to the fall of Adam and Eve (Fenwick Note, *PW* 4.464)

In the Ode he introduces the notion of preexistence not as a simile but a metaphor:

> Our birth is but a sleep and a forgetting:
> The Soul that rises with us, our life's Star,
> Hath had elsewhere its setting,
> And cometh from afar:
>
> (lines 58–61)

With these lines in mind, Gene Ruoff has observed that "what is missing in the Ode is that crucial 'may,' which would condition its overstatements, identifying its myth as conjecture" (Ruoff, 235). But do we really need the "may"? Wordsworth would have cumbersomely undermined the myth at one stroke, surely, in introducing it so tentatively. By allowing the poet the reorientational boldness of his fifth stanza, the elliptical transitions of the odal form allowed him to introduce an extended conceit in an effective manner. The opening lines of stanza five stage a metaphorical gambit, their abruptness underscoring their status as a venturous surmise offered self-consciously *as* surmise. Ruoff concedes that the Ode ultimately redefines its etiological myth as a "speculative instrument which has helped to uncover a truth more fundamental than the teleological certitudes it announced, which need no longer be credited" (Ruoff, 262)—and unquestionably the preexistence motif fades away, tellingly, as the poem proceeds. But the Ode was never intellectually committed to the motif to begin with. If others prefer to argue that, Wordsworth's personal disbelief in preexistence notwithstanding, his poem advocates the doctrine seriously, they may certainly do so. My own experience in reading the Ode is that—as with the animistic "Presences" of the Two-Part *Prelude*—

one easily reads past the cosmic declarations of stanza five, taking the inflation of its claims, its mythopoeic grandstanding, as the poet's strategically exorbitant gesture.

Within the transitions effected by stanza five, that gesture would help Wordsworth posit a connection between imagination and soul. The earlier stanzas of the Ode work to establish a connection between imagination and the mysterious effulgence Wordsworth elegizes. The poet's vanished "glory" unmistakably suggests "the heightened sensibility of childhood" manifesting itself as a capacity for wonder; it suggests the appeal of sensuous immediacy, "the ravishments of sense"; it suggests a sense of wholeness before individuation disrupts the unity of self and environment; and it suggests childhood unawareness of death, with nature garbed accordingly in "a garment of timelessness."[17] These suggestions are mutually implicated and corroborative. But what interrelates them as a constellation of motifs is their status as characteristics or consequences of mental power. They all testify to a perceptual re-creation of the world. Therefore the truly crucial point about the light imagery of Wordsworth's initial stanzas is that, as Cleanth Brooks wrote, "it is the child himself who confers the radiance on the morning world upon which he looks with delight."[18] Through such projections, the mind demonstrates its independence of sensation, exercising its creative ability to reorganize experience according to a logic of the emotions. So the radiance Wordsworth celebrates signifies a lost, only partly recoverable, mode of imagination.

Through the light imagery of the Ode Wordsworth harks back, again, to his Blessed Babe passage from the 1799 *Prelude*. Banishing the mother from its account of the infant's negotiations with its environment, the Ode simply makes the child himself the source of the "virtue which irradiates and exalts / all objects through all intercourse of sense" (*TPP* 2.289–90):

> No outcast he, bewildered and depressed:
> Along his infant veins are interfused
> The gravitation and the filial bond
> Of nature that connect him with the world.
> Emphatically such a being lives
> An inmate of this *active* universe;
> From nature largely he receives, nor so
> Is satisfied but largely gives again,
>
> . . . .

> . . . . .—his mind,
> Even as an agent of the one great mind,
> Creates, creator and receiver both,
> Working but in alliance with the works
> Which it beholds. Such verily is the first
> Poetic spirit of our human life,
> By uniform control of after years
> In most abated and suppressed, in some
> Through every change of growth or of decay
> Preeminent till death
>
> (*TPP* 2.291–98, 301–10)

Unlike the celestial visitant mythologized by the Immortality Ode, the child of the Two-Part *Prelude* enjoys a fostering connection with nature reminiscent of the mutual fittedness of the Prospectus. In other respects, however, the Blessed Babe lines directly clarify the perceptual drama of the Ode. Wordsworth's Babe wields a power which "irradiates" objects encountered through "the intercourse of sense." In part, his mind divinely creates the world, which conditions his perceptions but remains reflexively conditioned by those perceptions as well. These reciprocal exchanges illustrate imagination in action, disclosing the "Poetic spirit" inherent in human consciousness.

Due to this creative spirit, the pastoral realm of Wordsworth's opening stanzas wears—is "Apparell'd in" (line 4)—a luminosity not inherently its own. The natural beauties catalogued in stanza two expressly establish the vanished radiance as something other than a light of nature. Wordsworth likens this light to the "glory and freshness of a dream" not merely because it transmutes and intensifies in the manner of a dream, as Brooks suggested (Brooks, 172), but also because the comparison refigures the light as a mental phenomenon. Wordsworth implies the glory's imaginative affinities, similarly, by referring to it as a "visionary gleam" (line 56). The pansy's "tale" and the reawakened "Winds," connoting a no longer dormant inspiration, also help to associate the radiance with imagination. Now, the mental agency at issue here is merely a primal mode of imagination. All human beings share in it, so the universalizing imperative of the Ode suggests, and so Wordsworth contended in his Fenwick remarks: "to that dream-like vividness and splendour which invest objects of sight in childhood, everyone, I believe, if he would look back, could bear testimony" (*PW*

4.463–64]. Therefore the visionary brightness at issue differs from that skill with metaphor which Helen Vendler, for instance, rightly restricts to adult practitioners of the poet's craft (Vendler, 70). Yet the Ode seems to locate the child's power of perceptual illumination and the poet's more specialized control over language at disparate points on a single continuum. Poets must mature and discipline the light celebrated in the Immortality Ode in order to produce great poetry. But no great poetry could ever result without at least some fitful contact with the light.

Wordsworth intimates as much, surely, by allusively associating his transitory radiance with Miltonic inspiration. Wordsworth's conjuring of Milton enhances the spiritual resonance of his poem's imagery, and helps place the Ode's visionary claims in religious perspective, but it helps associate the vanished light with imaginative perception as well. Book 3 of *Paradise Lost* begins with the famous invocation,

> Hail holy Light, offspring of Heav'n first-born,
> Or of th' Eternal Coeternal beam
> May I express thee unblam'd? since God is Light,
> And never but in unapproached Light
> Dwelt from Eternity, dwelt then in thee,
> Bright effluence of bright essence increate.
> Or hear'st thou rather pure Ethereal stream,
> Whose Fountain shall tell? Before the Sun,
> Before the Heavens thou wert, and at the voice
> Of God, as with a Mantle didst invest
> The rising world of waters dark and deep,
> Won from the void and formless infinite.[19]

This "holy Light" glances at the "celestial light" of Wordsworth's opening lines, which appicals nature even as Milton's light covers the rising world "as with a Mantle." For Milton as for Wordsworth, moreover, the imaginatively vitalizing radiance has vanished: both Milton's invocation and Wordsworth's poem, Paul McNally points out, concern "lost powers of outward sight and renewed powers of insight" (McNally, 28). It is with Milton still in mind, very likely, that Wordsworth can at one point depict his child's immersion in the mundane as a form of blindness (line 125). The mysterious, fleeting radiance of Wordsworth's Romantic poem differs dramatically, of course, from the "Celestial Light" which Milton confidently implores to "Irradiate" all the powers of his mind (*Paradise*

Lost 3.51–53). The Miltonic recollections in the diction of the opening stanzas of the Ode nonetheless render Wordsworth's light a Miltonic legacy, helping to make it a figure for imaginative power.

Here we might notice that Coleridge had no difficulty in identifying Wordsworth's radiance as a trope for imagination. Taking its departure from the Ode's first four stanzas, the Verse Letter to Sara Hutchinson mourns "A Light, a Glory, and a luminous Cloud" (line 302) which once enveloped the earth but which has now departed. Coleridge names this evanescent quality "Joy," but clearly links joy with creativity, blaming his despondency for suspending "what Nature gave [him] at [his] Birth— / [His] shaping Spirit of Imagination!" (lines 240–41). The Verse Letter to Sara explicitly presents the fleeting light of the Ode as a capacity for imaginative responsiveness. Coleridge is equally explicit about the light's inwardness, characterizing it as a mental power that emanates outward to lend the world whatever secondary charm it acquires. In developing its own account of lost inspiration, the Verse Letter redirects implications established in the Ode's introductory stanzas. Coleridge may have conceivably misinterpreted those stanzas, misconstruing Wordsworth's intentions, but in 1802 no one knew Wordsworth's habits of mind or imagery better. If indeed the Verse Letter misrepresents the haunting luminosity of the Immortality Ode, the misrepresentation accords with Wordsworthian precedent. In the Two-Part *Prelude*, for example, Wordsworth had written of moments when

> . . . such a holy calm
> Did overspread my soul that I forgot
> The agency of sight, and what I saw
> Appeared like something in myself—a dream,
> A prospect in my mind. . . .
> . . . An auxiliar light
> Came from my mind which on the setting sun
> Bestowed new splendour.

> (2.397–401, 417–419)

Like the Ode, these lines commemorate a dream-like blurring of the boundaries between self and world, and here too a superabundant light of the mind dominates the outer scene to refashion it as a visionary prospect. Other Wordsworthian texts reveal a similar use of light imagery. The Immortality Ode merely gives culminating expression to Wordsworth's dependence on the traditional association of light and imagination.

Eventually, however, the imaginative theme of the Ode moves from light to darkness, developing beyond the pastoral brightness of the text's opening scenes. In stanza nine Wordsworth contemplates moments of blindness and estrangement. He praises the fugitive radiance of his earliest days while reserving his greatest gratitude

> . . . for those obstinate questionings
> Of sense and outward things,
> Fallings from us, vanishings;
> Blank misgivings of a Creature
> Moving about in worlds not realiz'd.

> (lines 144–48)

The most helpful glosses on these sudden darkenings remain Wordsworth's own comments as reported by R. P. Graves, Bonamy Price, and, again, Isabella Fenwick:

> I remember Mr. Wordsworth saying that, at a particular stage of his mental progress, he used to be frequently so rapt into an unreal transcendental world of ideas that the external world seemed no longer to exist in relation to him, and he had to reconvince himself of its existence *by clasping a tree,* or something that happened to be near him.

> The venerable old man raised his aged form erect . . . and then uttered these ever-memorable words: "There was a time in my life when I had to push against something that resisted, to be sure that there was anything outside me. I was sure of my own mind; everything else fell away, and vanished into thought."

> I was often unable to think of external things as having external existence, and I communed with all that I saw as something not apart from, but inherent in, my own immaterial nature. Many times while going to school have I grasped at a wall or tree to recall myself from this abyss of idealism to the reality.[20]

All three statements bear relevantly on the Immortality Ode. In Price's testimony about the poet's conversation, the "There was a time" locution and references to things falling away and vanishing verge on outright allusion to the Ode.

The sense of vertiginous absence reported in these remarks represents a Wordsworthian version of mysticism's negative way. The poet's "obstinate questionings" began, perhaps, as heightenings of an egotistically sublime absorption in his own thoughts, but ended, at least in his understanding, as glimpses of transcendent reality. Such rapt glimpses recall other visionary usurpations in Wordsworth's poetry. Indeed, they recall some of the most famous episodes in *The Prelude*: the "spots of time" reveal "that the mind / Is lord and master, and that outward sense / Is but the obedient servant of her will," after all, even as the rising of Imagination occurs as a negative epiphany extinguishing "the light of sense" (1805 *Prelude*, 11.271–73; 6.533). In all such moods of disorientation, "sense and outward things" fall away visually, become lost to consciousness, and leave the poet groping for them blankly amid the vestiges of their de-realization. So the Ode shows, as Vendler writes, that "besides the ecstatic component clothing the world in light and glory, there was another component [of childhood], dark, obscure, and subtractive" (Vendler, 82)—and she is entirely justified in stressing the differences between Wordsworth's two memories of childhood. For the "Blank misgivings" of stanza nine, a mystical darkening of mind and world, emerge as the apparent opposite of the luminous coloring of the Ode's opening tableaux.

The conceptual coherence of the Ode rests, however, on the interrelation of Wordsworth's visionary glory and blank misgivings. The two share a common mutability, obviously. More important, both the light and the darkness reveal the mind imposing itself upon the nominally external world. In these related impositions, the "poetic spirit" of human consciousness alternately modifies or, erupting at greater intensity, wholly appropriates nature. Each a visionary affront to empirical explanation, a natural world celestially illumined and a natural world mystically derealized equally demonstrate the human mind's independence of mere sensation. The religious claims of the Ode simply extend the mind's independence from its physical surroundings into an analogous freedom from temporal constraints. Traditionally paired, nature and time are transcended together, as the Ode affirms the imagination's affiliation with the absolute. Wordsworth's Fenwick note correlates his encounters with an "abyss of idealism"—his discoveries, as Blake might say, that "Mental Things are alone Real"—with his conviction "of the indomitableness of the spirit within [him]" (Fenwick note, *PW* 4.463). But the Ode itself correlates them on a grand scale by inferring the soul's immortality from the discrete but related experiences of a perceptually projective brightening, or a perceptually impositional erasure, of the natural world.

That progressively emergent correlation clarifies the importance of both the preexistence motif and Coleridge's Verse Letter to Wordsworth's case against materialism. Wordsworth's comparison of the glory of stanzas 1–4 to the heavenly visitant, "trailing clouds of glory" (line 64), in stanza five allowed him to reconfirm the glory's innateness, beauty, and evanescence. Yet that organizing comparison also allows him to compound the figural concentricity of the Ode. He can give the lost light of his initial stanzas—a metaphorical vehicle the tenor of which is "imagination"—a secondary vehicle of its own. In a manner reminiscent of the "stone is like sea-beast is like man" linkage of "Resolution and Independence," the Ode can thereby displace its controlling idea through an "imagination is like radiance is like preexistent soul" succession. This figural doubling introduces an additional vehicle through which Wordsworth can explore the fate of childhood vision. In doing so, moreover, it brilliantly justifies his introduction of "The Soul." Wordsworth's extended Romantic conceit allows the image of light to mediate between, and tacitly identify, imagination and soul. Again, the importance of the Verse Letter resided finally in the support it lent that identification. For Coleridge uses Wordsworth's light imagery, directly associating it with imagination, but also associates imagination with soul. He employs the word "soul" memorably and recurrently: "Ah! from the Soul itself must issue forth / A Light, a Glory, and a luminous Cloud"; "And from the Soul itself must there be se[nt] / A sweet & potent Voice, of its own Bir[th]"; "To thee would all Things live from Pole to Pole, / Their Life the Eddying of thy living Soul" (lines 301–2, 304–5, 334–35).

The example of Coleridge's Verse Letter helped Wordsworth extend the organizing religious claim of the Immortality Ode. Moving from luminous glory to mystical blankness, the Ode celebrates the mind's ability to transmute the naturalistic and temporal. Moving from imagination to soul, it associates this creative transmutation with the soul's transcendence of death. The transitions in stanza five from Boy, to Youth, to the Man who witnesses the light's fading, mark a temporal declension which conditions life tragically. Still, the process preserves a cyclical pathway back, grounding its hope for salvation in Wordsworth's faith that the discontinuities of human existence, while profound, are never complete: "O joy! that in our embers / Is something that doth live" (lines 132–33). What complements and completes this religious vision is Wordsworth's treatment of the redemptive child at the center of his poem.

DIVINE CHILD, MORTAL FATHER

Critics of the Immortality Ode often find it elegiac. In Vendler's opinion, for example, the Ode displays "the classic proportions of elegy" by descending to "that point of death which is reached by Wordsworth in the weight of custom," and then rising to an "apotheosis or transfiguration" (Vendler, 78). In reading the Ode elegiacally, I want to speculate that the elegy in Wordsworth's poem originates from his reflections on fatherhood. The Ode unquestionably displaces those reflections, which obtrude into the text only at a few revealing moments. The poem's epigraphs announce its interest in the relationship of fathers and sons. If the lines from "My heart leaps up" expressly declare that "The Child is Father of the Man," the poem's earlier Virgilian epigraph had similarly invoked the love and resistance binding son to father.[21] Within the Ode, Wordsworth at one point observes a father observing his son. This father enters the Ode as a surrogate Coleridge watching Hartley play, but Wordsworth assimilates these biographical references to a generalized model of the problems of fatherhood. Wordsworth's portrait of a son seeking paternal approval in stanzas 7–8 reveals his insights into masculine development as well as his anxieties about fatherhood. Those anxieties produce the passage describing the child's understanding of the grave as "a lonely bed without the sense or sight / Of day" (lines 121–22). Wordsworth finally deemed this image inessential for his poem, deleting it in response to Coleridge's strictures. It nonetheless affords a revealing perspective on the elegiac dynamics of the Ode. So does the *Hamlet* allusion of stanza nine, an allusion to the ghostly father who serves as a concealed motive force in Shakespeare's play—and Wordsworth's poem.

The Ode's elegiac meditation on family romance reflects Wordsworth's appreciation of the entanglement of immortality, death, and love. Discussing "the consciousness of a principle of immortality in the human soul" in the first *Essay on Epitaphs*, Wordsworth wrote,

> We may, then, be justified in asserting, that the sense of immortality, if not a co-existent and twin birth with Reason, is among the earliest of her offspring: and we may further assert, that from these conjoined, and under their countenance, the human affections are gradually formed and opened out. . . . for my own part, it is to me inconceivable, that the sympathies of love towards each other, which grow with our growth, could ever attain any new

strength, or even preserve the old, after we had received from the outward sense the impression of death . . . if the same were not counteracted by those communications with our internal Being, which are anterior to all these experiences, and with which revelation coincides. (*WPr* 2.51)

For Wordsworth, love is a matter of life *and* death. The prospect of love requires the presupposition of immortality. But death is the mother (or father) of immortality, an idea etymologically incorporating death as the reflex and ground of its own meaning. Fathers supposedly "die" sexually to be resurrected through their sons, sons who grant their sires a surrogate immortality—those "forward-looking thoughts" which deepened Michael's love for Luke. Yet this prospect of survival never nullifies entirely the connection of procreation with mortality.

Taking up that connection, the Ode explores the mutual implication of eternity and death as it conditions the love between father and son. By becoming a parent, a man perpetuates the generational sequence, assenting implicitly to his replacement by a son whose very existence figures the father's unavoidable finitude. "Sex is of the body," Ernest Becker observes, "and the body is of death":

animals who procreate, die. Their relatively short life span is somehow connected with their procreation. Nature conquers death not by creating eternal organisms but by making it possible for ephemeral ones to procreate. . . .
But now the rub for man. If sex is a fulfillment of his role as an animal in the species, it reminds him that he is nothing himself but a link in the chain of being, exchangeable with any other and completely expendable in himself. Sex represents, then species consciousness and, as such, the defeat of individuality, of personality.[22]

Moving metonymically from sex to procreation, we can add that parenthood also signifies the mortal defeat of the self. In fathering a son, a man initiates a relationship which promises the perpetuation of his identity, but which also reconfirms his mortality and symbolically delivers him to death.[23] The Ode attempts to unpack this paradox by distributing its elements into the discrete stages of a redemptive elegiac narrative. In the Immortality Ode, the identifications and rivalries of the father/son relationship move the father through successive responses to death—resistance, transference, acceptance—before allowing him his climactic affirmation of love for the son.

Haunted by the glory's transitoriness, the speaker of the Ode begins with resistance. To evade that fate presaged by the death of beauty, one can flee adulthood and nostalgically become a child again—a recovery of the past staged in several of Wordsworth's 1802 lyrics and again at times in the first four stanzas of the Immortality Ode. These stanzas—especially when taken in the context of the Ode as a whole—surely identify the ascendancy of the radiance with the period of childhood.[24] By turning to the joyful children of the May festival to seek his vanished glory, the poet bestows the glory upon childhood. In this ceremony of innocence, early days return and the speaker vicariously recovers his past: Wordsworth invokes the Shepherd Boy, as Paul Fry writes, "in order to make himself present to his own childhood."[25] It is a recovery W. B. Carnochan would consider typical of Romanticism. Carnochan distinguishes "the feelings of distance that Swift, Johnson, Gibbon, and Gray, for better or worse, put between themselves and their childhood" from the psychological proximity to childhood apparent in writers like Blake and Wordsworth.[26] "Even such a happy Child of earth am I," exclaims the speaker of "Resolution and Independence" as he identifies with nature's unselfconscious vitality. At the beginning of the Ode, Wordsworth can similarly tell the "Child of Joy," "My heart is at your festival, / My head hath its coronal" (lines 39–40). In both poems, the childlike mood dissolves quickly enough, and the strained tone of some of the Ode's avowals surely prefigures its dissolution. The voice dramatized in the Ode can nevertheless briefly identify with childhood to the point of repossession. The Ode's early stanzas include an "Already with thee!" moment in which the speaker seemingly shares the child's happy incomprehension of death, and would share it longer were that possible.

When the Immortality virtually re-begins with stanza five, Wordsworth elaborates upon the promise implicit in his early stanzas, and invokes a divine child embodying the assurance of immortality. This redemptive figure seems like a child of the sun, drenched with the light of heaven and replete with spiritual power:

> Our birth is but a sleep and a forgetting:
> The Soul that rises with us, our life's Star,
> Hath had elsewhere its setting,
> And cometh from afar:
> Not in entire forgetfulness,
> And not in utter nakedness,

But trailing clouds of glory do we come
From God, who is our home:
Heaven lies about us in our infancy!

(lines 58–66)

For just a moment, Wordsworth's visionary *topos* seems to insinuate him into the child's splendid immortality, the plural pronouns
indicating a common divinity, the "God, who is *our* home." Reaching a limit with this affirmation, unfortunately, the Ode immediately reverses field, insinuating the child into the speaker's mortality. It is a generational mortality, for the immortalizing power
summoned by the Ode at the beginning of stanza five remains shel-
tered in the "Soul," suffusing the collective, unindividuated state
of "our infancy" just slightly. When the "Soul" becomes a child,
the promise of immortality fades. The rest of stanza five charts the
temporal declension mentioned previously, a developmental
process in which the course of human life—from "Boy" to "Youth"
to "Man"—marches solemnly deathward. The succession unfolds
as if the speaker's solicitation of the boy worked to progressively
mortalize him. "The child is life, the man, death," G. Wilson
Knight remarked.[27]

The stanzas which follow contemplate the more specific proposition that the *father* is death, and that the father's deathliness taints
the son. For the "Soul" became a "child" only by acquiring a father
and entering a cycle of dying generations. The satirical stanzas of the
Ode explore death as a paternal legacy by reflecting, obliquely, on the
troubled filial experiences of Hartley Coleridge. Wordsworth brings
Hartley within the compass of the Immortality Ode through references to his diminutive stature and recent schooling, through echoes
of "To H. C., Six Years Old," and through allusions to other Coleridge
poems.[28] Mythologized as the quintessential Romantic Child, Hartley was to be reared by Nature's ministry and "wander like a breeze
/ By lakes and sandy shores," unlike his father, who spent his childhood "in the great city, pent 'mid cloisters dim" ("Frost at Midnight," lines 52–55). By 1802, however, the elegiac note Wordsworth
could strike in depicting Hartley's unfitness for life derived in part
from perceived similarities between the boy and his inspired, impossible father. In "To H. C., Six Years Old," the lines,

I thought of times when Pain might be thy guest,
Lord of thy house and hospitality;

And Grief, uneasy Lover! never rest
But when she sate within the touch of thee.
Oh! too industrious folly!
Oh! vain and causeless melancholy!

(lines 15–20),

seem overreactive unless read as Wordsworth's displaced analysis of a Coleridge cunning in his own overthrow. Through the connections it sketches, "To H. C." hints at family resemblances. But friends often noted the likeness of father and son, Anya Taylor remarks ("'A Father's Tale,'" 46–47), and Coleridge himself had written of Hartley in 1796, "He is the very miniature of me" (*CLSTC* 1.243).

By 1804 Wordsworth had greater reason to construe Hartley's worrisome oddities as filial inheritances. Coleridge's mounting personal problems aside, the developmental narrative of the Verse Letter—in which philosophical study ("abstruse research") deadens emotional resiliency—affords an obvious variation on what Lucy Newlyn calls the "fall into education" in stanza seven of the Ode (Newlyn, 153). Declaring "Hartley's 'endless imitation' . . . a repetition of his father's fall," Newlyn remarks that "it is tempting to think that [Coleridge] . . . perceived the analogy between Hartley and himself" (Newlyn, 154, 154n20). It is more tempting to think that Wordsworth intended the analogy. The Immortality Ode concentrates on transmissions between father and son by masculinizing the child's socialization. The boy of stanzas 7–8, Vendler astutely observes,

has discovered how to please his father—by imitating adult transactions. He is annoyed when his mother—who wishes he were still the baby on her lap—makes possessive forays on his attention. The father's approval is all he seeks. . . . Wordsworth keenly sees the child's own eagerness to "grow up," and emphasizes the paternal role in the socializing of the boy.[29]

When the process of growing up refashions the child as a "little Actor" increasingly out of touch with his own deeper being, the father's power to shape the son in his image appears deadening—a funeral pall "Heavy as frost, and deep almost as life!" (line 131). This mortal weight falls as if in realization of a family curse: the Ode glances at the vexed relationship of Coleridge and Hartley to present mortality itself as a fate conferred on sons by fathers.

Here we might note that several of Coleridge's 1796 sonnets contain seemingly unmotivated prophecies of Hartley's death. In the earliest, "Written on Receiving Letters Informing Me of the Birth of a Son," the prophecy becomes protectively wishful: "ere my Babe youth's perilous maze have trod," Coleridge prays to the Deity, may "Thy overshadowing Spirit . . . descend, / And he be born again, a child of God!" (lines 12–14). This prayer would make Coleridge a father no more. The next sonnet, the preexistence poem "Composed on a Journey Homeward," concludes similarly with the child's spirit springing "to meet Heaven's quick reprieve, / While we wept idly o'er thy little bier!" (lines 13–14). In the third sonnet, "To a Friend Who Asked," Coleridge so empathizes with Hartley—seeing "All I had been, and all my child might be!"—as to compound recollection and premonition in a "dark remembrance and a presageful fear" (lines 4, 10). These poems disclose the mobility of the term "death" in the economy of identification and resistance binding fathers and sons. When first informed of Hartley's birth, Coleridge described himself as "quite *annihilated*" (*CLSTC* 1.236; italics mine). While he meant stunned, his choice of diction appears powerfully revealing. Experiencing fatherhood, Coleridge seemingly intuited his mortality—as if, in anticipation of Ernest Becker's theories, the birth of a son symbolically *meant* his own death. Yet in the poems, the son becomes the endangered figure, and for reasons hardly demanding psychoanalytic explanation: infant mortality rates were high in the late eighteenth century. We know too much about the psyche's defensive inversions, however, not to feel suspicious of Coleridge's fears for his son. Surely those fears transpose the poet's own intimations of mortality. They take the prospect of death aroused in Coleridge by Hartley's birth and return it to the child, remade as a paternal benediction, a fatherly show of shielding the boy from threats originating, in truth, in Coleridge's own anxieties.

In a similar way, whether or not Wordsworth had Coleridge in mind, the Immortality Ode consigns its own child figure to death. In its original form, the Ode portrayed the child's actual death, although the vision undergoes complex displacement. Wordsworth depicts the boy as one

> To whom the grave
> Is but a lonely bed without the sense or sight
> Of day or the warm light,
> A place of thought where we in waiting lie.
>
> (lines 120–23)

Coleridge considered these lines "frightful" for the suffocating eeri-
ness they conveyed (*Biographia Literaria*, 2.141). Their disturbing
aspect arises from the fact, I propose, that obscurely embedded in
them lies the image of a dead child. I realize that the passage presents the living child's incomprehension of death and that the
poet's "we" makes the plight envisioned a shared one. But in rendering a child's conception of death, the image implies the child
proleptically visualizing his own death. The poem uncannily
depicts its "little Child" imagining himself, as William and
Dorothy once did, actually lying in a grave.[30] The lines literalize an
"analogy between death and sleep" habitual, Coleridge remarked,
to "all christian children" (*Biographia Literaria*, 2.141). The idea of
a grave as a darkened bed remains profoundly childlike, very much
an instance of what a child, drawing on familiar experience, might
imagine death to be. Framed by satirical commentaries which treat
the son's maturation as a journey into psychic death, Wordsworth's
"lonely bed" trades the radiance of immortality for funereal darkness, and momentarily inters its redemptive child.

The remainder of the Ode unfolds in recoil from this elegiac crisis. In the sequence from stanza five to stanza eight, the Ode dramatized a process of transference whereby its briefly immortal
child assumed the mortality of his earthly father. The poem reaches
its final phase by disassociating death from the son and transferring
it back to the father. As in the conclusion to *Adonais*, the elegiac
exchanges of Wordsworth's poem attempt to divide death and eternality between its two main characters—with the Ode's climactic
reimmortalizing of its child figures occurring as a reflex of the
father's deliverance to death. The poem's immortalizing drive produces an image of the dead father, in fact, as a reversive counterpart
of the dead child palimpsest in stanza eight. Wordsworth evokes
the death of the father by alluding to *Hamlet*:

> Blank misgivings of a Creature
> Moving about in worlds not realiz'd,
> High instincts, before which our mortal Nature
> Did tremble like a guilty Thing surpriz'd.
>
> (lines 147–50)

The lines echo Horatio's description of Hamlet's ghostly father
who, with daylight's return, "started like a guilty thing / Upon a
fearful summons" (1.1.148–49).[31] This richly suggestive echo

imprints the Ode equally with the father's demands upon the son and the father's guilt. Allusion seemingly identifies the child of the Ode with the spectral father, Wordsworth's immortal visitant allusively inheriting the gruesome deathliness of the Shakespearean father-figure.

Through this identification of child and ghost, life and death, the lines certainly stage Wordsworth's oblique confession, reduced to mere implication, of his poem's inability to truly liberate its child-figures from time. But the Ode disrupts the mortalizing connection which the *Hamlet* allusion draws between father and son, and it is that disruption, in my reading, in which Wordsworth seems most profoundly invested. The child lost in an "abyss of idealism," as Wordsworth termed it, and the ghost stalking the castle until daybreak are, after all, *obverse* instances of beings dispelled from their familiar worlds: the natural child groping amid an immaterial darkness, the immaterial shade prowling through the darkness of a natural night. Just so, the Shakespearean scene which Wordsworth recalls leaves Hamlet and the ghost on opposite sides of a border, with the son's capacity for action—and living possession of the morning—a distinction between them of enormous importance. The father may be dead; the son is alive. Wordsworth's allusion significantly recalls the moment of the ghost's banishment to the realms of death by "the light of common day." The allusion therefore acts as a cathartic icon in Wordsworth's elegiac plot. It is as though the Ode were obligated to a transvaluative logic demanding the death of the father. Wrested from eternity to life, the newborn son of the Ode inherits the father's mortality. The boy can be freed from death, it seems, only if the father will self-sacrifically reassume his dubious gift. In turning from the child thinking about inhabiting a grave to Shakespeare's spectral patriarch, the Ode seemingly enacts that reassumption, transferring death from child back to father.

One thing seems clear: what results from the Ode's *Hamlet* allusion is the poet's renewed ability to immortalize the children of his poem. When stanza nine begins, Wordsworth's Hartley-like boy has been a figure of the moribund for some time. Stanza eight may refer to his spiritual "heritage," but throughout the satirical tableaux all such references are ironic rather than celebratory, touchstones in a lament over the child's perverse complicity in his own mortalizing diminishment. They identify qualities lost to life's heavy changes. The "simple creed" of childhood, no creed at all, surrounds the boy with the lesser pleasures of a purely sensuous existence. Even his playing represents a form of enervating imitativeness. Only after Wordsworth allusively dispatches the father to death can the Ode invoke eternity in celebratory terms and position its "best Philosopher" near his originary immortality:

> Hence, in a season of calm weather,
> Though inland far we be,
> Our Souls have sight of that immortal sea
> Which brought us hither,
> Can in a moment travel thither,
> And see the Children sport upon the shore,
> And hear the mighty waters rolling evermore.

(lines 164–70)

Given "the thalassic depths of primal experience sounded by the images," in McFarland's phrase (McFarland, 61), this passage can seem like a mysterious dream-matrix for the Ode as a whole, its deepest memory. The poet can only imagine his children at the threshold of transcendence. Still, Wordsworth's vision grants them delighted contact with "that immortal sea," assimilating child's play and "mighty waters" as complementary aspects of an "evermore" the poem has authorized him to name.

Unfortunately, this redemptive *topos* excludes the poet himself, who remains stationed "inland far." That exclusionary distancing reiterates the costs of imaginatively giving the children this refuge. The visionary strangeness of Wordsworth's shoreline was noticed years ago by W. K. Wimsatt.[32] What struck Wimsatt as curious was precisely the children's seemingly gratuitous presence in these lines: the metaphorical function of Wordsworth's passage requires only that the poet, using a spatial trope for a temporal experience, be allowed sight of the waters. "Why," Wimsatt asked, "are the children found on the seashore?" (Wimsatt, 87). His answer was that Wordsworth's sporting children facilitate an exercise in revitalizing identification: "the travellers looking back in both space and time see themselves as children on the shore" (Wimsatt, 87). Yet I cannot feel that the lines allow poet and children psychic convergence, or that the speaker emotionally recovers his childhood in them. These children do not allow Wordsworth to trace his own way back. He seems resigned, rather, to his distant vantage point. Ultimately, the prodigal children of the Ode's ninth stanza embody a redemption available in some form to the poet and all adults. Nonetheless this shoreline no adults approach. It is a place where children play and Wordsworth refuses to intrude upon it. The lines are most moving for his absence from them.

That valedictory absence reconfirms the significance of the *Hamlet* allusion. It signifies a fatherly assent to death, the poet relinquishing his claims upon the children's seaside immortality in freeing them to their own experiences. Peter Manning has suggested, although hesitantly, that when the Ode commits its consolations to the image of the child, the poet briefly "appears as a mother."[33] For me, conversely, in the Ode Wordsworth writes as a father. The poem's various invocations of fathers and sons, of the problems of paternity, mediate Wordsworth's own authorial identification with the fatherly role. "Some extraordinary revaluation of [Wordsworth's] childhood experiences clearly occurred between the initial composition of the first four stanzas and the later completion of the poem," Vendler writes of the Ode, and most Wordsworthians would agree, even if they differed among themselves in explaining the reorientation (Vendler, 81). I would attribute the differences between the 1802 and 1804 sections of the Ode partly to Wordsworth's first authentic experiences of fatherhood. Either in Paris or already embarked for England, the poet had been absent when, and long after, Caroline was born in 1792. Johnny's birth in 1803 plunged him into the myriad immediacies of fatherhood. Between starting the Ode in 1802 and finishing it in 1804, Wordsworth had in an important sense become not only a husband but a father for the first time.

This experience of fatherhood, the Ode hints, moved him to thoughts of his son's mortality. The Ode seems motivated at points by his resistance to such thoughts, and by an impossible determination to liberate the child-figures of his poem from death—or rather, since the Ode acknowledges the impossibility, by the poet's fears of childhood death. To see those fears informing the text we need only return to Wordsworth's ocean scene, recasting Wimsatt's question and inquiring not about the children's presence by the sea but the sea's presence in the poem. For "it is not clear by what logic," Fry remarks of the Ode's development, "the celestial descent has become an aquatic emergence" (Fry, 149). The Ode moves to the sea, I suggest, because oceanic imagery could most effectively conflate the ideas of the poet's powerlessness and the children's vulnerability. The shore traditionally marks the limit of poetic vision. "The image of the drowned man," John Heath-Stubbs remarks, "haunts English poetry whenever the poet envisions imaginative failure through the overreaching of his powers."[34] At the same time, Wordsworth's surging waters unquestionably threaten the children themselves. We are so accustomed to the Ode's sublime assertions, so familiar with its celebration of celestial birthrights and glorious vestures, that we can easily overlook how insistently the poem concentrates its preoccupation with mortality upon the figure of the child. "Burial never seems far from Wordsworth's mind when he looks at water," Willard Spiegelman muses, adding justly, "Nor, for that matter, is death far from his mind when he looks at children."[35] So in a shoreline scene intended to propound the invulnerability of innocence, Wordsworth superimposes the children against the same sea which claimed Lycidas, recognizing their exposure to death even as he makes them geniuses of the shore.

The underlying fears of the Immortality Ode proved prophetic for Wordsworth. The deaths of their children ranked among the most agonizing events of William and Mary Wordsworth's life together. If Wordsworthians will think instantly of "Surprised by joy" in this connection, several other poems and letters reveal the Wordsworths' utter anguish over the deaths of both Catherine and Thomas in 1812. The deathly prefigurations of the Ode's ninth stanza look beyond childhood, however, to all human suffering occasioned by temporality. In that way Wordsworth's ocean scene also leads appropriately to the concluding stanzas of the Ode, with their chastened, clear-sighted resignation. I argue below that these minor chords nullify none of the poem's religious commitment. They simply remind us that the speaker of the Ode, no Dante touring heaven, attains his spiritual insights within the world of time and nature.[36] Offered as consolation, the faith of the Immortality Ode concedes the need for consolation, but also reaffirms the love which underlies human vulnerability, especially a father's love for his children.

THE ODE AND CHRISTIANITY

Wordsworth's meditation on childhood and death reflects the evolution of his faith from 1800–1804. To all appearances, his earlier attraction to the One Life had been based partially on an unconscious maternalizing of nature. Manning has shown, for example, how *The Ruined Cottage* transforms a "fantasy of reunion" with the mother into the Wordsworthian topos of "the solitary man communing with nature," even as Richard Onorato has shown how the complex evasions of "Tintern Abbey" disclose an "unconsciously held resemblance between the mother and Nature."[37] By the time of the Immortality Ode the lure of maternal reassimilation had seemingly lost its hold on Wordsworth. Trilling has of course made the exactly opposite claim, but I cannot agree with him. While honoring natural beauty and praising Nature for her "Mother's mind" (line 79), the Ode betrays no nostalgia for pantheistic immersion in a maternalized natural world. Here the poet speaks not as an Oedipally bereaved son—or so I have argued—but as a mature man who contemplates childhood from a fatherly perspective. This speaker privileges a supernatural order portrayed as masculine and patriarchal, addressing his appeals to "God, who is our home" (line 65). By 1804 Wordsworth had stopped wanting the mother, I suggest, because he had grown beyond seeing himself as a son. My further suggestion is merely that this "growing up," as Trilling put it, encouraged his drift toward Christian orthodoxy. Intellectually, Wordsworth had declined the One Life some years earlier. But not until he decisively outgrew an unconscious filial self-image—with its yearning for the mother and struggle against the father—could he turn decisively toward a religion in which "assurance of the trustworthiness of the Divine character," Norman Sykes remarks, rested in large measure on "the popular doctrine of the Fatherhood of God."[38]

It is hardly coincidental, then, that Trilling's reading of pre-existence in the Ode as a trope for prenatal union comes accompanied by an insistence on the poem's naturalism. Those differently minded critics who concede the Ode's religious interests usually dismiss its Christian associations. Or they agree that the Ode's frame of reference may be predominately Christian, but that Wordsworth's Christianity remains thoroughly vexed and hesitant, contributing essentially nothing to the poem's meaning. This Wordsworth surrendered the Ode to a radical secularism: to a determined humanism cautious of belief, prepared to flirt with the transcendental, if only as a figure for the enigmas of memory, but unprepared to affirm Christian truths even tacitly. That is the Immortality Ode which modern criticism offers; it is an offer I suggest we decline. Before accepting it, we should at least notice that nineteenth-century readers typically regarded the Ode as an expression of faith, often admiring the poem precisely for its revisionary Christianity. Wordsworth's undoctrinaire "religion in Poetry" never satisfied the fiercely zealous; almost predictably, when first published the Ode itself was accused of outright irreligiousness by one reviewer.[39] Scholars conversant with the Immortality Ode's reception know well, however, that most nineteenth-century readers approached Wordsworth's poem as a religious statement, and most typically as a Christian affirmation.[40] It was a favorite of both Evangelical reformers and Tractarian apologists, at times inspiring the reverence aglow in Hopkins' 1886 comment: "for my part I shd. think that St. George and St. Thomas of Canterbury wore roses in heaven for England's sake on the day that ode, not without their intercession, was penned."[41]

The Immortality Ode solicits these readings. For the poem's visionary gambits are framed by spiritually familiarizing diction, by images and motifs which presuppose and reinscribe the Christianity of the poet's projected audience. In the Ode Wordsworth "had dared to clothe the experience of his own childhood," Vendler remarks, "in the most sublime of literary modes, the mode of revealed religion," by drawing his language "from the most powerful cluster of poetic words, images, and concepts in English, the King James Bible," and from the literary tradition through which that religious rhetoric was further disseminated (Vendler, 72). The use of Christian diction and allusion begins in stanza one, becomes more overt in stanza two—Wordsworth's "there hath pass'd away a glory from the earth" (line 18) echoes Christ's words, "Heaven and earth shall pass away, but my words shall not pass away"—and never lags. The language of the Ode is massively inflected with Christian associations: there are Wordsworth's explicit references to God, Heaven, soul, immortality, "the eternal mind," and "the faith that looks through death"; his use of religious words such as "benediction," "blest," and "creed"; his various biblical and Miltonic allusions; his choice of biblical pronouns and forms of address ("Ye blessed Creatures"); and his recourse to such images as celestial light, glory, the rainbow, the rose, the lamb, the flowers of the field, and the "Tree, of many one," with its suggestion of the Fall. At the center of these constellated Christian motifs is, of course, Wordsworth's heavenly child.

The cyclical myth of the Immortality Ode makes this child at once a figure of memory and a harbinger of redemption. As a figure of the soul, the child of the Ode offers the promise of eternal life. He therefore recalls Christ as child, as the incarnated coincidence of childhood and divinity. Even his fifth stanza's Platonic conceit Wordsworth wrests to the purposes of a Christian mythmaking through an especially dense collocation of religious diction. Alan

Grob remarks that the very passage introducing Wordsworth's heavenly visitant "seems pointedly Christian in its language, referring literally to the 'Soul,' to 'God,' and to 'Heaven.'"⁴² This Christianizing of Plato produces a Platonized Christianity. Most orthodox members of Wordsworth's reading public could not endorse the notion of the soul's preexistence any more than he could. Fortunately, they could agree that the second person of the Trinity resided with the Father in heaven before beginning His earthly trials, and that Christ's ability to become a child again liberated the soul from the "second death" of damnation. Declared to have existed prior to his mortal probation, gendered as a son, and made the guarantor of eternal life, the redemptive child of the Immortality Ode becomes in implication a typological figure of Christ. For all its visionary boldness, Wordsworth's divinizing of the child of the Ode depended on a widespread cultural symbolism. In ways making example superfluous, Christ's insistence that children are closer to God—"Except ye be converted and become as little children, ye shall not enter the kingdom of heaven"—had prompted celebrations of childhood innocence that ramified through countless sermons, hymns, poems, and essays in the religious culture of Wordsworth's day.⁴³

The Christian associations of the Ode produce what Joseph Sitterson calls an "internalization of Incarnation" (Sitterson, 32). Discussing the bearing of "On the Morning of Christ's Nativity" on the Immortality Ode, Sitterson notes that Milton's poem foregrounds a religious context only implied by the Ode yet crucial to its meaning:

> Wordsworth's poem connects the child and his birth with the Incarnation itself—connects, not equates. "[W]e come," in words not to be glossed over as Christian excrescences in a dialectic of self and nature, "From *God*, who is our home: / *Heaven* lies about us in our infancy!" . . . And if "The Child is father of the Man," then the poet's wish that such a connection be maintained by "natural piety" becomes not only a familial and natural devotion but specifically a religious one. That is, the poet does not worship blindly and egotistically his earlier or preexistent self; instead he piously values his own nativity as a sign, however enigmatic, that there is something more than nature and self. (Sitterson, 32)

Wordsworth certainly forebears to "equate" the birth of the Ode's child "with the Incarnation itself": doing so would have been outlandishly presumptuous. And Sitterson rightly emphasizes that the

Immortality Ode merely likens its vision of nativity to the Incarnation. Later in his essay he notes further that the internalizing gestures of Wordsworth's poem are complicated by anxieties, unfelt by Milton, over the uncertainties of prophetic inspiration. Yet Sitterson is also right to insist that Wordsworth's internalization of Incarnation retains a specifically religious significance and seriousness. The hint of severity in his comment that the Ode's sublime affirmations should not "be glossed over as Christian excresences in a dialectic of self and nature" is entirely fair.

For if the Ode declines to equate "the child and his birth" with Christ's Incarnation, it similarly declines to equate the Incarnation with the saving power of recollection. As with the Prospectus, the internalizing project of the Ode promotes a rich humanism, yet not a humanism which casts away the divine and replaces it with the human. By no means does Wordsworth use his redemptive child for a full-scale psychological relocation of the Christian promise of salvation. Rather, through the inwardness of the Ode we witness the poet's spiritual imagination finding subtler imprints of divinity within human consciousness—exploring the religious mystery of human consciousness by reading God's displacement of Himself in the deepest recesses of memory. Wordsworth does not declare that God *is* the human mind and heart; he declares that God is *in* the human mind and heart. As an exercise in Christian mythmaking, the Immortality Ode refuses to endorse Church doctrines directly. At the same time, the poem's almost incessant Christian inflections strategically coordinate its religious outlook with Christian values. Wordsworth's evocations of Christianity place the Ode's supernaturalism in a metaphorical relationship to Christian tradition. They render the Ode's transcendent gestures not fully coincident with Christianity, certainly, but coterminous with it. Wordsworth summons the spiritual authority of the Christian tradition to bolster his own visionary claims. At the same time, those claims selectively reconfirm the Christian revelation and represent Wordsworth's prophetic innovations upon a tradition his poem honors.

Critics often caution that Wordsworth's use of religious imagery in the Ode is in effect Arnoldian, an imaginative expedient which enhances the text's breadth of implication without ceding it to literal belief. One of the most judicious and widely approved formulations of this position is Manning's. Reflecting on the sunset image of Wordsworth's last stanza, Manning comments that in the Ode the preservation of the past in memory emerges as a private spiritual analogue to the Christian's keeping alive the presence of Christ in his heart: the Kingdom of God is within you. The Christian resonance accords with the language of transcendence running throughout the poem: it strengthens, for example, the echoes in "Another race hath been, and other palms are won" of I Corinthians 9:24–25. . . . I would argue nonetheless that the indirectness of the reference to Scripture is as important to the success of the poem as the reference itself. . . . If the concluding movement of elegy is consolation, then it is the restraint of Wordsworth's final affirmations that is remarkable. The inclusive self-portrait that emerges from the disparate pictures of the Ode is that of "A meditative, oft a suffering man," to borrow the contemporaneous words of *The Prelude*, "temperate in all things," as in the Pauline exhortation. The closing emphasis is on the continuing "joys and fears" of this meditative mind, and not on a heavenly resolution. The poem exploits the resonances of Christian faith without committing itself to belief, to the conviction that would lessen its human uncertainty. (Manning, "Epigraphs," 538)

Manning is a Wordsworth critic I particularly admire, and yet I find myself deeply resistant to his treatment of the Ode's conclusion. For one thing, I do not think—and doubt that Manning truly thinks—uncertainty more fundamentally "human" than belief. But I am troubled further by the way this position verges on the indirect suggestion that religious faith dispels the pain of human life, so that if we find Wordsworth's restrained tone an admission of that pain, the only conclusion to be drawn is that his belief must be uncommitted and inauthentic.

The muted tones of the Ode's final meditation do not qualify or retract its affirmation of an immortal soul. Instead they foreground the existential problems of living with faith. Secular but not naturalistic, the Ode turns in closing to the speaker's worldly situation, to his awareness of how mortality conditions the possibilities of living long before death comes. That dramatically appropriate turn by no means nullifies the exalted claims which precede it. The Ode expressly avows the existence of God, Heaven, and the Soul: surely this is not the poem to serve as a textual exhibit of Wordsworth's inability to accept his culture's leading conceptions of supernatural truth. Religious faith requires assent to propositions about the nature of absolute reality; it does not provide for a humanly absolute experience of conviction. The crucified Christ confessed to feeling abandoned by God, and Christian apologists from Saint

Augustine on have depicted doubt as a contributory moment in the way of the soul. We all understand that doubt may so intensify as to destroy faith. Doubt itself, however, does not seem to trouble the Ode's conclusion, which appears emotionally chastened but not intellectually irresolute, the penetrative "thoughts too deep for tears" of Wordsworth's last line looking back to "the faith that looks through death." Faith has its moods, and "O dearer far," the 1824 poem discussed above, illustrates one of them. But the ending of the Immortality Ode does not disclose a wishful, wavering faith. It presents the self-portrait of a man who has lived on sufficiently intimate terms with faith to appreciate its inability to rid human life of suffering.

Despite that appreciation, it would be a mistake to belabor the elegiac restraint of Wordsworth's final stanzas. They counterbalance the lyrical exuberance of earlier passages, and render the Ode's religious affirmations more convincing. The poem's religious humanism underlies its insistence on the native spiritual dignity of humankind. I noted in beginning that the Immortality Ode mounts a displaced polemic against the Augustinian emphasis on original sin and, more specifically, the Calvinistic orientation of British Evangelicalism. Eighteenth- and nineteenth-century England witnessed thunderous denunciations of the inherent sinfulness of unsaved children in particular: "Great God, how terrible art thou," Isaac Watts had hymned, "To sinners ne'er so young!"[44] The persistence of such attitudes appears when one considers the popularity of Wilberforce's *Practical View* in light of the author's characteristically earnest exhortation,

> Remember that we are fallen creatures, born in sin, and naturally depraved. Christianity recognizes no innocence or goodness of heart but in the remission of sin, and in the effects of the operation of divine grace.[45]

We are born in glory, the Ode retorts. Wordsworth did not invent that response: images of childhood as a spiritually heightened time, a golden time, recur in sacred and secular writings from before the time of Christ. But the Ode gave the image culturally unprecedented power in nineteenth-century England. With the Immortality Ode, Wordsworth helped direct the philanthropic and humanitarian energies of his Victorian readers to the plight of children. By linking his assertion of the soul's immortality, demonstrated by the reconstitutive powers of the human imagination, to a celebration of a child's innate spiritual privilege, he used the idea of childhood to ease the spiritual disquietude of his age. He gave imperviousness to death a human form by making "our infancy," as he wrote in the 1799 *Prelude*, "A visible scene / On which the sun in shining" (*TPP* 1.463–64). He made the Romantic myth of natural innocence the guarantor of a supernatural heritage.

Politically, it is a conservative heritage in which the stabilities of mature wisdom assimilate youthful glory, so teasingly fleeting, and establish its genuine meaning. For, however glamorous "the visionary gleam," its ultimate import lies in the way it evokes and defers to underlying continuities—that "primal sympathy / Which having been must ever be" (lines 184–85)—reminiscent ideologically of the organic traditionalism of Edmund Burke. Citing Hazlitt's use of the Ode as a touchstone of revolutionary nostalgia in his review of *The Excursion*, Marjorie Levinson argues in fact that in the Ode "Wordsworth not only organizes his imagery in an ideologically specific fashion, he draws his denotative and iconic materials from the dictionary of eighteenth-century libertarian discourse,"and that the poem's revisionary program supplants Enlightenment notions of Nature and Reason with "a radical conservatism" (Levinson, 90, 95). So here, as throughout Wordsworth's 1802–1804 writing, the greater conventionality of his religious outlook coexists with greater nationalistic and patriotic leanings. We encounter the same entanglement of theological and political conservatism in the 1805 *Prelude*. There Wordsworth's builds his affirmation of the transcendental imagination, the "creative soul," into a developmental narrative assimilating the revolutionary upheavals of his epoch to the form of religious prophecy and myth.

CHAPTER FIVE

Soul's Progress:
The Faith of *The Prelude*

Scarce conscious, and yet conscious of its close
I sate, my being blended in one thought
(Thought was it? or aspiration? or resolve?)
Absorbed, yet hanging still upon the sound—
And when I rose, I found myself in prayer.

—Coleridge, "To William Wordsworth"

"*The Prelude,*" Stephen Gill asserts, "is a religious poem."[1] His matter-of-fact air renders the statement all the more strategically provocative. For the majority of modern academic critics, as Gill well knows, Wordsworth's human and historical interests so dominate his autobiographical epic as to reduce God to "an adventitious and nonoperative factor. . . . The purely formal remainder of His former self." These phrases come from a section of M. H. Abrams' *Natural Supernaturalism* where he memorably asked of *The Prelude,* "what does God *do* in the poem?"—and memorably answered, "nothing of consequence" (*NS,* 90). I entirely agree that we should not expect bold representations of divine agency from *The Prelude.*[2] We can gauge religion's contribution to *The Prelude* more effectively, testing Gill's assertion, simply by invoking the timeworn distinction between narrative subject and authorial point of view. *The Prelude* does not portray the poet's development from a viewpoint restricted to the concepts mind and nature. Rather, Wordsworth makes the influence of nature on his imagination the focal *subject* of *The Prelude*, then explores that subject from an authorial *viewpoint* which regularly mentions God. While Wordsworth's God occasionally acts in His own right, and exercises an enormous indirect agency through the ministry of nature, *The Prelude* remains a realistic autobiographical narrative. It depicts human life as most religions have understood it in recent centuries: as a sequence of earthly events lacking God's intervention in the world "outside" consciousness except at rare moments, and yet controlled by purposes emanating from Him. *The Prelude*, in short, is a modern religious poem.

The faith of *The Prelude* marries Wordsworth's assurance of spiritual purpose to his humanistic reverence for the "mind of Man." Acting on that reverence, he builds the Immortality Ode's interest in imagination as an internalization of divinity—the site of the soul—into a religious perspective enfolding the events of his life in a single, retrospectively revealed design. Evidence suggests that his commitment to a longer *Prelude* including the French Revolution followed partly from religious considerations. Certainly he makes his political experiences turn on a Fall occasioned by his related attractions to Power and the Sublime. His eventual progress beyond the Sublime typologically reenacts the historical progress of Christianity from punitive violence to a gospel of love. So the protagonist's development culminates quite appropriately in the implied Christianity of the poem's final book. As with the Christian mythmaking of the Immortality Ode, the Christian suggestiveness of the 1805 *Prelude* offers readers a culturally familiar context for understanding. The poem expressly affirms religious values; it then likens those values to orthodox tenets by allusively invoking Christianity in presenting the speaker's revelations. Again, Wordsworth stations individual prophetic insight and Christian tradition as complimentary, mutually corroborative variations on a common ground of truth. The resulting religious position qualified for most nineteenth-century readers as a form of revisionary Christianity—and that, my conclusion will suggest, is most probably how the poet himself intended matters. John Wordsworth's February 1805 drowning consolidated his brother's growing religious conventionality, confirming William in that conservative turn which would leave him, despite the heterodoxies recorded by Crabb

Robinson, committed to the established Church. Through the displacements of Christianity in the Thirteen-Book *Prelude* Wordsworth attempts to revitalize and reclaim the faith of his nation and his childhood.

RESHAPING *THE PRELUDE*, 1804

From one important perspective, accounting for the 1805 *Prelude* means accounting for the process by which Wordsworth discontinued the Five-Book *Prelude* of spring 1804 and began recasting his life story on epic scale. In the years following 1799, the poet occasionally composed passages for his autobiographical poem. But his first full-scale expansion of the Two-Part *Prelude* of 1799 dates from January-March 1804. At that time Wordsworth projected a *Prelude* in five books organized around the influence of nature and books on his imaginative development. This conception of the poem survives in drafts, some finished and some extremely rough, in MSS. WW and W. Editorial reconstructions of this planned poem by Jonathan Wordsworth and Mark Reed—with Robin Jarvis selectively dissenting—envision versions of Books 1 and 2 modeled closely on the two parts of the 1799 text, with the drowned man of Esthwaite and spots of time episodes from 1799 Part 1 repositioned, respectively, in 1804 Books 4 and 5; a Book 3 similar to Book 3 of the 1805 text; a Book 4 basically combining the material of 1805 Books 4 and 5; and a Book 5 beginning with the ascent of Snowdon, moving to a transitional passage, and concluding with the spots of time.[3] This Five-Book *Prelude* was abandoned on or around March 10, having enjoyed a life span of 6–8 weeks. By 18 March Coleridge, leaving soon for Malta, had been sent versions of Books 1–5 closely resembling 1805 1–5 and shortly thereafter Wordsworth had moved on to work intended for later sections.

Wordsworth recast his Five-Book *Prelude* apparently because his conception of it unraveled in Book 5. Reed believes, in fact, that MS. W displays the five-book poem's conceptual unraveling. At one point in MS. W Wordsworth shifts into lines which anticipate 1805 Book 11. For Reed, these drafts "seem oddly unconnected with the content of MS. W," but "make much readier sense against the background of . . . the poet's journey through the Alps and the AB Book VI descriptions of France at the outset of the second year of the Revolution."[4] He consequently infers that these MS. W prefigurations of the political concerns of 1805 Book 11 were intended for a poem that was to treat both the 1790 walking tour and a temporary but significant lapse in the poet's imaginative growth. The enlargement of plan would appear to have occurred logically as an outgrowth of Wordsworth's development of the "foes" theme on MS. W 45^r 47^r, and to be documented formally by the outset of the AB XI, 42 ff, passage on 47^r. . . . [which] almost certainly marks the point by which Wordsworth's intention to complete the poem in five books had succumbed before a paramount impulse to treat later events of the poet's progress to maturity, and to treat them on a scale beyond—probably indeterminably beyond—the compass of five books. (Reed, 34)

Below I return to Reed's suggestion that "the 'foes' theme"— Wordsworth's analysis of forces inimical to creativity—fostered the text's expansion beyond five books. For the moment, the salient point is simply Reed's conviction that MS. W incorporates the textual site of Wordsworth's abandonment of the five-book poem—a claim of far-reaching significance. Identifying the apparent textual locus of the 1804 poem's dissolution, Reed implicitly identifies the imaginative matrix of the Thirteen-Book *Prelude*.

It is an identification confirmed by Jonathan Wordsworth's analysis of MS. W, despite his apparent dissent from Reed's reconstruction of the compositional progress of Wordsworth's fifth book. Unlike Reed, Jonathan Wordsworth finds it "easier to believe," if impossible to prove, that the poem was essentially finished. Having summarized its structure, he comments,

it remains to ask how near it was to completion. On present evidence no satisfactory answer can be given. There is, however, no reason why the five-book *Prelude* shouldn't in fact have been finished. Time was short, but Wordsworth had only to tidy up 200 or so lines of existing draft. . . . Though it is not a point on which great emphasis should be laid, the nature of Wordsworth's tidying up in Books XI and XII suggests that it is more likely to belong to the original period of composition. . . . It seems easier to believe that he got beyond the fragmented drafts of *W* and achieved some sort of connected whole, the previous March, while the phrases and ideas were still fluid in his mind. ("Five-Book *Prelude*," 23–24).

The ramifications of this position for Reed's reconstruction of the imaginative genealogy of the 1805 *Prelude* can seem striking. After all, MS. W cannot formally incorporate the textual site of the five-book poem's breakdown, as Reed argues, if the poem in fact achieved completion. For critics interested in the genesis of the thir-teen-book poem of 1805, however, it finally matters little whether or not the Five-Book *Prelude* was provisionally finished. For "if the climbing of Snowdon was one of the first passages to be composed for the five-Book poem," Duncan Wu reminds us, "those connecting it with the spots of time were evidently the last" (*FBP*, 9), and the five-book scheme collapsed immediately thereafter. So the two posi-tions broadly agree. It makes no real difference whether we locate Wordsworth's cancellation of the five-book plan during or directly after the writing done towards the end of MS. W. In either case, MS. W allows us to speculatively reconstruct Wordsworth's dissatisfac-tion with his Five-Book *Prelude* and his reasons for expanding it.

Why then did Wordsworth drop the Five-Book *Prelude*? Jonathan Wordsworth argues that "two factors seem especially to have influenced Wordsworth's decision to work towards a longer poem: dissatisfaction at having left out important biographical material and unwillingness to make a further attempt on the cen-tral philosophical section of *The Recluse*" ("Five-Book *Prelude*," 24). Elaborating on a point made by Ernest de Selincourt, Reed adds a third factor in noting that Wordsworth's expansion of the Five-Book *Prelude* followed upon his decision "to make 'higher minds,' as such—rather than natural effects analogous to those produced by higher minds—his primary subject."[5] As Reed's phrasing implies, his claim rests partly on the evidence of what Wordsworth scholar-ship has agreed to call the Analogy Passage. This 140–line passage consists of six illustrations of the "analogy betwixt / The mind of man and Nature," all of which dramatize the power of nature, and even "the powerful ascendancy of nature over men."[6] As if in rec-ollection of the Prospectus, Wordsworth's subsequent removal of the Analogy Passage demoted nature and left "the mind of Man" as his poem's central subject. The inclusion and almost immediate withdrawal of Wordsworth's six analogies betrayed the eroding coherence of his conception of the five-book poem, and forecast its dissolution and replacement by a new structure. So Wordsworth's 10 March turn to a lengthier narrative for *The Prelude* represents the formal corollary of a philosophical turn from nature to con-sciousness. All told, Wordsworth's restiveness about *The Recluse*, interest in supplementing the biographical record, and concern with "higher minds" spurred his expansion of the Five-Book *Pre-lude*. My argument is that these three considerations were interre-lated aspects of a single revisionary ambition: Wordsworth's desire to clarify and foreground the religious implications of *The Prelude*.

Wordsworth's restiveness about *The Recluse* influenced the spiritual scope of the 1805 *Prelude* by encouraging him to adapt his autobiography to Coleridge's interests as much as possible. Apparently, Wordsworth's 1804 labors on the reconceived *Prelude* were prompted by his reading "the second Part of his divine Self-biography" to Coleridge "in the highest and outermost of Grasmere" on 4 January 1804.[7] Yet the figure of Coleridge was inseparably associated not merely with *The Prelude* but with *The Recluse* as well. In fact, Wordsworth's worries about *The Recluse* would have brought Coleridge instantly to mind in early 1804 because Coleridge had been championing *The Recluse* so incessantly. By pressuring Wordsworth to work on it, Coleridge encouraged a certain defensiveness on Wordsworth's part for any dereliction of duty. Thankfully, Wordsworth could defend his attention to *The Prelude*—in both its five-book and subsequent longer format—by basing the poem on an approved Coleridgean project. These considerations help explain why Wordsworth evidently developed his plan for *The Prelude* from advice offered by Coleridge in a September 1799 letter:

> I wish you would write a poem, in blank verse, addressed to those, who, in consequence of the complete failure of the French Revolution, have thrown up all hopes of the amelioration of mankind, and are sinking into an almost epicurean selfishness, disguising the same under the soft titles of domestic attachment and contempt for visionary *philosophes*. It would do great good, and might form a part of "The Recluse." (*CLSTC* 1. 527)

In the context of Coleridge's letter, Wordsworth could invoke *The Recluse*'s greatest advocate in defending his labors on *The Prelude* as secondary contributions to *The Recluse*. That connection would also allow *The Prelude* to engage issues previously reserved for treatment in *The Recluse*, such as the key issue Coleridge mentioned in later setting forth his understanding of the scope of *The Recluse*: the poem was "to have affirmed a Fall in some sense" and to have traced the operation of "a manifest Scheme of Redemption from this Slavery" (*CLSTC* 4.574–75). So if Wordsworth could not fulfill Coleridge's hopes by producing *The Recluse*, he could at least placate his friend by producing a *Recluse*-related text on a suggested topic. Through that concession—with both poems entangled complexly in Wordsworth's relations with Coleridge—the longer *Prelude* of 1805 inherited some of the religious ambitions of the *Recluse* project.

Eventuating in the adaptation of his "Self-biography" to this Coleridgean redemptive scheme, Wordsworth's 1804 anxieties about *The Recluse* dovetailed with his interest in extending the biographical scope of the five-book poem. Wordsworth apparently realized that a religious reconception of his poem answered equally to the demands of *The Recluse* and the problem of biography. It is entirely possible, in fact, that considerations of biographical amplitude remained subordinate to considerations of prophetic mythmaking as Wordsworth carried the story of his life beyond his Cambridge years. For the material Wordsworth added to his Five-Book *Prelude*, as we have seen, consisted basically of the poet's experiences in France and England during his period of revolutionary partisanship. These experiences gravitate toward the longer text's moral nadir, when Wordsworth "Sick, wearied out with contrarieties, / Yielded up moral questions in despair" (1805 *Prelude* 10.899–900). They gravitate toward those experiences of imaginative enervation which stand in Wordsworth's construction of himself as his own Miltonically resonant Fall. In 1804, Wordsworth could recall the dependence of *The Recluse* on "a Fall in some sense," then recall Coleridge's advocacy of political disillusionment as a topic appropriate for *The Recluse*, and he would stand on the verge of the very identification which dominates the later books of the Thirteen-Book *Prelude*: the protagonist's disillusionment with the French Revolution conceived as a personal Fall.

Scholarship on the paradigm of a lost and recovered paradise in *The Prelude*, especially the work of M. H. Abrams and Jonathan Wordsworth, has proven so influential, and has identified *The Prelude* with the idea of a Romantic Fall so memorably, that Wordsworthians can easily forget that the poem did not always include one.[8] Yet "the two-Part *Prelude* of 1798–9," Jonathan Wordsworth notes, "contains no version of the Fall" (*Borders of Vision*, 235). Wordsworth first incorporated the Fall as a structural principle in *The Prelude* during his 1804 recasting of the poem in five-book form—or, crucially, that was his first such *attempt*. Previously I cited Reed's point that the Five-Book *Prelude* turns at one juncture to consider forces which impair poetic creativity. In the five-book text, these "foes" of imagination never become terribly formidable: they consist primarily of Cambridge distractions and certain habits of superficial association encouraged by the picturesque. Worse, the five-book text continually vacillates in its presentation of them, producing what Jonathan Wordsworth calls "a see-saw movement" between admissions of lapse and assertions of enduring power (*Borders of Vision*, 238). Thus the poet's confession,

In truth, this malady of which I speak,
Though aided by the times whose deeper sound
Without my knowledge sometimes might perchance
Make rural Nature's milder minstrelsies
Inaudible, did never take in me
Deep root or large action,

comes as a rehearsal of the self-evident.[9] Reading the Analogy Passage scenarios as "metaphors for Wordsworth, ringed round with fatal dangers," Kenneth Johnston remarks likewise that their "metaphorical force does not correspond to any concomitantly impressive image in the text of Wordsworth's danger or impairment" (Johnston, Wordsworth and "The Recluse," 109). So a key limitation of the 1804 Five-Book Prelude was its failure to authenticate the Fall to which Wordsworth had structurally and intellectually obligated it. He reorganized the poem, enlarging it beyond five books, to make the speaker's rationalization of revolutionary violence into the vehicle of an imaginatively credible Fall.

The Fall paradigm itself dovetailed with Wordsworth's final motive for expanding the Five-Book Prelude: the turn from nature to human consciousness marked by his abandonment of the Analogy Passage. For the "higher minds" celebrated in the 1805 Prelude are precisely the sites of a redemptive power capable of reversing the effects of the Fall. The Thirteen-Book Prelude depicts the debasement and recovery of the mind's "genial Spirits," in Coleridgean phrase (Verse Letter to Sara Hutchinson, line 44).[10] For the Fall of The Prelude Wordsworthians have usually assigned the coldly rationalistic Godwin to the role of serpent. I suggest that Wordsworth's representation of imaginative impairment in The Prelude in some ways relies more on Coleridge than Godwin, and that it depends in particular on the Verse Letter. Although written on 2 April 1802, the Verse Letter would have recurred to Wordsworth's mind almost inevitably in March 1804. Of course, Coleridge independently become a presiding presence in the expanded Prelude. Yet the Verse Letter was entangled with the Immortality Ode in a debate over the mundane fate of imaginative "glory"—and Wordsworth had returned to complete the Immortality Ode in March 1804, the very month which witnessed the collapse and reconception of the Five-Book Prelude. Mediated by Wordsworth's work on the Immortality Ode, the Verse Letter gave Wordsworth an enormously pertinent Coleridgean reference point for a higher mind's creative Fall. Coleridge's attribution of lost inspiration to the deadening effects of "abstruse Research" (Verse Letter, line 265) stands as a scaled-down variation on the Fall of *The Prelude*. The Immortality Ode would proclaim that the embers remained alive. Still, the presentation of imaginative enervation in the Verse Letter remained so vivid and challenging that, apparently, it finally demanded an extended response. In part, the Thirteen-Book *Prelude* of 1805 took shape as a vastly elaborated rejoinder to the moral and imaginative pessimism of Coleridge's plaint to Sara.[11]

The pressure exerted on Wordsworth's 1804 reshaping of *The Prelude* by his recollections of the Verse Letter acquires specific textual confirmation. Working to complete his Five-Book *Prelude* in early 1804, Wordsworth faced a specific compositional challenge. For his culminating book he had his beginning—the recently written climbing of Snowdon—and his ending—the two spots of time, relocated from the first part of the 1799 poem. He merely needed appropriate connecting lines. After discarding his first attempt at a connection in the Analogy Passage, he turned in MS. W to lines praising the creative power lodged in the human mind. Asking, "Oh who is he that hath his whole life long / Preserved, enlarged this freedom in himself?" Wordsworth replies that he has, and describes himself as "A meditative, oft a suffering, man, / And yet I trust with undiminished power."[12] Defending this trust, he proceeds to discuss the "various foes" arrayed against the imagination in "unremitting warfare," a warfare which grows

> With growing life and burdens which it brings
> Of petty duties and pressing cares,
> Labour and penury, disease and grief,
> Which to one object chain the impoverished mind
> Enfeebled and defeated, vexing strife
> At home, and want of pleasure and repose,
> And all that eats away the genial spirits,
> May be fit matter for another song;
> Nor less the misery brought into the world
> By the perversion of this power misplaced
> And misemployed, whence emanates
> Blinding cares, whence ambition, avarice,
> And all the superstitions of this life—
> A mournful catalogue. Gladly would I then,
> Entering upon abstruser argument,
> Attempt to place in view the diverse means
> Which Nature strenuously employs to uphold
> This agency. . . .[13]

"No one reading this passage," Lucy Newlyn justly asserts, "can fail to connect it with Coleridge."[14] This Coleridgean palimpsest resembles the veiled censure of Coleridge in "Resolution and Independence," but it recalls the Verse Letter unmistakably. Wordsworth's specific reference to "genial spirits" eaten away alludes to Coleridge's famous claim, "My genial Spirits fail" (line 44); Wordsworth's glance at "vexing strife / At home & want of pleasure and repose" recalls Coleridge's complaint that his "household Life, / It is, & will remain, Indifference or Strife—" (lines 163–64); finally, Wordsworth's "abstruser argument" phrase echoes Coleridge's awareness of the debilitation caused by "abstruse Research" (line 266).

Submerged in MS. W, then, immediately preceding the site of the five-book poem's abandonment, lies a verbal recollection of the Verse Letter to Sara. Such textual proximity implies that the Verse Letter, which clearly recurred to Wordsworth's mind, influenced his decision to retract his Five-Book *Prelude* in favor of a longer narrative depicting a loss of creativity. In fact, the Coleridgean associations of the Fall he was contemplating lingered in Wordsworth's mind, evidence suggests, as he approached even closer to the disintegration of the five-book plan. For Wordsworth moves from the lines above to an actual address to Coleridge on MS. W 47^r (1805 *Prelude* 2.300), and then on to the first surviving draft of the new transition between the two spots of time incidents in 1805 Book 11:

> Oh mystery of man, from what a depth
> Proceed thy honours! I am lost, but see
> In simple childhood something of the base
> On which thy greatness stands—but this I feel:
> That from thyself it comes that thou must give,
> Else never canst receive. The days gone by
> Come back upon me from the dawn almost
> Of life; the hiding-places of my powers
> Seem open; I approach, and then they close.[15]

Wordsworth's MS. W reference to "very fountains"[16] a few lines later derives from Coleridge's "The Passion & the Life whose Fountains are within!" (Verse Letter, line 51). Above all, the claim about giving and receiving in MS. W plainly alludes to Coleridge's declaration, "Oh Sara! we receive but what we give, / And in *our* Life alone does Nature live."[17] So Wordsworth's mind turned to Coleridge, and to the problem of imaginative debility in its

Coleridgean associations, as he neared what proved to be the limit of his five-book plan.

The figure of Coleridge and the vocational myth of the Verse Letter proved no more important for Wordsworth's religious reconception of the Five-Book *Prelude*, however, than the Immortality Ode itself. The Ode's influence on the development of *The Prelude* has long been recognized. Wordsworth's portrait of "old Grandam Earth" in 1804 Book 4 (4.429) resembles the sixth stanza of the Ode. In a similar vein Wordsworth evokes—and in this instance discreetly declines—the Ode's Platonic fiction in the lines,

> Our childhood sits,
> Our simple childhood sits upon a throne
> That hath more power than all the elements.
> I guess not what this tells of being past,
> Nor what it augers of the life to come,
> But so it is.

> (*FBP* 4.613–18)

Finally, the similarity of the Hartley-like child of the Ode to the infant prodigy of *The Prelude*, an issue explored by Newlyn, serves as an extended link between the two poems (Newlyn, 154–58). With respect to the compositional history of *The Prelude*, the most relevant facet of Wordsworth's allusions to the Ode may reside in their occurrence together, densely clustered, in 1805 Book 5. The fourth section of the Five-Book *Prelude*, this book was the last section indisputably finished before Wordsworth canceled his five-book plan. The constellation of Ode allusions closely preceding the collapse of the five-book poem takes on a prefigurative aspect—as if pressures exerted by the Ode, and localized in the echoes of 1804 Book 4, helped divert Wordsworth's ideas into the longer form required to dramatize an imaginative loss and recovery of paradise.

Certainly the Ode bears on Wordsworth's main reason for expanding the Five-Book *Prelude* of 1804, his shift from nature to the saving power of "higher minds." I have argued previously that Wordsworth's worries about death in the aftermath of *The Ruined Cottage* required him to reauthenticate the idea of personal immortality, and that he achieved reauthentication through an identification of soul and imagination in the Immortality Ode. That identification allowed him to ground a religious affirmation of the soul on his own visionary experiences. There can be little doubt, I believe, that his 1804 reorientation of *The Prelude* towards "higher minds" draws on and continues the Ode's identification of soul and imagination. The idea seems to have been in his mind as he struggled to conclude his five-book poem. Consider the crucial lines which replaced the analogy passage as Wordsworth, dilating upon his Snowdon vision, began to move his poem to its conclusion:

> To this one scene which I from Snowdon's breast
> Beheld might more be added, to set forth
> The manner in which ofttimes Nature works
> Herself upon the outward face of things,
> As if with an imaginative power—
> . . . .
> Such minds are truly from the Deity
> For they are powers, and hence the highest bliss
> That can be known on earth—in truth, a soul
> Growing, and still to grow, a consciousness
> Of whom they are, they habitually infused
> Through every image and through every being,
> And all impressions have religious faith
> And endless occupation for the soul,
> Whether discursive or intuitive.[18]

Wordsworth begins by contemplating the Snowdon landscape as a figure of "imaginative power." The draft then refers to such an imagination as "a soul," notes that creatively empowered minds "are truly from the Deity," and likens the expansive consciousness of such a mind to the ability of "religious faith" to provide "endless occupation for the soul." These lines equate soul with imagination in an expressly religious context.

The *Prelude* born from the wreckage of the five-book plan arose as Wordsworth glimpsed the spiritual logic of his imaginative development, the greater story lurking within his initial concentration on books and nature. The reasons given for Wordsworth's reconception of the five-book poem all show him striving to expand upon the religious potential of his material. If we look to factors ordinarily cited as motives for the 1804 text's expansion, and put aside guilt over *The Recluse* in favor of issues intrinsic to *The Prelude* itself, we are left, first, with the biographical additions necessary for adequate representation of a Fall and, second, with his turn from nature to the redemptive power of "higher minds." These two concerns represent complementary aspects of a single religious reconception of his life story: what redeems the poet's Fall in *The Prelude*, again, is the fact that he genuinely *is* a poet, a chosen son. He is saved by his possession of a "higher Mind" compounded equally of soul and imagination. Wordsworth's allusions to the Immortality Ode and the Verse Letter to Sara in MSS. W and WW represent verbal traces of his intellectual re-engagement of the debate over the creative soul staged by those poems. The 1805 *Prelude* is a complex, various poem dominated by historical representation and explorations of memory and emotion. It is nonetheless a profession of faith in which the spiritual affirmations of the Ode, autobiographically relocated, place the poet's development in religious perspective.

THE CREATIVE SOUL:
SIMPLON PASS TO MOUNT SNOWDON

Book 6 of *The Prelude*, with its apostrophe to Imagination and journey through the Ravine of Arve, was Wordsworth's first endeavor after deciding to reorganize and expand the Five-Book *Prelude*. Drafts towards the Simplon crossing and address to Imagination exist in MS. WW, and by the end of March 1804 the poet was developing them into a coherent narrative for his sixth book.[19] The Simplon adventure and apostrophe to Imagination were especially important for his reconceived *Prelude*, for these passages permitted Wordsworth a useful framing strategy. The 1805 *Prelude* relegates most of its newly added material to an intermediate position between Book 6 and Book 13, 13 being the new location of the Snowdon episode: the result is an account of the Fall framed by depictions of imaginative power. Wordsworth could thereby invoke the corruption of creativity by abstruse rationalization and still anchor his poem's darker episodes within a supervening optimism. At the same time Book 6 complexly portrays both triumph and failure. Due to its breadth of implication, Book 6 "has become one of a handful of paradigms capable by itself of representing the poet's work," Alan Liu justly declares, and matters change little in moving on to the complexities of Book 13.[20] With these rich, difficult books, I will restrict my argument to two main points. First, I will argue that Wordsworth's celebrations of imagination clearly presuppose religious values. Second, I will reconsider the narrative logic connecting the apostrophe to Imagination to the Ravine passage, and Book 6 as a whole to Book 13, in order to argue that the

mystical disorientation of Book 6 dangerously prefigures the protagonist's subsequent Fall.

As with the Immortality Ode, the religious resonance of Book
6 rests on the identity of imagination and soul which Wordsworth
posits. That resonance has not always been given its due. In our two
most powerful readings of the Simplon crossing, the text's ostensible revelations of transcendence are restaged as revelations of
merely an apocalyptic *desire* for transcendence and of an elided his-
toricity scattering political traces in its wake.[21] To these readings,
with their displacements of the supernatural as mind and history,
can be added Jonathan Wordsworth's respected claim that "the
sense of 'something evermore about to be' is infinitely valuable, but
not a religious experience" (*Borders of Vision*, 34). Fair enough, one
might respond, but it is an experience of imaginative potentiality
with manifest religious implications. Wordsworth's Simplon
episode draws on a familiar religious *topos*. This *topos* portrayed
the soul expanding inwardly to encounter its own infinitude as a
result of encountering God's infinitude in a natural prospect—and
the succession of Alpine mountains had long provided a preferred
prospect. Actually, Wordsworth's Book 6 passage may have been
prompted by one of Coleridge's early theological reflections:

> But we were not made to find Happiness in the complete gratifica-
> tion of our bodily wants—the mind must enlarge its sphere of
> activity, and progressive by nature, must never rest content. For
> this purpose our Almighty Parent hath given us Imagination that
> stimulates to the attainment of real excellence, by the contempla-
> tion of splendid possibilities, that still revivifies the dying motives
> within us, and fixing our eyes on the glittering Summits that rise
> one above the other in Alpine endlessness, still urges us up the
> ascent of Being. . . . The noblest gift of Imagination is the power of
> discerning the *Cause* in the *Effect* a power which when employed
> on the works of the Creator elevates and by the variety of its plea-
> sures almost monopolizes the Soul. We see our God everywhere—
> the Universe in the most literal Sense is his written Language.[22]

The Berkeleyan close occurs elsewhere in Coleridge, but its occurrence here may lie behind Wordsworth's "Characters of the great
Apocalyps" (6.570). For Coleridge's comments bring together the
idea of a verbally inscribed natural world, the motif of unending
progression, an Alpine scene, claims of the inadequacy of nature to
human aspiration, and the celebration of imagination as the vehicle of spiritual infinitude.

Wordsworth's apostrophe to Imagination certainly contends, with Coleridge, that the liberation of imagination produces a revelation of the soul. Wordsworth begins by addressing "Imagination," describes its visionary eruption, and then, in direct response to the resulting experience of loss and recovery, applauds the glory of his "Soul":

> Imagination!—lifting up itself
> Before the eye and progress of my Song
> Like an unfather'd vapour; here that Power,
> In all the might of its endowments, came
> Athwart me; I was lost as in a cloud,
> Halted without a struggle to break through,
> And now recovering to my Soul I say
> I recognize thy glory; in such strength
> Of usurpation, in such visitings
> Of awful promise, when the light of sense
> Goes out in flashes that have shewn to us
> The invisible world, doth Greatness make abode,
> There harbours whether we be young or old.
>
> (6.525–37)

Suspended vertiginously between contending realities, consciousness momentarily loses its way, unable to break through or even struggle effectively against the supernatural power encompassing it. Here the imagination rises "like an unfather'd vapour" because it has no natural origin, no father, and because it encloses the poet in a cloud which nullifies his visual contact with the world, extinguishing the "light of sense." Although placed in the moment of composition in Wordsworth's 1805 text, this nullification still implicates the Alpine setting of Wordsworth's narrative. Losing not merely the "progress" but the "eye" of his song, Wordsworth briefly misplaces his poem's narrative thread *and* natural setting, vicariously losing nature in consequence. So these lines confirm again the importance of the Immortality Ode for Wordsworth's expansion of *The Prelude*. They reclaim for early manhood those "Blank misgivings" which the Ode locates in childhood, and which Wordsworth glossed in remarking, "Many times while going to school have I grasped at a wall or tree to recall myself from this abyss of idealism to the reality" (Fenwick note, *PW* 4.463). The apostrophe dramatizes an Ode-like usurpation of time and place, the present moment of composition and the text's natural setting, by the visionary imagination.

This appropriative power illustrates nature's ontological subordination to spirit. It discloses the existence of supernatural realities and, even here, implies the soul's immortality. Wordsworth's lines associate "Greatness" with the "invisible world" conceived as a final "harbour" to which the voyaging soul returns. This "harbour" will become the soul's "home"—recall the soul's arrival "From God, who is our home" (Ode, line 65)—in the next lines of Wordsworth's meditation:

> Our destiny, our nature, and our home
> Is with infinitude, and only there;
> With hope it is, hope that can never die,
> Effort, and expectation, and desire,
> And something evermore about to be.
> The mind beneath such banners militant
> Thinks not of spoils, or trophies nor of aught
> That may attest its prowess, blest in thoughts
> That are their own perfection and reward,
> Strong in itself, and in the access of joy
> Which hides it like the overflowing Nile.

> (6.538–48)

These lines prefigure and justify Wordsworth's Book 13 assertion that his story of imaginative progress substantiates "The feeling of life endless, the one thought / By which we live, Infinity and God" (13.183–84). In Book 6 the portrait of imaginative aspiration as the soul's internalization of "infinitude" moves similarly to the soul's endless being, its "hopes that can never die" and desires "evermore about to be." The closing image of the Nile, another emanation from a mysterious source, transposes the visionary scenario the passage began with: here the mind's emergence hides rather than discloses it. Enacting that return to nature which Geoffrey Hartman finds so profoundly Wordsworthian, the images reassert seasonal cycles and natural experience. Those reassertions nonetheless naturalize beatitude. The blessedness and joy which flow like the Nile are legacies of the imagination's transcendence of nature: they lull apocalypse while remaining linked to the apocalyptic motif of inundation.

The religious resonance of that motif helps Wordsworth move to the more overtly religious portrayal of the Arve Ravine:

The immeasurable height
Of woods decaying, never to be decay'd,
The stationary blasts of waterfalls,
And every where along the hollow rent
Winds thwarting winds, bewilder'd and forlorn,
The torrents shooting from the clear blue sky,
The rocks that mutter'd close upon our ears,
Black drizzling crags that spake by the way-side
As if a voice were in them, the sick sight
And giddy prospect of the raving stream,
The unfetter'd clouds, and region of the heavens,
Tumult and peace, the darkness and the light
Were all like workings of one mind, the features
Of the same face, blossoms upon one tree,
Characters of the great Apocalyps,
The types and symbols of Eternity,
Of first and last, and midst, and without end.

(6.556–72)

Moving from the illimitable to the undecaying, and on to "symbols of Eternity," the lines follow the apostrophe to Imagination in developing from infinitude to eternality. They advance beyond the Ode by staging a Romantic theophany, as Book 6 shifts from the gloriously aspiring soul to an all-comprehending Deity. Wordsworth found assistance for this transition, we know, in the tradition of Christian apologetics concerned with geographical manifestations of divine power. His efforts to draw out the religious meaning of the Arve Ravine found independent assistance in Milton and the Bible. For Wordsworth's passage ends by merging Adam and Eve's call "to extol / Him first, him last, him midst, and without end" (*Paradise Lost* 5.164–65) with a biblical allusion to "the Lord God, who is and who was and who is to come" (Rv. 1.8).

Wordsworth's naturalized theophany has usually been taken as the terminus of a corrective progression, with the lost poet finding his way morally as well as literally. Properly reoriented, this Wordsworth moves from visionary isolation to natural harmony, healed by his understanding "that it is the eternal mind, the face of God, that reconciles the warring features of the landscape" (Jonathan Wordsworth, *Borders of Vision*, 33). This reconstruction of the narrative logic of Book 6, however, grants Wordsworth's Arve tableau greater reconciliatory import than in my view it possesses.

For this passage, I prefer critics like Alan Bewell and Isobel Armstrong, who consider Wordsworth's representation of the Arve Ravine deeply problematic. Noting the "suffering" of Wordsworthian locales which "have not yet been made habitable," Bewell reads the Arve Ravine as a traumatized landscape struggling toward a humanized articulation it never achieves.[23] Noting its blockage of power, Armstrong reads Wordsworth's passage for its "irreconcilable opposites . . . simultaneous but disjunct," its chaotic combination of violence and paralysis.[24] Such readings seem truer to the disturbing excessiveness of Wordsworth lines. Here nature is self-conflicted—"Winds thwarting winds"—and threatening. It raves and sickens. It dwarfs the human in its immeasurability and assumes an almost hallucinatory quality, with "rocks that mutter'd close upon our ears" and crags that *seem* to speak (*"As if* a voice were in them"). Harmony is the province of beauty; in its main thrust Wordsworth's passage unveils the sublime. His conclusion attains a tenuous unity ("Were all *like* workings of one mind") which lasts barely a moment before lapsing incrementally into discrete plural elements: features, blossoms, characters, types. The Ravine of Arve leaves nothing harmonized. It is less reconciling in affect than it is fearful and disorienting.

Consequently, the apostrophe to Imagination and Arve tableau should be construed less as progressive phases than as complementary perspectives on a single problem. For despite the grand avowals, a problem exists: the temptations of power mistaken as a hallmark of spiritual and political heroism. In *Prelude* 6 this is the danger of the apocalyptic. Wordsworth's two visionary climaxes are joined by their respective treatments of apocalypse as an event in consciousness and nature. Both passages disclose appropriative agencies of mind: the power of the poetic imagination to transcend, and perceptually negate, its mundane environment at moments of mystical epiphany; the power of God's "one mind" to suffuse, wreck, and remake the fallen world of nature. One sees the power, but, as Armstrong asks, "where is peace?" (Armstrong, 37). For the religious argument of *The Prelude*, then, it is not that the Arve lines correct the glorious but threatening autonomy of the apostrophe to imagination, for the Arve passage merely translates those threats into another register. Rather, the climbing of Snowdon in Book 13 corrects the interrelated errors of Book 6.

The appealing visionary power of Book 6 facilitates Wordsworth's Fall by extending the seductions of power into the political sphere. For the poet's attraction to power encourages, if not endorsements

of violence, then rationalizing equivocations about it. His fascination with power he directly acknowledges. Confessing his tempta-
tion to regard the violence of the times as "consummation of the
wrath of Heaven" (10.408), Wordsworth remarks,

> So did some portion of that spirit fall
> On me, to uphold me through those evil times,
> And in their rage and dog-day heat I found
> Something to glory in as just and fit,
> And in the order of sublimest laws;
> And even if that were not, amid the awe
> Of unintelligible chastisement,
> I felt a kind of sympathy with power.

> (10.409–16)

This sympathy remained tied to controlling moral values,
Wordsworth quickly adds (10.418), but an attraction to power
remains implicated in the Fall which organizes *The Prelude* as a crisis autobiography. Wordsworth scholarship has long recognized
that *The Prelude* draws an "explicit parallel," in Harold Bloom's
phrase, between Wordsworth's "Alpine expedition and the onset of
the French Revolution."[25] More recent criticism has lent that parallel detailed illustration. Pointing to the poet's association of Godwin's rationality with Robespierre's politics, for example, Nicholas
Roe isolates a sympathy with Jacobin decisiveness latent in
Wordsworth revolutionary activism: he isolates the "sympathy
with power," that is, which effectively hastened Wordsworth
toward his moral and poetic nadir.[26] The political subtext of imaginative apocalypse is an overreaching revolutionary ambition.

   If the apostrophe to Imagination and Ravine of Arve sections of
Book 6, legitimate but incomplete revelations, do not precipitate
Wordsworth's crisis, they prepare the ground for it. Wordsworth
suggests as much by giving his great Imagination passage a displaced political significance. The "banners militant" of the apostrophe to Imagination strategically glance at Napoleon's addresses
to his army and usurping aspirations to cross the Alps.[27] The
"flashes" exposing "the invisible world" ironically anticipate "the
light of circumstances, flash'd / Upon an independent intellect" in
Prelude 10 (10.828–29), phrases borrowed from *The Borderers* to
denote the amorality of Godwinian ethical autonomy. In these
ways, the language of *Prelude* 6 tacitly connects visionary aspira-

tion with political overreaching, hinting at the hidden violence of even the religious imagination when love fails to master power. Since, for Wordsworth, the Reign of Terror took place because Robespierre's "imagination had slipped the control of love" (Roe, 218), the meditation on Snowdon ends appropriately as a celebration of spiritual love. It is because Wordsworth needs his Snowdon ascent to counterbalance the excesses of his Alpine crossing that Book 13 echoes Book 6 so often. Moving to Snowdon from the Simplon Pass, we again encounter a mountain, mist which intensifies self-consciousness, an illuminating "flash" and accompanying usurpation ("Usurp'd upon as far as sight could reach"—13.51), and affirmations of both the mind's infinitude and "the invisible world" (13.105).

The Snowdon vision stages Wordsworth's grandest affirmation of spiritual and imaginative plenitude. The emphasis on plenitude can seem ill considered, admittedly, because the elisions and dissonances of the Snowdon scene seem so utterly apparent. Their disruptive power only intensifies when the central feature of Wordsworth's mistscape—a "blue chasm" formed by a "fracture" in the vapors—appears to ground presence disconcertingly in absence. The relationship of nature to mind, of the visual features of the scene to the poet's interpretation of them, of the creative mind to the divine Creator, and of the various stages of composition interlayered in the 1805 text, all resist easy Symbolic closure. Yet if the Snowdon prospect virtually solicits deconstructive reflection, such reflection can make the poetry appear more darkly problematic than it is. Certainly I cannot agree with Mary Jacobus that Wordsworth's "troping of metaphor as analogy" in *Prelude* 13 renders "emptiness . . . the most powerful presence in the Snowdon landscape."[28] Nor can I feel that a supplemental logic ultimately inimical to Wordsworth's celebrations of God, immortality, and love generates any discernible unease in the voice speaking the poem. For the poet himself, the rifts and errancies of the Snowdon passage at most suggest a subliminal recognition of absence—of death as the horizon of loss—as a motive contributing to both poetic endeavor and religious faith.

In proclaiming that faith, Wordsworth begins by invoking the divine. While describing the moonlit mistscape as the "genuine Counterpart" of the human imagination in its interaction with nature, Wordsworth also depicts the imagination's omphalic connection with divinity (13. 88–89). That connection occurs through the fracture in the mist. In an especially detailed reading of the

Snowdon ascent, W. J. B. Owen argues that Wordsworth's "blue chasm," while suggestive of the unconscious, signifies principally the natural or empirical matrices of consciousness, the flow of "data from various sources—notably the senses."[29] From this perspective, the mind "feeds upon infinity" through its openness to an endless series of sensory impressions. For me, conversely, the darkened sea audible in the distance represents not material but spiritual infinitude. Wordsworth wrote of an "immortal sea" in the Ode, and viewed the ocean as an image of God's "eternal motion" in other poems. Here the distant sea symbolizes supernatural origins, with the mountain scene stationed above it depicting a mind

> that feeds upon infinity,
> That is exalted by an underpresence,
> The sense of God, or whatso'er is dim
> Or vast in its own being.
>
> (13.70–73)

The "blue chasm" (13.56,) through which the voice of many waters surges upward, Wordsworth calls "The Soul, the Imagination of the whole," then, because it allows the mind access to the divine. No locus of absence, it teems with superabundant energies, recalling the upsurging of the sacred waters in "Kubla Khan" even as it adds sound to sight, recalling as well "the mighty world / Of eye and ear" in "Tintern Abbey" (lines 106–7). Wordsworth's tunnel in the mist can serve as the locus of "the sense of God" and still retain its associations with the unconscious because it is amid the mind's mysterious depths that God's presence survives. As in the Ode, such contact underlies both ordinary human perception and the poet's special ability to express ideas through images—mist serving Wordsworth as an image of visionary power, as in Book 6, and moonlight connoting creative illumination.

Wordsworth's concentration on poetic power explains the qualifications of his invocation of the divine. The imagination, he declares, can be uplifted to infinitude through the intimation of God *or* whatever is dim and vast in its own being. Indicating alternatives, Wordsworth acknowledges moments in which "the soul / . . . retains an obscure sense / Of possible sublimity" (1805 *Prelude* 2.334–36) or experiences a sublimity distinct from the religious sublime. It is nonetheless the religious implications of its opening vision that Book 13 subsequently develops. Actually, it is not always perfectly clear that the natural spectacle of Book 13 symbolizes merely the higher mind of the poet. Nudged by Wordsworth's commentary, readers ultimately take the poetic imagination as the referent of the speaker's vision. Jonathan Wordsworth concedes the accuracy of that inference but still adds, "not that the mind is initially taken to be the poet's: at first—and again the confusion is useful, enhancing—one assumes that it is God's" (*Borders of Vision*, 323). God appeared as an "omniscient Mind" in *Religious Musings*, as specifically a "mighty Mind" in both Young and Milton, as a Mind variously described in numerous eighteenth-century poems. Wordsworth's contemporary readers could hardly have missed the theophanic suggestiveness of a "mighty Mind, / . . . [feeding] upon infinity" or, for that matter, of the Miltonic allusions concentrated in the initial passages of Book 13. When Wordsworth's "huge sea of mist" is disrupted as "A hundred hills their dusky backs upheaved / All over this still Ocean" (13.45–46), *The Prelude* conjures up Milton's description of the separation of land and water during the creation:

> Immediately the Mountains huge appear
> Emergent, and their broad backs upheave
> Into the Clouds, their tops ascend the Sky:
> So high as heav'd the tumid Hills, so low
> Down sunk the hollow bottom broad and deep,
> Capacious bed of Waters.

(Paradise Lost 7.285–90)

This Miltonic vision of God's creation will modulate, in the course of Book 13, into Wordsworth's vision of the poet's creation: but the poetry which carries us to the imagination begins with God. So the prospect from Snowdon at once replicates the divine Mind in the act of creation and, through the comparison Wordsworth posits, symbolizes that same creative power in the register of the human mind.

Characteristically Wordsworthian, the secularizing gestures of the Snowdon vision are equally profound and incomplete. The mountainous mistscape does not effect outright substitutions, replacing God with the imagination, but connections, substantiating the poet's analogy between divine and human creativity. A commonplace of eighteenth-century aesthetics, that analogy has a long history in both Wordsworth and Coleridge's understanding of imagination. It recalls chapter 13 of the *Biographia Literaria*, where the secondary imagination acts as the hierarchically demoted type of "the infinite I AM." But we also find it in 1798 in "Frost at Midnight" and, as noted previously, in the Blessed Babe passage of the Two-Part *Prelude*, where the child's perceptual orchestrations make him "an agent of the one great mind" (*TPP* 2.301). The Snowdon tableau advances the claims of the Blessed Babe portrait by showing, as Abrams observes, that "the mature poetic mind, whose infant perception had been a state of undifferentiated consciousness, has acquired self-consciousness, and is able to sustain the sense of its own identity" (*NS*, 287). The higher minds of *Prelude* 13 are those fit

> To hold communion with the invisible world.
> Such minds are truly from the Deity;
> For they are Powers; and hence the highest bliss
> That can be known is theirs, the consciousness
> Of whom they are, habitually infused
> Through every image, and through every thought,
> And all impressions: hence religion, faith,
> And endless occupation for the soul,
> Whether discursive or intuitive.
>
> (13.105–13)

Imagination raised to self-consciousness provides understanding not only of the self but also the universe. Here Wordsworth sketches his own theology of the imagination.

For the scene on the mountain's summit inspires a meditation recurrently theological in its reflections and claims. The lines cited above afford only one example of religious discourse, religious argument, in the concluding book of Wordsworth's poem. One aspect of the religious orientation of Book 13 is its continual reference to an existing God. Another aspect involves Wordsworth's inference of spiritual immortality—"The feeling of life endless, the one thought / By which we live, Infinity and God" (13.183–84)—from his insight into imagination's link to the divine. The culminating religious revelation of *The Prelude*, however, emerges when Wordsworth identifies imagination and love. Wordsworth praises the passion felt by lovers, but insists,

> there is higher love
> Than this, a love that comes into the heart
> With awe and a diffusive sentiment;

Thy love is human merely; this proceeds
More from the brooding Soul, and is divine.
This love more intellectual cannot be
Without Imagination, which in truth
Is but another name for absolute strength
And clearest insight, amplitude of mind,
And reason in her most exalted mood.
This faculty hath been the moving soul
Of our long labour. . . .
. . . .
Imagination having been our theme,
So also hath that intellectual love,
For they are each in each, and cannot stand
Dividually.

(13.161–72, 185–88)

This spiritual love originates in "the brooding soul" precisely because it both arises and grows imaginatively, emerging from a soul which broods creatively as Milton's God "Dove-like satst brooding on the vast Abyss / And mad'st it pregnant" (*Paradise Lost* 1.21–22). So the ultimate affirmations of Book 13 elaborate on an underlying identification of soul and imagination, alternate names for an excursive creative power which is spiritual love in action.

Framing Wordsworth's Fall, the great visions of *Prelude* 6 and 13 foreground this foundational identification. As Wordsworth discovers "The Soul, the Imagination of the whole" on the summit of Snowdon (13.65), so did his confrontation with Imagination in Book 6 move him to remark similarly that "now recovering to my Soul I say, / I recognise thy glory" (6.531–32). In its long form, *The Prelude* pursues a protracted narrative incorporating passages written long before 1804. Such a poem cannot sustain—and *The Prelude* clearly does not sustain—a rigorous terminological consistency or establish an unfailing equation of the terms "soul" and "imagination." Robert Langbaum has even argued the that synonymity of the words "soul" and "imagination" remains entirely casual throughout *The Prelude*.[30] But I must agree with Jonathan Wordsworth's comment on the Snowdon episode:

> One responds to the terms soul and imagination as radically opposed, as bringing together and momentarily equating the religious principle in man (with the implication of communion with an ultimate power outside the self) and human creativity.

Wordsworth was perfectly capable of a slovenly use of language in which no such distinction would be intended. It is disconcerting, for instance, to discover his willingness to cross out "heart" and write "soul," "soul" and write "mind," simply to avoid repetition. In this case, however, the equation seems to have been more considered. (*Borders of Vision*, 321)

In the poet's most philosophically ambitious passages after 1804, the equation ordinarily seems considered and deliberate. Is it coincidental that Wordsworth, defining the importance of the spots of time in his transition to them, declares that they revealed him "A sensitive and a *creative* Soul" (11.256; italics mine)? First formulated in the Immortality Ode, his association of soul and imagination remains highly traditional.[31] But it justified Wordsworth's determination to seek spiritual truth in his own poetic experiences, allowing him an existentially authentic faith that could explain his life.

SUBLIMITY, BEAUTY, AND THE TYPOLOGY OF REDEMPTION

Seduced by sympathy with power into enervating polemics, and then rescued by his understanding of imagination as reciprocal interchange and spiritual love, the protagonist of the 1805 *Prelude* undergoes moral development from the sublime to the beautiful. The sublime and the beautiful had been variously conceived, not to say much discussed, by eighteenth-century theorists. But Wordsworth's understanding of these terms rests principally on Edmund Burke's famous *Philosophical Enquiry*. "By the sublime," Owen helpfully generalizes, "Burke means things which are large, imposing, rugged; by the beautiful he means things which are small, delicate, smooth."[32] Burke's analysis touches on both the natural and rhetorical sublime—on landscape and poetic style—and shares his century's interest in the emotional dynamics of a spectator's divergent responses to the sublime and beautiful. Whereas some earlier theorists construed sublimity as a higher beauty,[33] Burke placed the beautiful and sublime in antithetical relation by associating sublimity with fear and beauty with love. While "the link between sublimity and terror had been suggested before"—in not only Burnet but Dennis and Thomson, for example—"Burke was the first to convert it into a system" (James Boulton, "introduction," lvi). In the *Philosophical Enquiry*, Wordsworth found an emotional and moral dissociation of the sublime and beautiful answering to his own imaginative responses to nature.

Wordsworth's conceptual reliance on the categories of the sublime and beautiful in *The Prelude*, long recognized in Wordsworth studies, begins with the 1798–1799 text. He invokes sublimity and beauty in Part 1 of his poem, in this case taking his cue from Akenside's glance, in *The Pleasures of Imagination*, at the contrary inclinations of different minds. One kind of person, Akenside avowed, seeks "The vast alone, the wonderful, the wild" while "Another sighs for harmony, and grace, / And gentlest beauty."[34] In the Two-Part *Prelude* Wordsworth similarly stresses his own temperamental affinity with the sublime:

> . . . there are spirits, which, when they would form
> A favored being, from his very dawn
> Of infancy do open out the clouds
> As at the touch of lightning, seeking him
> With gentler visitation; quiet Powers!
> Retired and seldom recognized, yet kind,
> And to the very meanest not unknown;
> With me, though rarely, [in my early days]
> They communed: others too there are who use,
> Yet haply aiming at the self-same end,
> Severer interventions, ministry
> More palpable, and of their school was I.
>
> (*TPP* 1.69–80)

While leading specifically to the stolen boat incident, these lines implicate all the 1798 spots of time, presenting them as episodes in the protagonist's progressive introduction to the sublime. If both spiritual agencies contribute, one wields far greater influence—or so Wordsworth claims initially. But as the 1799 *Prelude* develops from Part 1 to Part 2, it exchanges visionary disquietude for the predominating love and joy of the Blessed Babe and the One Life. The Pedlar's experiences had carried him too from natural "communion, not from terror free" to "the lesson deep of love" (*MH*, lines 27, 89). Only with the 1805 *Prelude*, however, does Wordsworth dilate upon these structural implications and explicitly correlate a progression from terror to love with the categories of the sublime and the beautiful.

The idea of such a progression is one of the leading claims of Theresa Kelley's study of Wordsworthian aesthetics. "Because the sublime is primitive and incomplete" in Wordsworth, Kelley contends, "it needs the beautiful as its successor."[35] In fact, the notion of a diachronic relationship between sublimity and beauty seems to be the poet's own adaptation of the theories known to him. If Burke's contrast between authoritarian sublimity and domesticated beauty struck Wordsworth in part for "its suggestion of a progress from sublimity to beauty," as Kelley surmises (Kelley, 24), he built upon that suggestion in revising his poetic autobiography beyond five books. In the Thirteen-Book *Prelude*, the idea of a progression from sublimity to beauty emerges in Wordsworth's use of the Simplon and Snowdon visions to frame his Fall. He presents his Simplon crossing as a disruptive confrontation with the sublime, and the Snowdon revelation as a saving return to the beautiful.

The vision in the Ravine of Arve, I realize, has been interpreted as a reconciliation of power and peace, sublimity and beauty, and it certainly (and quite unavoidably) contains elements of the beautiful within it. In the awesome vision on Snowdon, similarly, nature assumes symbolic form with "circumstance most awful and *sublime*" (13.76; italics mine). But the presence of beauty in an essentially sublime prospect, or of sublimity in a scene ultimately dominated by the beautiful, was theoretically unobjectionable in the context of the *Enquiry*. "If the qualities of the sublime and beautiful are sometimes found united" Burke asked, "does this prove, that they are the same, does it prove, that they are in any way allied, does it prove even that they are not opposite and contradictory?" (*Enquiry*, 124–25)—and the point of these rhetorical questions was not lost on either the Wordsworth of the fragmentary essay on "The Sublime and the Beautiful" or the earlier Wordsworth of *The Prelude*. So power and sublimity merely dominate the passage on the Ravine of Arve, while the ascent of Snowdon, as Kelley writes, "secures the ascendancy of values that belong to the beautiful over those of the sublime."[36] I argued previously that the interaction of mountain, sky, and water in the Arve ravine seems violently majestic, a threatening, superabundantly energized *topos*. The interaction of natural elements on Snowdon finally appears reconciling and reciprocal, the appropriate inspiration for a meditation on spiritual love. The contrary emphases of these Wordsworthian scenes make them each other's antithetical complement. They also permit *The Prelude* to enact a pilgrimage from the sublime to the beautiful in moving formally from Book 6 to Book 13 (1805).

But we need not argue over the mix of sublimity and beauty in these two framing books. Finally, Wordsworth summarizes his development in terms which make the sublime-to-beautiful progression unmistakable. In Book 13 he tells Dorothy,

> And true it is
> That later seasons owed to thee no less;
> For, spite of thy sweet influence and the touch
> Of other kindred hands that open'd out
> The springs of tender thought in infancy;
> And spite of all which singly I had watch'd
> Of elegance, and each minuter charm
> In nature or in life, still to the last,
> Even to the very going out of youth,
> The period which our Story now hath reach'd,
> I too exclusively esteem'd that love,
> And sought that beauty, which, as Milton sings
> Hath terror in it.
>
> (13.214–26)

If Milton sang it, Satan said it, and who was Satan but the first revolutionary? Wordsworth's attraction to the sublime, to sublimity as the manifestation of power, had the Reign of Terror in it. His recovery from the resulting Fall declares itself in his development beyond the turbulence of the sublime to the serenity of the beautiful. So he gratefully informs Dorothy:

> Thou didst soften down
> This over sternness: but for thee, sweet Friend,
> My soul, too reckless of mild grace, had been
> Far longer what by Nature it was framed,
> Longer retain'd its countenance severe,
> A rock with torrents roaring, with the clouds
> Familiar, and a favorite of the Stars:
> But thou didst plant its crevices with flowers,
> Hang it with shrubs that twinkle in the breeze,
> And teach the little birds to build their nests
> And warble in its chambers.
>
> (13.226–36)

Dorothy "beautified" his soul by tempering its isolation and, as connoted by the image of the rock rendered habitable, readying it for domestic life. Wordsworth's celebration of love in Book 13 merely raises to self-consciousness the course of his own moral education.

This developmental paradigm implies a particular spiritual history. For the poet's progress from sublimity to beauty refigures Christianity's construction of its own historical development. We have long understood that Wordsworth's recourse to the sublime and beautiful helped to place the events of *The Prelude* in religious perspective. In an influential section of *Natural Supernaturalism* Abrams showed that "behind this familiar eighteenth-century aesthetic dichotomy lay centuries of speculation about the natural world—speculation whose concerns were not aesthetic but theological and moral, and which in fact constituted a systematic theodicy of the landscape" (*NS*, 98). But I would suggest further that the apocalyptic scars borne by the mountains were in Christian tradition the topographical legacies of a specifically Old Testament violence, the sublime testimonials of Jehovah's awesome power, whether left by the Creation or the Flood. Moreover, the Hebraic associations of the natural sublime were recurrently echoed in critical investigations of the rhetorical sublime. The Old Testament struck many critics as the preeminent example of an imaginative or stylistic sublimity. The eighteenth century recurrently claimed that religious texts had inherent advantages for representation of the sublime. Some commentators on the sublime accordingly privileged Milton; others declared for the sublimity of both the New and Old Testaments. From the time of Longinus, in fact, theorists of the sublime had been consistently impressed, Samuel Holt Monk remarks, "with the abundance of that quality in the Psalms, Job, and the writings of Isaiah."[37] By the time of *The Prelude* Robert Lowth's studies of Hebrew poetry offered the Old Testament as the supreme example of the rhetorical sublime, and the association of sublimity with primitivism championed by Blair secondarily encouraged appreciation of a Hebraic Sublime. "Sublimity," Coleridge could declare, "is Hebrew by birth."[38]

Burke himself had associated sublimity not merely with terror but with the anger of Jehovah and the imagery of the Old Testament. In a culturally characteristic gesture, his analysis of the fear provoked by imaginative responsiveness to divine power reverts to the Old Testament in seeking illustrations, turning to David's cry, "fearfully and wonderfully am I made!" in Psalm 139 as an instance of "divine horror." After nodding to similarly terrified astonishment in Horace and Lucretius, Burke continues on to assert,

But the scripture alone can supply ideas answerable to the majesty of this subject. In the scripture, wherever God is represented as appearing or speaking, every thing terrible in nature is called up to heighten the awe and solemnity of the divine presence. The psalms, and the prophetical books, are crouded with instances of this kind. (*Enquiry*, 69)

Disavowing theories which attributed the rise of religion to fear and superstition, Burke nevertheless insists that

dread must necessarily follow the idea of such a power, when it is once excited in the mind. It is on this principle that true religion has, and must have, so large a mixture of salutary fear; and that false religions have generally nothing else but fear to support them. Before the christian religion had, as it were, humanized the idea of divinity, and brought it somewhat nearer to us, there was very little said of the love of God. (*Enquiry*, 70)

Burke's commentary shows how the ideas of terror, sublimity, and the Old Testament were mutually associated in eighteenth-century aesthetic discourse. But Burke's reference to Christianity redirecting religious experience from fear to love also shows, with great pertinence for Wordsworth, the way in which this constellation of motifs impinged upon traditional conceptions of the history of Christianity.

When engaged with historical problems, eighteenth-century apologists for Christianity ordinarily insisted on the essential unity of the Old and New Testaments. This insistence survived Deist polemics against typological interpretation, as well as the skepticism underlying many Enlightenment studies of comparative mythography, and flourished in the intellectual life of the time. In Wordsworth's day, admittedly, claims for the mutual congruence of the Old and New Testaments were still a hallmark of historical defenses of the Scriptures. It remains true nonetheless, as Ernest Tuveson succinctly observes, that "Christian history tends to be *developmental*."[39] It certainly proved developmental in its genealogical demotion of Hebrew tradition: from the time of Saint Paul, Tertullian, and Saint Augustine, defenders of Christianity declared Old Testament law the mere childhood, or shadowy type, of the true faith. Fundamental to the belief of any Christian, this subordination of the Old Testament to the New Testament enjoyed a long history in Western civilization, underwrote the logic of typological interpretation,[40] and shaped various intellectual and artistic traditions. Moreover, one common representation of the relationship of Old and New Testament ideas of God involved exactly the notion of a progression from wrathful power to peaceful love.

Allowing for both the mercy of Jehovah and the wrath of the Lamb, this traditional distinction rarely became absolute. It survived its qualification, however, retained its place in several eighteenth-century discourses, and was part of the cultural background available to any poet grappling with spiritual mysteries. So Isaac Watts' "The Law and the Gospel" can make a familiar appeal in beginning,

> "Curst be the man, for ever curst,
> That doth one wilful sin commit;
> Death and damnation for the first,
> Without relief, and infinite."
>
> Thus Sinai roars; and round the earth
> Thunder, and fire, and vengeance flings;
> But, Jesus, thy dear gasping breath,
> And Calvary, say gentler things.[41]

The distinction between a potentially apocalyptic violence—as in Watts' Burnet-like thunder and fire flung round the earth—and gentle love recurs in the "unobtrusive but forceful transition from Old to New Testament conceptions of divine power" which, for David Morris, organizes Smart's "On the Power of the Supreme Being."[42] Blake relies on the same distinction, Morton Paley shows, in depicting the tiger as an "expression of the Wrath of God in the Bible, particularly in the Old Testament," as opposed to the lamb as an expression of Christian gentleness and love.[43] Wordsworth himself, Bewell argues, relies on a similar distinction in dramatizing Peter Bell's conversion.[44]

Eighteenth-century aesthetic discourse on the sublime, with its latent biblical associations, mediates Wordsworth's use of this same developmental paradigm for *The Prelude*. Depicting the sublime in *The Prelude*, Wordsworth evokes an idea commonly connected with divine wrath and Old Testament grandeur, and specifically reconfirms Burke's association of sublimity with terror. When he then places the sublime and beautiful in developmental succession, he constructs a personal history which reiterates Christianity's historical self-representation.[45] The typological progression from Old Testament law to New Testament love serves in itself as a type, writ large in cultural history, of Wordsworth's own

development from power to love. These developmental associations merely inflect the poet's story because the psychological real-
ism of *The Prelude* displaces and secularizes them. Yet his "sympathy with power," he confessed in Book 10, encouraged him to see
"The consummation of the wrath of Heaven" in the spectacle of
revolutionary violence, a violence descending "in the order of sub-
limest laws," and in fulfillment of warnings issued by "the ancient
Prophets" (10.416, 408, 413, 401). At one point, then, *The Prelude*
expressly associates violence, sublimity, and the Old Testament.
The sublimity of the Ravine of Arve culminated similarly in "Characters of the great Apocalyps" (6.570) engraved by the Old Testament God. Moving from Simplon to Snowdon, Wordsworth moves
from prophetic violence to moral love. He enhances the suggestion
of a development beyond Old Testament misconceptions when he
internalizes the promise of redemption after first looking to political violence, Jacobin rather than messianic, to establish the kingdom of God on earth. In all of these ways Wordsworth's moral
progress from the sublime to the beautiful in *The Prelude* subtly
recapitulates the history of Christianity.

The connections Wordsworth sketches between that history and
his own life work two ways. They justify his concentration on personal experience because his experience makes him a representative
figure, a spiritual hero whose struggles and victories reflect on every
Christian's situation. But if the Christian paradigms underlying *The
Prelude* confirm Wordsworth's importance, Wordsworth's personal
experiences, as they fall into final form, reconfirm the Christian
paradigms they personalize and displace. The very idea of a historically progressive revelation demands that believers look at particular biblical and doctrinal formulations as potentially inessential
encumbrances, the vestiges of the transitory cultural traditions
through which the Word made its way. Encoded in typological conceptions of the collective progression of the faith, the poet implies,
is a pattern which continues to govern individual moral development. Through the typology of redemption in *The Prelude*
Wordsworth creates a modern religious myth, a secularized reaffir-
mation of Christian insights into the way of the soul.

THE PRELUDE AND CHRISTIANITY

The Excursion, Aubrey De Vere thought, announces a theism
which finds its necessary complement in revelation, in "that Chris-

tianity so zealously asserted in Wordsworth's maturer poetry, and so obviously implied in the whole of it."[46] The related questions with which I will conclude are, does the visionary humanism of *The Prelude* also imply Christianity, and if so are the poem's Christian analogues, images, and allusions intellectually functional or merely ornamental? For readers willing to acknowledge the poetry's preoccupation with religious issues, the final question raised by the 1805 *Prelude* is precisely the question of the text's Christian affiliations.

Wordsworth scholars generally deny that the 1805 *Prelude* invokes Christianity as a significant conceptual background. Most of those denials rest on arguments first presented by Ernest de Selincourt in his great 1926 facing-page edition of the 1805 and 1850 texts; subsequent accounts of the theological differences between these versions of the poem ordinarily just restate de Selincourt's conclusions. For de Selincourt, the 1805 *Prelude* reaffirms "that religious faith which is reflected in all the poet's greatest work" and which, calling it "Hartley transcendentalized by Coleridge," he describes in terms reminiscent of the One Life (*EdS*, lxviii, lxix). In his opinion, Wordsworth's faith underwent no real changes from "Tintern Abbey" to the Thirteen-Book *Prelude*. The poet's beliefs were never positively or self-consciously opposed to Christianity, but Christian doctrine interested him little, failing to engage his deepest needs and intuitions. After 1805 Wordsworth "turned more consciously to the Christian faith" (*EdS*, lxx), altering *The Prelude* accordingly. While some of the revisions involve mere "embroidery," others, de Selincourt argued, reveal Wordsworth obscuring his earlier religious views:

> By changes such as these, the last [1850] Book in particular, which is the philosophical conclusion of the whole matter, leaves a totally different impression from that created by the earlier text. The ideas he has introduced are from the brain that wrote *Ecclesiastical Sonnets*; they were entirely alien to his thought and feeling, not only in that youth and early manhood of which *The Prelude* recounts the history, but in that maturer period when it was written; and they have no rightful place in the poem. (*EdS*, lxxiii)

De Selincourt's analysis of the religious changes made in *The Prelude* is finely responsive to the language of the poem and generally persuasive. Wordsworth clearly labored to make the 1805 *Prelude* more recognizably Christian in the decades following its initial composition, and ultimately produced a more conventionally pious poem. Yet de Selincourt's references to "totally different" impressions and "entirely alien" ideas insinuate that the 1805 text contains no Christian associations at all. Although it further encouraged the poet's return to the Anglican Church, even John's drowning, in de Selincourt's judgment, did not prevent the Wordsworth of 1805 from finishing *The Prelude* "in the spirit in which it had been begun, with no sign of wavering from his early faith" (*EdS*, lxxiv).

De Selincourt substantiates these claims by juxtaposing lines from the 1805 and 1850 versions of the poem. As an example of the contrasts he typically points out, we might take the lines,

> I worshipp'd then among the depths of things
> As my soul bade me: . . .
> I felt, and nothing else. . . .
>
> (1805, 11.234–35, 238)

"Nothing could be more significant," de Selincourt remarks, "than the change" in this passage's 1850 variant:

> Worshipping then among the depths of things
> As piety ordained, . . .
> I felt, observed, and pondered. . . .
>
> (12.184–85, 188)

The spiritual self-reliance and trust in personal feeling proclaimed in 1805 relent in 1850 to the ordinations of piety and the discipline of observation and thought. Yet can we fairly say that the 1805 text, lacking these solemnities, lacks any recognizably Christian qualities? We need read back only a few lines in the 1805 *Prelude* to find Mary Hutchinson characterized as someone in whom "God delights / . . . for her common thoughts / Are piety, her life is blessedness" (11.221–23). If thoughtful in its way, Mary's piety appears spontaneous rather then doctrinally ordained. The point remains, however, that her instincts move her to something Wordsworth will approvingly call "piety" even in 1805, and in lines which, mentioning God and blessedness, encourage conventionally religious understanding. Wordsworth's description of Mary then moves immediately to the lines de Selincourt cites, which I will now quote at slightly greater length:

I had not at that time
Liv'd long enough, nor in the least survived
The first diviner influence of this world
As it appears to unaccustom'd eyes;
I worshipp'd then among the depths of things
As my soul bade me: could I then take part
In aught but admiration, or be pleased
With any thing but humbleness and love;
I felt, and nothing else; I did not judge,
I never thought of judging, with the gift
Of all this glory fill'd and satisfied.

(1805, 11.230–40)

Since these lines evoke the Immortality Ode, the speaker's reference to his "soul" qualifies as a religious assertion. He also portrays his appreciation of natural beauty as an act of worship, and the beauty itself as a "gift" and a "glory" in which unjaded sensibilities enjoy the world's "diviner influence." As always, Wordsworth's lines avoid doctrine, preferring "the religion in Poetry" to "versified Religion." Their generality notwithstanding, the sentiments are commonplaces of Christian devotional reflection. One can justly ask, then, how profoundly the 1805 text's omission of the phrase "as piety ordained" dissociates it in tone and import from the Christianity de Selincourt discerns in the 1850 version?

In my view, the greater moralism of the 1850 *Prelude* represents merely the rhetorical ossification of Christian affinities scattered everywhere in the religious language of the 1805 poem. Here is another example:

In the midst stood Man,
Outwardly, inwardly contemplated,
As of all visible natures crown, though born
Of dust, and Kindred to the worm, a Being
Both in perception and discernment, first
In every capability of rapture,
Through the divine effect of power and love,
As, more than any thing we know, instinct
With Godhead, and by reason and by will
Acknowledging dependency sublime.

(1850, 8.485–94)

In a Norton Critical Edition note keyed to line 488, Jonathan Wordsworth calls this passage "one of the most extreme of the Christian revisions of *The Prelude*" (*NCP* 301n.8). De Selincourt would have doubtless agreed; he too mentions these lines and stresses the orthodoxy of other *Prelude* passages which, like this one, posit contrasts "between the body and the spirit of man" (*EdS*, lxx, lxxi n.1). So how dramatically do the lines differ from their 1805 counterparts?

> Then rose
> Man, inwardly contemplated, and present
> In my own being, to a loftier height;
> As of all visible natures crown; and first
> In capability of feeling what
> Was to be felt; in being rapt away
> By the divine effect of power and love;
> As more than any thing we know, instinct
> With Godhead, and by reason and by will
> Acknowledging dependency sublime.
>
> (8.631–40)

The 1805 lines celebrate emotional susceptibility and ignore humankind's dust-like creatureliness, a biblically resonant image tinged with the humility of Wordsworth's later orthodoxy. But do the resulting differences indicate a revolution in spiritual outlook? Wordsworth's 1805 reflections declare humanity the crown of creation, a biblically resonant image in its own right. The poet then ascribes that preeminence to our rational and emotional recognition of divine power and love—an awareness rendering us "instinct / With Godhead"—and concludes by acknowledging his dependence on God with sincere humility.

One can similarly challenge de Selincourt's contention that "the last Book in particular" undergoes a drastic change in religious orientation in the 1850 version. De Selincourt makes Wordsworth's two descriptions of redemptive love the chief exhibit for this claim:

> thou call'st this love,
> And so it is; but there is a higher love
> Than this, a love that comes into the heart
> With awe and a diffusive sentiment;
> Thy love is human merely; this proceeds
> More from the brooding Soul, and is divine.
>
> (1805, 13.160–65)

There linger, listening, gazing with delight
Impassioned, but delight how pitiable!
Unless this love by a still higher love
Be hallowed, love that breathes not without awe;
Love that adores, but on the knees of prayer,
By heaven inspired; that frees from chains the soul,
Bearing in union with the purest, best
Of earth-born passions, on the wings of praise
A mutual tribute to the Almighty's Throne.

(1850, 14.179–87)

With admirable restraint, de Selincourt simply comments that

> the change in the text here, with the introduction of a definitely
> Christian interpretation of the character of that "higher love," is
> noteworthy, as is the change in the next line of "intellectual" to
> "spiritual." Wordsworth would not, in 1804–5, have denied that
> the love was spiritual, but he prefers to emphasize his belief that
> it is essentially a part of the natural equipment of man as man,
> and does not depend, as in the later text, upon a definitely Chris-
> tian faith and attitude to religion. (EdS, 628–29)

I entirely agree that the 1850 passage is heavy-handed and impositional. I merely suggest that here too Wordsworth's 1805 meditation depends—if not on a definite—on an *implied* "Christian faith
and attitude to religion." The "higher love" Wordsworth praises in
1805, after all, is seemingly not "part of the natural equipment of
man as man": the text expressly states that it informs the heart and
Soul as a divine legacy. The greater naturalism of the 1805 version
hardly renders it unreligious, or divests Wordsworth's references to
the "divine" and the "Soul" of their conventionally religious implications, particularly as those references echo within the rhetorical
and dramatic context of Book 13 as a whole. Obtrusively Christian
the 1805 passage certainly is not—but would anyone cite it as evidence of Wordsworth's intellectual rejection of Christian belief?
Surely the changes distinguishing the 1805 from the 1850 *Prelude*,
even in this worst-case instance, are not substantive enough to war-
rant the conclusion that Christianity remained "entirely alien" to
the poet's moral imagination in 1805.

"We have too often been led," Robert Barth remarks, "to
believe that the differences between the 1805 and 1850 versions,
in terms of their religious attitudes and values, are greater than

they actually are" (Barth, 18). Indeed we have, and the prevalence of the belief is no less instructive than it is welcome, frankly, for my argument. For once de Selincourt demonstrated the religious chasm ostensibly separating the 1805 and 1850 texts, he paved the way for widespread recognition of the Christianity of the 1850 *Prelude* by allowing that recognition to arise in the form of disapproval. So Herbert Lindenberger, participating in the panel discussion mentioned in a previous note, declares of Wordsworth's "Dust as we are, the immortal Spirit grows / Like harmony in music" (1850 1.340–41), "this is much too stiff—abstract, formal, too obtrusively Christian for a modernist sensibility."[47] So Harold Bloom writes that the 1850 *Prelude* "manifests an orthodox censor at work, straining to correct a private myth into an approach at Anglican dogma" (Bloom, 141). Lindenberger's and Bloom's admissions of the Christian quality of the 1850 text articulate a position prevalent in Wordsworth studies. Consequently, any demonstration that the religious differences between the 1805 and 1850 texts have been exaggerated, that Wordsworth's texts manifest an overriding similarity of spiritual emphasis and outlook, raises the possibility that the 1805 *Prelude* is itself significantly Christian. The very possibility may make Wordsworthians less quick to concede the 1850 text's Christian aspects, but for the moment I will disallow such backpedaling. *The Prelude* could only become "somewhat more explicitly or assertively [religious] in the 1850 version," Barth writes, "because it was deeply religious from the beginning."[48] The 1805 text lent itself to Christianizing revision, I would add, only because of Christian affinities latent in it from the beginning.

Initially, those affinities are deliberately understated. What Abrams terms the "circuitous" structure of *The Prelude* obliges Wordsworth to unveil only in concluding "a principle which was invisibly operative from the beginning" (NS, 76), or which was at first obscurely operative. As a result, one common response to the Christian qualities of Wordsworth's Snowdon meditation, for instance, has been to deplore them as inconsistent with the preceding books of *The Prelude*. The poem's faith in immortality can serve as a case in point. Jonathan Wordsworth annotates Wordsworth's assertion of "life endless" (1805, 13.183) as "a reference to the afterlife which emerges very suddenly in the context of the poem as a whole, but which is explained by Wordsworth's urgent need to believe in the survival of his brother John" (NCP 468n.6). Yet Wordsworth prefigures his Book 13 allusion to "life endless" in earlier books. The claim is clearly anticipated, I suggested, in Book 6. And additional examples come easily to mind: in Book 4 Wordsworth thinks about "How Life pervades the undecaying mind, / How the immortal Soul [creates] with Godlike power" (4.155–56); introducing the dream sequence of Book 5, he praises the "sovereign Intellect" for diffusing through the human body "A soul divine which we participate, / A deathless spirit" (5.14–17). The affirmation of immortality in Book 13 should seem neither precipitous nor unanticipated. It acts as Wordsworth's more declamatory (and more pointedly theological) reassertion of one of his poem's established convictions.

The immortality lines afford merely one example of how Christian motifs in Wordsworth's Snowdon episode expand upon previous points. The glad preamble leaves the poet "cloth'd in priestly robe" as if intended "For holy services" (1805 1.61, 63) so that Wordsworth's Romantic self-fashioning can from the beginning look ahead to his prophetic election. In the dawn dedication lines from Book 4 he similarly reflects,

> My heart was full; I made no vows, but vows
> Were then made for me; bond unknown to me
> Was given, that I should be, else sinning greatly,
> A dedicated Spirit. On I walked
> In blessedness, which even yet remains.
>
> (1805 4.334–38)

Here Wordsworth gives his vocational mythmaking a distinctly Christian aspect by allusively restaging the baptismal rite from the Book of Common Prayer.[49] In like manner, Wordsworth's Simplon crossing and apostrophe to Imagination prefigure the religious claims—and the biblical and Miltonic phrasing—of his epiphany on Mount Snowdon. As his poem approaches Snowdon, Wordsworth's language becomes more self-consciously Christian in spiritual ambience. Confessing his intention to celebrate outwardly humble people who honor human nature through their selflessness, he declares in 1805 Book 12:

> it shall be my pride
> That I have dared to tread this holy ground,
> Speaking no dream but things oracular,
> Matter not lightly to be heard by those

> Who to the letter of the outward promise
> Do read the invisible soul. . . .
> . . . .
> . . . . This I speak
> In gratitude to God, who feeds our hearts
> For his own service, knoweth us, loveth us
> When we are unregarded by the world.
>
> (12.250–55, 274–77)

In lines praising the watchful love of a personal God, Wordsworth accommodates Christ's transvaluation of the lowly and humble to the moral office of poetry. Yet the biblical and Christian sanctions this passage bestows on the poet's labor merely concentrate, for privileged summation, Christian associations subtly woven throughout the 1805 text.

Despite this associative pattern, the religious vision which culminates in the Snowdon episode does not *depend* on biblical revelation or Church doctrine. Wordsworth's vision is his own, anchored in his experience and validated by his exalted conception of humankind's potential for goodness and love. The 1805 *Prelude* is dominated by secular issues and eventuates in an insistent, deeply felt humanism. As Book 13 draws to a close, Wordsworth praises Coleridge precisely for helping him humanize his nature worship:

> And so the deep enthusiastic joy,
> The rapture of the Hallelujah sent
> From all that breathes and is, was chasten'd, stemm'd,
> And balanced by a Reason which indeed
> Is reason, duty and pathetic truth;
> And God and Man divided, as they ought,
> Between them the great system of the world
> Where Man is sphered, and which God animates.
>
> (13.261–68)

But here too, in a passage balancing the moral claims of Man and God, the poet's belief in God finds straightforward expression. By no means the earthbound anthropocentrism of a "*Semi*-atheist," the humanism of even the 1805 *Prelude* is a religious humanism. It is simply not the case that the poem divests its theological paradigms of any significant reference to the divine. Critical accounts of a

Wordsworthian humanism separate from spiritual reality—grounded strictly in human consciousness—read tendentiously and slight important essentialist continuities. Certainly one could argue that *The Prelude* anticipates contemporary insistence that the traditional ideas "God" and "Man" are so deeply complicit as to be unthinkable apart—that Wordsworth anticipated recent claims that we cannot have "Man" without "God." Yet we cannot accord Wordsworth's religious affirmations the seriousness they deserve without also crediting his persistent invocations of Christianity.

Like the Immortality Ode, the Thirteen-Book *Prelude* presents its religious insights not as coincident but as coterminous with the Christian revelation. Without claiming the poem for orthodoxy, one can claim that the Christian suggestiveness of Wordsworth's language remains intellectually pertinent and strategic. Implying that Romantic prophecy and religious tradition are mutually corroborative, Wordsworth positions his spiritual autobiography on the brink of the doctrinally explicit Christianity his text both reinscribes and creatively revises. The question of whether the text's similarity to Christianity outweighs its dissimilarity from Christianity depends, as always, on how one understands "Christianity." For some critics, no doubt, the Christian affinities of the 1805 *Prelude* do not dominate its heterodox aspects sufficiently to allow for an overall endorsement of Christianity. Certainly Wordsworth seems less interested in endorsing than transforming orthodox values. Even so, the metaphorical approximation to Christianity in *The Prelude* remains an intellectually contributive element of Wordsworth's poem, and as such a part of its religious meaning. Summoning up the convictions which define him, the Wordsworth of the 1805 *Prelude* calls upon God with rapture and gratitude, dramatizes a providential order shaping his life, insists that the creativity and immortality of the soul are a divine legacy, and centers his final prophecy on an apotheosis of love—an apotheosis reenacting the progression from Old Testament sublimity to New Testament beauty, and celebrated in language filled with spiritually familiarizing allusions to Christian texts and attitudes. We have grown skilled of late at reading the displacements of Wordsworth's poetry. It should not prove too difficult, I hope, to read the displacement of Christian promise informing Wordsworth's vision of a life "centring all in love, and in the end / All gratulent if rightly understood" (13.384–85).

Wordsworth's dialogue with Christianity in the Thirteen-Book *Prelude* envisions a faith capable of accommodating modern humanism. As innovative as that vision can appear, Wordsworth's allusions to Christian tradition signify a profound accommodation in their own right. In the conclusion which follows, I speculate that Wordsworth's poetics were modeled, whether consciously or not, on the revaluative traditionalism of the Higher Criticism—and that his intentions as a religious poet were to circumscribe innovation within tradition. The Immortality Ode and the Thirteen-Book *Prelude* attempt to preserve Christianity by assuming its status as a progressive revelation and prefiguring its future form. For all the liberating energies of Wordsworth's Romantic gospel, it would be a mistake to undervalue his traditionalism, then, or imagine him agreeing in 1805 that his revisionary engagement of Christianity thrust him beyond its pale. The poet who wrote the Thirteen-Book *Prelude* had renewed his commitment to an Anglican Church associated in his mind with his nation, his family, and his childhood. In recent years critics have argued—one thinks of James Chandler and Kenneth Johnston—that Wordsworth's political viewpoint and imaginative purposes became fundamentally conservative earlier than has often been thought.[50] The Christian affiliations of the 1805 *Prelude* represent the religious dimension of this conservative reorientation.

CONCLUSION

The Christian Wordsworth

My commentaries on the Immortality Ode and the Thirteen-Book *Prelude* glanced at Wordsworth in offering their explanations, unavoidably enough, but concentrated on the texts themselves. Here I want to reverse that protocol and conclude by interposing the author himself in the issue of his poetry's meaning. More specifically, I want to reconsider the question of Wordsworth's "religion in Poetry" from the vantage point provided by my readings of the Ode and *The Prelude*. The entanglement of Romantic natural theology and Christian tradition in these texts, my opening chapter suggested, places their religious outlook in irreducibly metaphorical relation to institutional Christianity per se. I continue to think that one cannot reformulate that outlook fairly without lingering over its intellectually contributive incorporation of Christian values. Ultimately, however, the supplemental economy of similarity and difference in metaphorical structure allows scholars to privilege, by turns, either the poetry's convergence with or divergence from Christian doctrine as its controlling commitment. So I want to conclude by speculating about the poet's own commitments and likeliest intentions. How did Wordsworth himself most probably understand the religious rhetoric his texts employ? If he had aligned himself with the Church of England by 1804, why would he have been content, given the enhanced possibilities of misreading, with a merely implied Christianity?

Wordsworth's acceptance of a religious rhetoric of implication,

I contend, reflects above all his historicist conception of Christianity. He owed his understanding of Anglican Church doctrine largely to the methods of the Higher Criticism. Historians working from Higher Critical premises, Elinor Shaffer shows, conceive religious tradition "in a totally new way: it is neither the unquestioned authority of the Church nor the unquestioned authority of the Biblical text on which tradition rests, but the perpetually shifting sense within the Christian community of what has the power to persuade its members and strengthen them in the faith."[1] The most advanced biblical scholarship of the time, the Higher Criticism was widely discussed in intellectual circles, including Wordsworth's own. Higher Critical influence explains Southey's portrait of himself as "*not* believing in the inspiration of the Bible, but believing in the faith which is founded upon it"—the faith, that is, of the Church's evolving evaluation of the Gospels.[2] But both *The Rime of the Ancient Mariner* and *Peter Bell* display a similar conversancy with Higher Critical attitudes. Citing Coleridge's interest in Herder, Shaffer claims that "in 'The Ancient Mariner,' Coleridge drew a visionary character belonging clearly to the primitive milieu in which apostolic credulity could flourish," and Jerome McGann has extended this claim into a full-scale reading of the poem's dependence on Higher Critical ideas in order to explore the historicality of reception.[3] Coleridge's interest in the narrative dissemination of conversion experiences helps connect his poem to *Peter Bell*. However we read that connection, it is clear, thanks to Alan Bewell, that *Peter Bell* also engages the arguments of the Higher Criticism, that the poem is an anthropologically conceived treatment of the "Natural History of Religion."[4] So Wordsworth knew something of the Higher Criticism as early as 1798.

That knowledge encouraged the undoctrinaire indirections of his religious poetics. For Higher Critical scholarship not only subordinated doctrine to history but, by that subordination, cast particular dogmas as the (arguably) outmoded residues of a historical process which may well have advanced beyond them. Finally, one needed to test apparent doctrinal obsolescence through an appeal to the religious community, but what is poetry if not one way of making such an appeal? So Higher Critical hermeneutics diminished the poet's obligations to Church doctrine through its innovative reconception of tradition. But it licensed prophetic individualism while reserving a place—in ways comforting to a "Catholic" Anglican sensibility—for the community's spiritual heritage.[5] The Higher Criticism exemplified a way of accepting orthodoxy while accommodating change. As further enactments of the historical process underlying the Church's spiritual authority, a poet's revisionary conjectures could function as tradition-confirming extensions of that authority. That is precisely how Wordsworth intended his poetry's secularizing gestures to function, I believe. The poetry's humanistic and naturalistic elements comprise a revisionism continuous with the tradition it aspires to revise. Wordsworth's intention was not to engage spiritual tradition in an extrinsic and subversive way—transforming its supernaturalism from without into an intellectually inimical naturalism—but to reaffirm the values of his Christian heritage by acting within its compass. In his religious poetry, Wordsworth typically attempts to expand that compass by projecting a reimagined Christianity answerable to modern secular imperatives.

So Wordsworth's religious poetics strategically mix tradition and innovation. Higher Critical methods supplied a model for his prophetic traditionalism because their own revisionism was grounded on a historically motivated deference to Christian tradition. Usually Wordsworthian "religion in Poetry," let me caution, involved no direct or conceptually specific dependence on biblical hermeneutics. Wordsworth simply came to understand, no doubt with Coleridge's assistance, that justifications of faith through a fundamentalist appeal to origins had given way among informed thinkers to justifications based on the notion of Christianity as a historically progressive revelation.[6] Modern defenses of Christianity had to be historically prosecuted. The *Ecclesiastical Sketches* aside, the historical self-consciousness of Wordsworth's approach to religious issues is perhaps clearest in a text such as the Prospectus to *The Recluse*. For the revisionist ambitions of the Prospectus are by no means confined to the epic example of Milton: Wordsworth expressly declares his intention to transvalue historically obsolescent ideas of God ("Jehovah with his thunder") and Paradise. A similar historicist orientation emerges when the 1805 *Prelude* stages its concluding theodicy as the speaker's response to the revolutionary upheavals of the European scene. Here is the spiritual vision, Wordsworth's Book 13 implies, which history has rendered necessary for modern heirs of the Christian tradition.

If Wordsworth meant to write in defense of a reimagined Christianity, why then was he content in 1804–1805 with poetic language qualifying at most as suggestively Christian? Later in life he was not content with his poetry's lack of doctrinal specification. His Fenwick note to the Immortality Ode laments a misreading "which has given pain to some good and pious persons" due to their inferences of heterodoxy (PTV, 428); his January 1815 letter to Catherine Clarkson similarly worries over her pantheistic interpretation of The Excursion (LMY 2.188). Vexed by the apparent ambiguities of his poems, the Sage of Rydal would sometimes revise them towards a more conspicuous orthodoxy. Yet Wordsworth never viewed the presentation of doctrine as his artistic metier. Also, he was convinced that his genuine audience would read the poetry appropriately in the end—even if dullards such as Charles Lamb and Sara Hutchinson at times required prompting![7] His conviction of his poetry's power of morally educating readerly sensibilities required him to trust his readership. In matters of religion, the only alternative was a dogmatic explicitness which would carry him beyond the scope of his talent and, as he notes in Essay, Supplementary to the Preface, threaten to divisively narrow his audience.[8] The appeal to audience mandated by his historicist poetics made publication an effort to construct a reciprocally legitimating community of readers. The prestige of Wordsworthian prophecy among nineteenth-century readers followed from Wordsworth's rhetorical success, as Thomas Pfau writes, in "gradually enfranchising himself and his audience as a novel, imagined community"—for Pfau a middle-class community fashioned as the social reflex of the poetry's defining values.[9]

Finally, it was a religiously conservative community. What I have described as the tradition-confirming force of Wordsworth's religious rhetoric becomes clearer, in fact, if we consider the cultural work performed by that poetry for its own historical community. That gradually enfranchised body of readers consisted of Wordsworth's Victorian admirers. Most of those readers honored Wordsworth as a Christian sage whose spiritual insights justified even the length of The Excursion, in Victorian eyes Wordsworth's most important religious poem. The Excursion sheds valuable light on Wordsworth's poetics of faith precisely because readers cannot now take its Christian stoicism at face value. For contemporary critics, the poem deconstructs all systematic orders of truth, including theological orthodoxy. In The Excursion Wordsworth may proclaim "his new identity as a religious teacher, a consecrated prophet embarking on a public mission," Robert Ryan comments, but the poet finally leaves his readers with "a complex of discordant impressions arising from the conflict of three different conceptions of ultimate value" (RR, 100, 113). Just so, Alison Hickey reads The Excursion as a poem of "epistemological uncertainty" and "multiple dead-end plots" notable for their "deviation and deferral, usurpation, broken lineages, and unfulfilled promises" (Hickey, 16, 8, 14). For her too, Wordsworth's glances at "the Christian paradigm are interesting for the dynamic of choice they invoke, rather than for the clear superiority of one of the choices" (Hickey, 28).

But asking "to what extent were the features I have detected visible to nineteenth-century readers," Hickey must admit that those features mostly went unrecognized, adding that during the century "admirers increasingly value Wordsworth's poetry for upholding moral and spiritual values" (Hickey, 167). Not every nineteenth-century reader seized instantly on the Christianity of *The Excursion*. Initially the poem's religious position puzzled Lamb, prompting his question to Wordsworth: "are you a *Xtian*? or is it the Pedlar & the Priest that are?" (*Lamb Letters* 3.112). Despite this reviewer's request for useful clarification, however, Lamb finally had no doubts about the text's basic religious orientation: Wordsworth's spiritual responsiveness to nature, working "in friendly alliance and conjunction with the religion of his country," sponsored a theological outlook which Lamb likened alternately to a "generous Quakerism" and a "Natural Methodism," but which he deemed indisputably Christian.[10] In a similar vein, James Montgomery's well-known disapproval of the elision of dogma in *The Excursion* arose only because the poem's spiritual reflections established the *expectation* of dogma—and even then Montgomery objects merely to Wordsworth's disinclination to draw the implicit into the explicit, to dilate prophetic suggestion into doctrinal confirmation.[11] Lamb and Montgomery aside, there can be no doubt about the nineteenth-century consensus that *The Excursion*, despite the Solitary's skepticism, vindicated the spiritual truth as well as the modern social necessity of Christianity. It is facile to account for that consensus by declaring the Victorians inattentive readers. For Victorian interpretive practice, the problems of action and belief probed in *The Excursion*—many hard to miss, surely, in Wordsworth's far from cheerful poem—simply qualified as problems *of* faith rather than as problems exposing faith as a delusion.

What proves true of *The Excursion*, furthermore, proves true for the entire Victorian construction of Wordsworth: it displays a supervening identification of the poet's spiritual vision with Christianity. Wordsworth's writings unquestionably served diverse agendas and inspired conflicting interpretations in the nineteenth century. As late as 1842, John Wilson could write that Wordsworth "certainly cannot be called a Christian poet," and similar denials occasionally surfaced.[12] Some readers valued Wordsworth's poetry for its doctrinally unmediated evocation of a living God; others looked to Wordsworth for a mental renewal unallied to spiritual conversion; yet others saw him as a humanistic thinker and humanitarian defender of the humble, as a poet whose affective power was encumbered by unnecessary philosophical pretensions, or as an aesthetic celebrator of intense, fleeting moments. Stephen Gill's recent *Wordsworth and the Victorians* repeatedly shows the need for qualification in generalizing about the nineteenth-century's cultural appropriation of "Wordsworth." But throughout the Victorian period, Gill also shows, "the commonest way of dealing with the direct pretensions of Wordsworth's philosophical utterances was to interpret them in the light of revealed religion, to gather him within the Christian fold of whatever denomination" (*Wordsworth and the Victorians*, 171). Gill's portrait of Wordsworth as "England's Samuel" documents Wordsworth's Christian reputation ramifying through a truly extraordinary range of cultural practices: comparisons of his work to the Bible, pilgrimages to Rydal Mount, recourse to Wordsworthian epigraphs to ease the reception of scientific arguments, veneration of Wordsworthian souvenirs in the manner of religious relics, personal testimonies to the poetry's spiritual comfort, and more. Underlying all of these activities, of course, was an energetic collective reading of Wordsworth for his elaboration of Christian truths.

It is true that this reading often privileged texts composed after 1805. Yet it reserved pride of place for the Immortality Ode, which most Victorian readers revered for its Christian mythmaking. The Thirteen-Book *Prelude* went unpublished during the Victorian era, needless to say. I have argued in chapter 5, however, that the 1805 version of *The Prelude* seems less solemnly pious but otherwise similar in religious outlook to the 1850 version, and that text Victorian readers effortlessly assimilated to prevailing notions of Wordsworth's faith.[13] No response merely to the later poetry, the nineteenth-century Christian construction of Wordsworth accommodated his whole career. That construction took shape in part, therefore, as a response to the undoctrinaire "religion in Poetry" found in Wordsworth's most characteristic and admired work. In that response we witness the poetry's metaphorical relation to orthodox Christianity signifying as meaningfully Christian in the poet's contemporary cultural milieu. For nineteenth-century readers, the normative and reinscriptive force of Wordsworth's religious rhetoric outweighed its more radically innovative aspect, which remained encompassed, they mostly thought, by the poetry's traditionalism. We may prefer to regard the Wordsworth of 1798–1805 as a humanistic ironist unable to find either religious questions or their Christian answers even remotely compelling. But the fact that his own century regarded him so differently surely bears on any critical project flying the banners of the return to history.

It certainly bears on the questions of Wordsworth's personal faith and poetic motives. For the nineteenth-century Christian construction of Wordsworth, I argue, unfolds reflexively from the authorial self-fashioning undertaken in the poems: it is a construction that the poet projected and the poetry invites. We know well that Wordsworth was an uncommonly busy interventionist in his poetry's social reception. Those interventions involved numerous publication and presentational issues. Yet they began, we should recall, with the expressive decisions responsible for the verbal and ideational form of the poems, both in the case of work issued and work withheld. If the construction "Wordsworth" has no existence outside the cultural field, the artistic choices and intellectual intentions informing Wordsworth's poems impinge on that field, I think, as actively as it reciprocally positions the poems. These reciprocities lend the Victorian public image of Wordsworth considerable prestige as a culturally proximate reading of Wordsworth's motives for writing. By no means am I retreating into the bald assertion that Wordsworth wrote a Christian poetry. The instability of evaluative criteria for gauging orthodoxy more than justifies Gill's observation that "there is no such thing as orthodox Christianity"[14] and creates insurmountable difficulties for anyone tempted to flatly declare the Ode, for instance, a Christian text. The unproductive, even unanswerable question, "is Wordsworth's poetry Christian in import?" needs reformulation so that we can ask in what sense, or better, to *whom* the poems qualified as Christian. An extrapolation from the Victorian Wordsworth, my contention is that in all probability the poet *himself*, even in 1804–1805, understood his poems as the vehicles of a revisionary Christianity.

Wordsworth's challenge in pursuing his career, Pfau writes, was to "continually renegotiate the fundamental antagonism between his grounding hypothesis of a unique yet representative self and the inherited aesthetic and political languages required for reconfirming that hypothesis" (Pfau, 13). We must extend this claim to include inherited religious language, but we must above all retain

Pfau's emphasis on the author's active negotiations with the normative discourses of his society. As rhetorical overtures to that society, the Immortality Ode and Thirteen-Book *Prelude* presuppose Wordsworth's sense of the cultural codes—the connotative registers, public idioms, textual precedents, and habits of interpretation—underlying the performative potential of language in his world. Wordsworth's career illustrates Jon Klancher's point that "readers are *made*, created as a public through a network of circulatory channels"used by writers to anticipate, extend, and redirect readerly habits of response.[15] With the glorious child of the Ode, as he trails God and Heaven after him, and the biblical and Miltonic resonances of the Snowdon meditation, Wordsworth inscribes his texts with a socially recognizable frame of reference facilitating Christian understanding. In ways familiar from Church liturgy, sermons, hymn books, and the religiously inflected language of various discourses, the poems incorporate the coordinates necessary for a nineteenth-century reader to map out a Christian response. My argument is simply that the poetry's reinscription of Christian conventions was Wordsworth's deliberate gambit. He knew that his work's religious affirmations would ordinarily be viewed as reclamations of Christian truths; he assented to that response because of his own Christian faith.

Noting "the view, widely held in the previous generation, that literary history wrote the poems," and the subsequent views that language or "property" wrote Wordsworth's poems, David Bromwich has wittily offered his contrary "view that a man wrote them."[16] It is my view as well, though I understand it, without Bromwich's sanction, to involve a respect for authorial agency which extends unavoidably to the notion of intentionality. When the field of textual criticism, long a bastion of scholarly conservatism, routinely sees the idea of intention called into question, the problems posed by that idea are surely recognized sufficiently—and no conceptual defenses of intentional meaning will be offered here. Instead I submit Jack Stillinger's observant remark that in the "world of academic discourse, in spite of extremely influential theoretical efforts to the contrary, individual historical authorship continues to be an essential element in opinions about reading, interpreting, and editing—even when those opinions begin with proclamations about the death of the author."[17] In contemporary Romantic studies, it is the uncommonly bold reader who turns to a text prepared to disregard or overrule available information about likely authorial motives, and I am no such reader. I believe that neither the problematics of language or representation, nor the institutions of cultural reception, nor history conceived as an absent cause, shaped Wordsworth's poetry as profoundly as the man's compositional intentions did. I believe further that Wordsworth's consciously held beliefs consistently informed those intentions. With all apologies if I seem to take the long way round to an unremarkable end, Wordsworth's poetry can be read as an expression of Wordsworth's ideas.

That unremarkable point is an especially important one for this book. For my approach to Wordsworth's religious poems specifically seeks a reintegration of the man and his writing. Wordsworth himself has been escorted from his poetry, I think, whenever critics encountering references to a tenet of religious faith declare the lines in question to have been written by Wordsworth's spectre—or by Wordsworth the "*Semi*-atheist" (*CLSTC* 1.216). It is obviously possible to regard the early Wordsworth as a radical humanist left imaginatively moribund by his retreat into Christianity after John's drowning. But that biographical myth cannot stand up to contextual analysis of the pertinent evidence. Wordsworth almost certainly never lost his faith in God for any sustained period of time. The most probable explanation of the "*Semi*-atheist" phrase—once it is repositioned among Coleridge's letters to Thelwall—lies with Wordsworth's spiritual reverence for nature or his aversion to the idea of eternal punishment. Moreover, Coleridge's correspondence significantly describes the Wordsworth of 1797 as "more inclined to Christianity than to Theism, simply considered" (*CLSTC* 1.327). If temporarily fierce, Wordsworth's political unhappiness with the Anglican establishment had eased considerably by 1798: thus his resistance to Unitarian proselytizing despite the attractions of a religious poetry celebrating the One Life. That resistance illustrates the poet's emotional loyalties to the Christian norms of his social world and personal upbringing. My argument that residual Christian sympathies undermined his 1798 expansion of *The Ruined Cottage* MS. B remains purely speculative. Still, those sympathies had evolved into recommitment to the Anglican Church by 1803, in Ryan's judgment, and certainly by 1804: so Wordsworth's faith consisted of an occasionally troubled but supervening Anglicanism by at least the time he finished the Immortality Ode and Thirteen-Book *Prelude*.[18]

If we concede the conservatism of Wordsworth's spiritual temperament, how do we integrate the man with a body of work which affirms key religious ideas in poetic contexts rich in Christian associations? Exactly by reading the poetry as a displaced expression of the man's private allegiances to Christianity. The incomplete convergence of Wordsworth's poems and Christian orthodoxy is not due principally to any incomplete faith on the poet's part, although his hesitancies and heterodoxies were quite real at times. It is due rather to his particular artistic purposes. Again, Wordsworth's sense of his talent, the taste he acquired through familiarity with the British loco-descriptive tradition, and his historicist understanding of Anglican Church doctrine, all combined to divert him from a doctrinally explicit religious poetics. That divergence was his imaginative right. At the same time, it was something he could afford precisely *because* his 1804–1805 poems crucially presupposed Christian spiritual conventions as a conceptual backdrop—a backdrop which alone rendered his prophetic innovations meaningful and even possible. The Christian interpretive coordinates encoded in his poetry, its Christian promptings, were eagerly recognized by the majority of his nineteenth-century readers. If we acknowledge the poet's investment in those promptings, we are left with a way of reconciling the poetry's Christian moral climate with both Wordsworth's need for imaginative independence and his deference to the truth of Christianity.

The importance of Christianity for Wordsworth's 1798–1805 poetic development can of course be overstated. Even Wordsworthian poems most dependent on religious motifs remain, despite that dependence, the complexly mediated productions of a poet impressively myriad-minded in his own right. No one should underestimate the assimilation of moral traditions underlying Wordsworth's sympathetic depictions of human suffering; no one should reduce the visionary and transcendental in Wordsworth to a projection of his theological convictions. But both the Wordsworth who insisted "That we have all one human heart" ("The Old Cumberland Beggar," line 146) and the Wordsworth of visionary defamiliarization are figures moved to insight partly by their religious attitudes. The virtual certainty that Wordsworth believed sincerely in spiritual realities, in a transcendent God of love and an immortal soul, and that he formed those beliefs within a Christian culture he deeply valued, left an indelible mark on his poetry—on most of his greatest poetry, in fact. No doubt we find that poetry fascinating for the several portraits of the artist it offers us. If the Christian Wordsworth, 1798–1805 represents just one of those portraits, it nonetheless captures an aspect of the poet deserving of closer attention, and greater respect, than it has often received.

NOTES

NOTES TO PREFACE

1. James Chandler, *Wordsworth's Second Nature: A Study of the Poetry and Politics* (Chicago: University of Chicago Press, 1894), xviii; Kenneth Johnston, *The Hidden Wordsworth: Poet, Lover, Rebel, Spy* (New York: Norton, 1998), 669. Regina Hewitt rightly notes that a conservative Wordsworth also emerges from new historicist critiques—such as the work of Jerome McGann and Marjorie Levinson—which stress the erasure of (revolutionary) politics and history in the poetry, in *The Possibilities of Society: Wordsworth, Coleridge, and the Sociological Viewpoint of English Romanticism* (Albany: State University of New York Press, 1997), 185n.1.

NOTES TO CHAPTER 1.
WORDSWORTH'S FAITH

1. Cited in Peter Gay, *The Enlightenment: An Interpretation*, 2 vols. (New York: Norton, 1966–1969), vol. 1, *The Rise of Modern Paganism*, 122. Gay's account of this incident draws on the lengthier version in Alfred Noyes, *Voltaire* (New York: Sheed and Ward, 1936), 554–55. See *The Enlightenment* (385–96) for a synopsis of Voltaire's Deistic allegiances and heated opposition to institutional Christianity.

2. Thomas Carlyle, *Sartor Resartus*, in *The Works of Carlyle*, ed. H. D. Traill, The Centenary Edition, 30 vols. (London: Chapman and Hall, 1896–1899), 1.154.

3. Roland N. Stromberg, *Religious Liberalism in Eighteenth-Century England* (Oxford: Oxford University Press, 1954), 4.

4. Donald J. Greene, "Augustinianism and Empiricism: A Note on Eighteenth-Century Intellectual History," *Eighteenth-Century Studies* 1

(1967): 37. Greene's comment comes in the course of an argument that the eighteenth century in Britain was dominated intellectually by the two value systems of his title.

5. Basil Willey, "Wordsworth and the Locke Tradition," in *English Romantic Poets: Modern Essays in Criticism*, 2nd ed., ed. M. H. Abrams (New York: Oxford University Press, 1975), 121.

6. See James Downey, *The Eighteenth Century Pulpit: A Study of the Sermons of Butler, Berkeley, Secker, Sterne, Whitefield, and Wesley* (Oxford: Clarendon Press, 1969).

7. Gordon Rupp, *Religion in England: 1688–1791* (Oxford: Clarendon Press, 1986), 493.

8. Robert Ryan, *RR*, 20, 21. See Ryan's first chapter, "'A sect of dissenters,'" for a richly detailed synopsis of the politics of religion in these decades.

9. "In face of the formal abolition of orthodox Christianity in the French republic and the worship of the goddess of Reason, attachment to the Established Church in England became more widespread and cordial," comments Norman Sykes in *Church and State in England in the XVIIIth Century* (Cambridge: Cambridge University Press, 1934; Reprint Hamden, Conn.: Archon Books, 1962), 407. G. R. Cragg discusses this conservative reaction in *Reason and Authority in the Eighteenth Century* (Cambridge: Cambridge University Press, 1964), 262–63.

10. In this connection it seems worthwhile mentioning Sykes's respected claim that "the eighteenth century witnessed a steady and progressive laicisation of religion, which is the keynote of its ecclesiastical development. Hostile critics have preferred to describe the process as the secularisation of the Church; but it may be contended that the laicisation of religion is a more accurate phrase; for albeit the clerical order generally was characterised by a markedly unprofessional temper, the laity not only deemed themselves a proper and necessary part of the organisation of the Christian Church but acted upon that persuasion with vigour and conviction" (Sykes, 379).

11. Gay, 543. As he acknowledges, Gay takes his definition of secularization from the seminal work of Ernst Troeltsch.

12. Horton Davies' phrases summarizing the "characteristic marks of the theology" of early- to mid-eighteenth-century Britain, in *Worship and Theology in England: From Watts and Wesley to Maurice, 1690–1850* (Princeton: Princeton University Press, 1961), 3.

13. Geoffrey Hartman, *Wordsworth's Poetry 1787–1814* (1964; New Haven: Yale University Press, 1971), 338. Alan Liu discusses the Hegelian presuppositions of Hartman's approach to Wordsworth in *Wordsworth: The Sense of History* (Stanford: Stanford University Press, 1989), 513–15n.3.

14. John Hodgson, *Wordsworth's Philosophical Poetry, 1797–1814* (Lincoln: University of Nebraska Press, 1980), xiii, xvi.

15. Paul H. Fry, "Green to the Very Door? The Natural Wordsworth," *SIR* 35 (1996): 535. Fry contends that, despite the critical diversity he mentions, "all the most influential rereadings have but one refrain: Wordsworth was not a nature poet" (535). Because Wordsworth as a nature poet was the poet of nature's spiritual power, the refrain Fry mentions can be rephrased, "Wordsworth was not a religious poet." As with Fry's claim, this generalization pertains only to the dominant tradition of Wordsworth criticism, "the most influential rereadings."

16. Jerome McGann's phrase, from *The Romantic Ideology: A Critical Investigation* (Chicago: University of Chicago Press, 1983), 1. For criticism of new historicist dismissals of Romantic religion, see Ryan, *RR*, 2, 5, 23.

17. Stephen Gill, *William Wordsworth: The Prelude*, Landmarks of World Literature (Cambridge: Cambridge University Press, 1991), 39.

18. Nancy Easterlin, *Wordsworth and the Question of "Romantic Religion"* (Lewisburg: Bucknell University Press, 1996), 9; Ryan, *RR*, 11.

19. Ryan, *RR*, 83, 90, 96. Ryan also argues, let me add, that "in reality this unsystematic metaphysician seems from the start not to have noticed any important theological discrepancy—whatever the political difference—between his own natural religion and Christianity," and that "the poet's return to Christian practice and belief required no significant recantation of his earlier metaphysics," being "a return in which he brought his 'nature religion' with him almost intact" (*RR*, 94, 94–95).

20. *The Notebooks of Samuel Taylor Coleridge*, ed. Kathleen Coburn, 2 vols., vol. 1: *1794–1804, Text* (Princeton: Princeton University Press, 1957), entry 1616f74.

21. Mary Moorman, *William Wordsworth: A Biography*, 2 vols., vol. 1: *The Early Years, 1770–1802* (Oxford: Clarendon Press, 1957–65), 583–84. Stephen Prickett also concludes that Wordsworth's "argument is not that Paley, Ray, or Derham are guilty of any kind of philosophic error, but simply that they are a lot of 'pedants,'" in *Romanticism and Religion: The Tradition of Coleridge and Wordsworth in the Victorian Church* (Cambridge: Cambridge University Press, 1976), 84. As Prickett remarks, another problem with this approach for Wordsworth was its tendency to remove God from nature.

22. Legouis quoted Coleridge's letter to Thelwall on behalf of the claim that the Wordsworth of 1798 "had broken with" all "religious creeds," in *The Early Life of William Wordsworth 1770–1798: A Study of "The Prelude,"* trans. J. W. Matthews, 2nd ed. with additional appendix (1897; London: J. M. Dent and Sons, 1921), 470 and 470n.4. In his detailed considera-

tion of Wordsworth's opinions, Hoxie Neal Fairchild concludes, conversely, that "such remarks reveal less about Wordsworth than about Coleridge," and urges that Coleridge's description of Wordsworth as "a *Semi*-atheist" "should be observed with interest and heavily discounted: for Coleridge, atheism consisted in disagreement with his own peculiar ideas" (*HNF* 3.189, 155). Wryly comparing Coleridge's term to the phrase "moderate atheist," Edith C. Batho justly remarks that "the term itself, though taken seriously and solemnly repeated by later biographers, is almost meaningless," in *The Later Wordsworth* (Cambridge: Cambridge University Press, 1933), 267.

23. Mark Philp, *Godwin's Political Justice* (London: Duckworth, 1986), 34.

24. See the discussion of this issue in the "Death and the Soul" section of chapter 3 (98–104).

25. In a letter to Quaker author Joseph John Gurney, Southey remarked, "but for an eternity of torments—I *cannot* believe it,—and God forgive me if I am wrong, but I cannot in this case call upon him to help mine unbelief," cited in Geoffrey Carnall, *Robert Southey and His Age: The Development of a Conservative Mind* (Oxford: Clarendon, 1960), 219. Others who rejected the idea of Hell were Rousseau, Hartley, and F. D. Maurice.

26. From *The Table Talk and Omniana of Samuel Taylor Coleridge*, as cited in Thomas McFarland, *Coleridge and the Pantheist Tradition* (Oxford: Clarendon Press, 1969), 169.

27. Alan Bewell, *Wordsworth and the Enlightenment: Nature, Man, and Society in the Experimental Poetry* (New Haven: Yale University Press, 1989), 119. This position is common: Basil Willey, for example, argues similarly that Coleridge's comments reveal him lamenting "Wordsworth's lack of Christian faith," in "Coleridge and religion," in *S. T. Coleridge: Writers and Their Background*, ed. R. L. Brett (Athens: Ohio University Press, 1972), 232.

28. Richard E. Matlack, "Classical Argument and Romantic Persuasion in 'Tintern Abbey,'" *SIR* 25 (1986): 107.

29. Matlack, 107. Readings of Coleridge's patronizing of Wordsworth in this letter need to weigh the letter's evidential force against "Coleridge's own chameleon-habit, which lasted for life, of adjusting his mental colour to that of his correspondents" (Willey, "Coleridge and religion," 228). E. P. Thompson interprets Coleridge's "manner of modifying (almost helplessly) his views to suit an audience" as outright political equivocation in "Disenchantment or Default? A Lay Sermon," in *Power and Consciousness*, ed. Conor Cruise O'Brien and William Dean Vanech (New York: New York University Press, 1969), 153.

30. From Keats's well known 21, 27 (?) December 1817 letter to his brothers, in *The Letters of John Keats*, 2 vols., ed. Hyder E. Rollins (Cambridge: Harvard University Press, 1958), 1.193.

31. Gill, *William Wordsworth: The Prelude*, 42. De Selincourt commented that "when Coleridge described his friend as a semi-atheist he was not objecting to his positive faith, but rather reflecting on what he regarded as its incompleteness," in *The Prelude: or, Growth of a Poet's Mind*, ed. Ernest de Selincourt, 2nd ed., rev. Helen Darbishire (1926; Oxford: Clarendon Press, 1959), lxix–lxx (hereafter *EdS*); see note 22 above for the comments of Batho and Fairchild.

32. See the 31 May 1812 entry in *HCR* 1.90: "Wordsworth spoke in defence of Church establishment, and on the usual grounds said he would shed his blood for it. He declared himself not virtuous enough for a clergyman."

33. Christopher Wordsworth, *Memoirs of William Wordsworth*, 2 vols. (Boston: Ticknor, Reed, and Fields, 1851), 1.90.

34. Probably the best known instance of Wordsworth's capacity for boorish remarks in company is his "very pretty piece of Paganism" response to Keats's recitation of the Hymn to Pan from *Endymion*, as reported by Benjamin Robert Haydon in a 29 November 1845 letter to Edward Moxon, from *The Keats Circle: Letters and Papers, 1816–1879*, ed. Hyder E. Rollins, 2 vols. (Cambridge: Harvard University Press, 1965), 2.143–44. But other instances can be adduced: Crabb Robinson's 8 May, 1812 entry reports Wordsworth speaking to Robinson himself in a manner "by no means flattering or courteous" of a pamphlet he had written, and making statements about Coleridge which Robinson, hoping to see the two poets resume their friendship, "was careful not to repeat, as they could not tend to the reconciliation so desireable" (*HCR* 1.74–75).

35. R. D. Havens, *The Mind of a Poet*, 2 vols., vol 1: *A Study of Wordsworth's Thought* (Baltimore: The Johns Hopkins University Press, 1941), 189.

36. Jonathan Wordsworth, "Wordsworth's Borderers," in *English Romantic Poets: Modern Essays in Criticism*, 2nd ed., ed. M. H. Abrams (New York: Oxford University Press, 1975), 185, 183. As noted above, Ryan finally places Wordsworth's return to the Anglican Church in 1803, when the birth of Johnny, assisted by the poet's growing conservatism, reorganized life at Dove Cottage in ways promoting the family's reintegration into both the local and extended Anglican communities (*RR*, 96). In light of Ryan's reconstruction of Wordsworth's development, we should note Jonathan Wordsworth's acknowledgment that John Wordsworth's drowning, in its influence on the poet's faith, merely consolidated a drift toward Christianity already in progress: "the signs had all been there the previous

year," Jonathan Wordsworth comments in *William Wordsworth: The Borders of Vision* (Oxford: Clarendon, 1982), 33.

37. Judson Lyon's phrase, from *The Excursion: A Study* (New Haven: Yale University Press, 1950), 113. Fairchild summarizes reservations about the Christianity of *The Excursion* among Wordsworth's contemporaries (*HNF* 3.208–9). The reviews which challenged the poem's Christianity most directly were by J. Montgomery, *The Eclectic Review*, n.s. 3 (1815): 131–39, and John Wilson's article, "Sacred Poetry," in *Blackwood's Edinburgh Magazine* 24 (1828): 917–28. It is generally agreed that this article, as reprinted in Wilson's *Recreations of Christopher North* (1842), prompted the heavy-handed accentuation of Christian doctrine in Wordsworth's 1845 revisions of *The Excursion*, but see Gill's account of Frederick William Faber's religious influence on the older Wordsworth, in *Wordsworth and the Victorians* (Oxford: Clarendon, 1998), 70–80.

38. Richard E. Brantley, *Wordsworth's "Natural Methodism"* (New Haven: Yale University Press, 1975), 22. For the interrelated emergence of Methodism and Romanticism within an encompassing cultural reorientation, see Henry Abelove's claim that to study "the spirituality of the Methodist people is to gain a potentially useful perspective on the origins of Romanticism. The discovery of grace at everyday places; the internalization of apocalypse; the privileged and continuous self-exploration and self-expression: these are the basic features of the Methodist appropriation of the Puritan tradition, and they may also have been among the basic features of the poetry that Wordsworth and Coleridge introduced in 1798," in *The Evangelist of Desire: John Wesley and the Methodists* (Stanford: Stanford University Press, 1990), 95n.73.

39. William Wilberforce, *A Practical View of the Prevailing Religious System of Professed Christians, in the Higher and Middle Classes, Contrasted With Real Christianity*, The Evangelical Family Library, vol. 2 (New York: The American Tract Society, n. d.), 68.

40. See Sykes's comments on "the retrograde intellectual influence" of the Evangelical movement, especially its extreme "depreciation of the intellectual study and criticism of the Bible," and Cragg's similar remark that "one consequence of the practical strain in Evangelical thought was a tendency to depreciate intellectual effort" (Sykes, 398; Cragg, 180).

41. The emphasis on community was, again, typically Anglican. The Evangelicals, notes Cragg, "were intensely preoccupied with the conversion of the individual; they were little interested in his sacramental incorporation into the Church" (Cragg, 180). Sykes remarks similarly that "Evangelicalism might speak of fellowship, but it was not referring to the unity of the Church Triumphant in heaven with the Church Militant upon earth. More often, it was thinking chiefly of the vertical relationship between the individual soul and God" (Sykes, 58).

42. Joseph C. Sitterson, Jr.'s phrase, from "The Genre and Place of the Intimations Ode," *PMLA* 101 (1986):32.

43. Gill, *William Wordsworth: A Life* (Oxford: Oxford University Press, 1990), 111; the phrase Gill quotes is Coleridge's, from his "Fragments of Theological Lectures" (Gill, *William Wordsworth: A Life*, 445n.89).

44. My four quotations come respectively from "I only look'd for pain and grief" (lines 3 and 59–60) and "Distressful gift! this Book receives" (lines, 38, 41–42) (*PTV*, 611–14, 617–18). The elegies written for John Wordsworth include numerous additional instances of Christian diction and sentiment.

45. *British Critic*, 2nd Series, 3 (May 1815): 455; reprint, *The Romantics Reviewed: Contemporary Review of British Romantic Writers*, ed. Donald H. Reiman, 9 vols. (New York: Garland, 1972), Part A, 1.141.

46. For Tillotson, L. P. Curtis remarks, "the principles of natural religion, accordingly—belief in the existence of God, the immortality of the soul, and a future state—had by logic and of necessity to take precedence of revelation," in *Anglican Moods of the Eighteenth Century* (Hamden, Connecticut: Yale University Press, 1966), 39. An expression of weariness with the doctrinal controversies of the seventeenth century, this privileging of natural theology was a hallmark of Latitudinarian moderation.

47. Aubrey De Vere, *Essays, Chiefly on Poetry*, 2 vols. (London: Macmillan, 1887), 2.283.

48. Robert Longbaum, *The Poetry of Experience: The Dramatic Monologue in Modern Literary Tradition* (New York: W. W. Norton & Company, Inc., 1957).

49. J. Robert Barth, S.J., "Cross Examination: 3: Robert Barth," *WC* 17 (1986): 21.

50. Lionel Trilling, "Wordsworth and the Iron time," in *Wordsworth: A Collection of Critical Essays*, ed. M. H. Abrams (Englewood Cliffs: Prentice-Hall, 1972), 46, 45. See page 46 of this essay for Trilling's synopsis of Wordsworth's Christian qualities.

51. Jeffrey Baker, *Time and Mind in Wordsworth's Poetry* (Detroit: Wayne State University Press, 1980), 157.

NOTES TO CHAPTER 2.
VAIN BELIEF: WORDSWORTH AND THE ONE LIFE

1. Jonathan Wordsworth, *MH* (1969); "Wordsworth Borderers" (1969), in *English Romantic Poets: Modern Essays in Criticism*, ed. M. H. Abrams,

2nd ed. (New York: Oxford University Press, 1975), 170–87; and "The Two-Part *Prelude* of 1799" (1970), in *NCP*, 567–85. On the idea of the One Life, its philosophical and scientific background, and the question of Wordsworth's pantheism, also see H. W. Piper, *The Active Universe: Pantheism and the Concept of Imagination in the English Romantic Poets* (London: Athlone Press, 1962). As indicated by the parenthetical identifications in the body of this chapter, most of Wordsworth's texts are cited from volumes in the Cornell Wordsworth Series. *The Excursion* and Wordsworth's comments to Isabella Fenwick are cited from *PW*; and, for the convenience of citing a reading text, the Pedlar narrative from *MH*, 172–83.

2. "Two-Part *Prelude*," 575. Jonathan Wordsworth tacitly reconstructs the grounds for Wordsworth's turn from the One Life by noting the humanist perspective and "flirtation with the transcendental" in the Two-Part *Prelude* of 1798–1799 ("Two-Part *Prelude*," 576). John Hodgson has argued that Wordsworth renounced the One Life because "the immortality it promises . . . comes at the expense of human individuality, awareness, and intelligence," but this claim, as compelling as I find it, has not elicited much response from Wordsworthians (*Wordsworth's Philosophical Poetry, 1797–1814* [Lincoln: University of Nebraska Press, 1980], xv).

3. Coleridge's 11 December 1794 letter (*CLSTC* 1.137). While Coleridge expressed passing reservations about Necessity well before 1797–1798, his final break with the idea may have come as late as 1801, at which time he claimed to have "overthrown . . . the doctrine of Necessity" in his 16 March letter to Thomas Poole (*CLSTC* 2.706). I assume Coleridge's willingness to defend the idea of Necessity until at least 1799 on the authority of Lewis Patton and Peter Mann, who argue merely that "by 1799 [Coleridge's] disenchantment with the doctrine of necessity was *virtually* complete," in their introduction to *Lectures 1795 on Politics and Religion*, *CWSTC* 1.lxvi (italics mine). For Necessity as the causal principle of events, an ontological or historical rather than merely psychological principle, see the discussion in Piper, 22–27, and Kenneth Neill Cameron, *The Young Shelley: Genesis of a Radical* (New York: MacMillan, 1950), 272–73.

4. *CLSTC* 2.1037. The primary evidence concerning Wordsworth's attitudes toward Necessity is conveniently gathered by Melvin Rader in *Wordsworth: A Philosophical Approach* (Oxford: Clarendon Press, 1967), 17–21, 60–62. My view of Wordsworth's presentation of Necessity in *The Ruined Cottage* draws on Paul D. Sheats's account of the conflict of naturalism and humanism in the poem, especially his comment that the poet-figure's "human compassion for Margaret . . . implicitly compensates for the 'chearful' necessitarianism of the pedlar," in *The Making of Wordsworth's Poetry* (Cambridge: Harvard University Press, 1973), 179.

5. James Chandler, *Wordsworth's Second Nature: A Study of the Poetry and Politics* (Chicago: University of Chicago Press, 1984), 258–63.

6. William Godwin, *Enquiry Concerning Political Justice and Its Influence on Morals and Happiness*, 3rd ed., ed. F. E. L. Priestley, 3 vols. (1793; Toronto: University of Toronto Press, 1946), 1.384. Due to this "systematical arrangement [of] the universe," Godwin adds, "it [is] impossible for him [man] to act in any instance otherwise than he has acted" (Godwin 1.384).

7. Mark Philp, *Godwin's Political Justice* (London: Duckworth, 1986), 90.

8. *The Notebooks of Samuel Taylor Coleridge*, ed. Kathleen Coburn, 2 vols., vol. 1: *1794–1804, Text* (Princeton: Princeton University Press, 1975), entry 174. These early reservations target merely the notion of Necessity in its irreligious, Godwinian form, but nonetheless look ahead to Coleridge's conviction of the notion's inherent liabilities.

9. Godwin, from an Abinger manuscript, deposit b 228/9, at the Bodleian Library, Oxford; as cited by Philp (34).

10. William Hazlitt, "On the Doctrine of Philosophical Necessity," in *The Collected Works of William Hazlitt*, ed. P. P. Howe, 21 vols. (London: J. M. Dent and Sons, 1931), 20.60.

11. *LB*, 309 (lines 11–26). James Butler and Karen Green place the composition of these lines in Wordsworth's Goslar period, dating them between 6 October 1798 and late April 1799. Duncan Wu dates them to February-March 1798 in *Romanticism: An Anthology*, 2nd ed. (Malden, MA: Blackwell, 1998), 298.

12. R. D. Havens, *The Mind of a Poet*, 2 vols., vol. 1: *A Study of Wordsworth's Thought* (Baltimore: Johns Hopkins University Press, 1941), 186.

13. Sheats, 211–212. The philosophical eclecticism of "Tintern Abbey" militates against simply characterizing it a One Life poem. In this regard, see the discussion of Wordsworth's dependence on the empiricist and idealist philosophical traditions in "Tintern Abbey" by Alan Grob, in *The Philosophic Mind: A Study of Wordsworth's Poetry and Thought, 1797–1805* (Columbus: Ohio State University Press, 1973), 13–45; and by Keith G. Thomas, in *Wordsworth and Philosophy: Empiricism and Transcendentalism in the Poetry* (Ann Arbor: UMI Research Press, 1989), 65–84. Before agreeing that Wordsworth's poem confronted its original readers with any distinctive or innovative philosophical doctrine, we should also recall Robert Mayo's remark that "Tintern Abbey is one of the most conventional poems in the whole [*Lyrical Ballads*] volume," in "The Contemporaneity of the 'Lyrical Ballads,'" *PMLA* 69 (1954): 493.

14. Which is why Daniel Dombrowski argues that Wordsworth should be regarded as a panentheist: "Wordsworth's Panentheism," *WC* 16 (1985): 136–42.

15. Although its relevance is merely suggestive, we might note Coleridge's quotation of a version of "Not useless" (lines 1–18) in illustration of his own beliefs in his 10 March 1798 letter to his brother George (*CLSTC* 1.397–98)—which implies, given Coleridge's opposition to pantheism, that he hardly interpreted Wordsworth's lines as pantheistic. While the passage Coleridge cites does not touch directly on the One Life, the quotation immediately follows his statement that his poetry attempts to render "the beauty of the inanimate impregnated, as with a living soul, by the presence of Life." So we indeed see Coleridge invoking a Wordsworthian One Life meditation to clarify implications of his own sense of a spiritual ("as with a living soul") presence in nature.

16. See, for example, the notes to "Lines written in early spring" (*LB*, 349–50). James H. Averill discusses Wordsworth's conversancy with this scientific material in "Wordsworth and 'Natural Science': The Poetry of 1798," *JEGP* 77 (1978): 232–46; more recently, Richard E. Matlack has argued for the profound influence of Darwin's *Zoonomia*, in particular, on the representations of a living nature in the *Lyrical Ballads* poems of natural communion, in *The Poetry of Relationship: The Wordsworths and Coleridge, 1797–1800* (New York: St. Martin's, 1997), 111–19.

17. Stephen M. Parrish, "Michael and the Pastoral Ballad," in *Bicentenary Wordsworth Studies in Memory of John Alban Finch*, ed. Jonathan Wordsworth (Ithaca: Cornell University Press, 1970), 57.

18. Coleridge, *Aids to Reflection*, ed. Henry Nelson Coleridge, with a preliminary essay by John M'Vickar (New York: Swords, Stanford, and Co., 1839), 316. Coleridge specifically laments the tendency of "Tintern Abbey" to confirm superficial readers in a heterodox natural religion at odds with Wordsworth's own beliefs and intentions.

19. Mary Jacobus, *Tradition and Experiment in Wordsworth's "Lyrical Ballads" (1798)* (Oxford: Clarendon Press, 1976), 129.

20. G. R. Cragg, *Reason and Authority in the Eighteenth Century* (Cambridge: Cambridge University Press, 1964), 161.

21. Gene Ruoff, "Religious Implications of Wordsworth's Imagination," *SIR* 12 (1973): 688–89.

22. Harold Bloom, *The Visionary Company: A Reading of English Romantic Poetry* (Ithaca: Cornell University Press, 1961), 139.

23. Mark Foster, "'Tintern Abbey' and Wordsworth's Scene of Writing," *SIR* 25 (1986): 93.

24. Richard E. Matlack's phrase, from "Classical Argument and Romantic Persuasion," *SIR* 25 (1986): 107.

25. "Even the dialogues introduced in the present volume are soliloquies of the same character, taking different views of the subject," Hazlitt quipped, adding that "the recluse, the pastor, and the pedlar are three persons in one poet," in "On Mr Wordsworth's Excursion," *Complete Works*, 4.113.

26. T. S. Eliot, "Tradition and the Individual Talent,"in *Selected Prose of T. S. Eliot*, ed. Frank Kermode (New York: Harcourt Brace Jovanovich, Strauss and Giroux, 1975), 43.

27. See Alan Bewell's brilliant discussion of *Peter Bell* in *Wordsworth and the Enlightenment: Nature, Man, and Society in the Experimental Poetry* (New Haven: Yale University Press, 1989), 109–41.

28. We can grant the implication of the One Life in Wordsworth's plan for, and commitment to, *The Recluse* and still envision his commitments to the One Life itself as tentative. To *The Recluse* he was certainly committed, and the poem would probably have celebrated some form of Unity. But no evidence suggests that the philosophical presuppositions of *The Recluse* ever achieved full clarity in Wordsworth's mind. See his March 1804 letters to Coleridge asking for a redaction of the plan of the poem (*LEY*, 452, 464).

29. Geoffrey Hartman, *Wordsworth's Poetry 1787–1814* (New Haven: Yale University Press, 1964), 135.

30. Stephen Gill, *William Wordsworth: A Life* (New York: Oxford University Press, 1990), 135. My understanding of "Not useless" relies on the thorough discussion in James H. Averill's *Wordsworth and the Poetry of Human Suffering* (Ithaca: Cornell University Press, 1980), 125–36, 138–43; and on Chandler (124–30).

31. *Political Justice* 1.420–21. See Philp's discussion of Necessity, perfectibility, and free will in Godwin (Philp, 89–95).

32. Thomas McFarland, *Coleridge and the Pantheist Tradition* (Oxford: Clarendon Press, 1969), 88.

33. Reeve Parker, "'Finer Distance': The Narrative Art of Wordsworth's 'The Wanderer,'" *ELH* 39 (1972): 110. David Pirie writes eloquently on the Pedlar's inhumanity, his "comfortable largesse," and specifically contrasts Wordsworth's depiction of the Pedlar with Coleridge's claim in *Religious Musings* "that pantheism was not just compatible with humanitarianism, but actually the source of human sympathy," in *William Wordsworth: The Poetry of Grandeur and Tenderness* (London: Methuen, 1982), 84, 82. Sheats also differentiates the Pedlar's and the poet-narrator's viewpoints and reads that difference as a compensation for "the paradoxical inhumanity of the pedlar's optimism" (Sheats, 180). Some critics, let me add, notice the Pedlar's own susceptibility to grief and on that basis emphasize the philosophy's inability to console its own advocate.

34. Cleanth Brooks, "Wordsworth and Human Suffering: Notes on Two Early Poems," in *From Sensibility to Romanticism*, ed. Frederick W. Hilles and Harold Bloom (New York: Oxford University Press, 1965), 385, 386.

35. Edward Bostetter, *The Romantic Ventriloquists* (Seattle: University of Washington Press, 1963), 65.

36. Helen Darbishire notes the modifying addition of free will to the idea of Necessity in this passage, in *The Poet Wordsworth* (Oxford: Clarendon Press, 1950), 163.

37. Albert O. Wlecke, *Wordsworth and the Sublime* (Berkeley: University of California Press, 1973), 65; my emphasis. Keith Thomas remarks similarly that in these lines "faith finds confirmation through sight" as "the bible's promise of 'the life which cannot die' becomes here a visible activity in nature" (Thomas, 53).

38. David G. Riede, *Oracles and Hierophants: Constructions of Romantic Authority* (Ithaca: Cornell University Press, 1991), 138.

39. Susan Wolfson, *The Questioning Presence: Wordsworth, Keats, and the Interrogative Mode in Romantic Poetry* (Ithaca: Cornell University Press, 1986), 108; Averill, *Wordsworth and the Poetry of Human Suffering*, 133. Averill reads this analogue as wholly ironic: "Wordsworth is not at all Christian but very nearly blasphemous in his equation of mere humanity with God the Son" (Averill, 133–34). Karl Kroeber notices the mutual accommodation of immanentism and Anglicanism—"a mixing of naturalism with the numinous"—in Wordsworth's poetry, in *Ecological Literary Criticism: Romantic Imagining and the Biology of Mind* (New York: Columbia University Press, 1994), 58.

40. Mary Moorman notes a similar emotional-religious reflex on Wordsworth's part in "Ruth": "the last verse, visualizing a Christian funeral 'in hallowed mould' for the poor vagrant, strikes a new note in Wordsworth's poetry. The dead Lucy had been consigned, without apparent concern for her 'immortal part,' to be 'Rolled round in earth's diurnal course, / With rocks and stones and trees.' Perhaps the solitude and wretchedness of Ruth created in him a reaction towards the comfort and kindness which Christian humanity can offer even to a poor dead body"— in *William Wordsworth: A Biography, The Early Years, 1770–1804* (Oxford: Clarendon, 1957), 427–28. As I mentioned above, and will emphasize in the following chapter, the Lucy poem Moorman quotes depicts the estranging objectification of death conceived as One Life reassimilation; so the final stanza of "Ruth," particularly since Ruth "is like another Margaret of *The Ruined Cottage*" (Moorman, 427), may replay the more subtle evocation of Christian consolation in *The Ruined Cottage* MS. D. Butler and Green date "Ruth" "between October 6, 1798, and February 23, 1799; almost certainly before [Wordsworth] left Germany in late 1799" (*LB*, 191).

NOTES TO CHAPTER 3.
FAITH'S PROGRESS, 1799–1804

1. Jonathan Wordsworth's annotations in *NCP* indicate both Wordsworth's recourse to the theory of the sublime and allusions to Akenside, but see W. J. B. Owen's "The Sublime and the Beautiful in *The Prelude*," *WC* 4 (1973): 67–86; and, for Akenside, the discussions in Abbie Findlay Potts, *Wordsworth's Prelude: A Study of Its Literary Form* (Ithaca: Cornell University Press, 1953), 244–78; and Mary Jacobus, *Tradition and Experiment in Wordsworth's "Lyrical Ballads" (1798)* (Oxford: Clarendon Press, 1976), 111–12. My fifth chapter argues that Wordsworth's characterization of himself as temperamentally inclined to the sublime develops a passage in *The Pleasures of Imagination*. Due to my dependence on Jonathan Wordsworth's annotations, this chapter cites the Two-Part *Prelude* from *NCP* rather than from the Cornell edition. Other Wordsworth texts are cited from the relevant Cornell volumes, except in the case of *The Excursion*, which is cited from *PW*.

2. Jonathan Wordsworth, "The Two-Part *Prelude* of 1799," in *NCP*, 573.

3. The one exception is the rigorously pantheistic passage from DC MS. 33 discussed in chapter 2.

4. F. R. Leavis, *Revaluation: Tradition & Development in English Poetry* (London: Chatto & Windus, 1936), 160; cited in *NCP*, 21n.3.

5. Kenneth Johnston, *Wordsworth and "The Recluse"* (New Haven: Yale University Press, 1984), 16–19.

6. Peter Manning, review of *Wordsworth and "The Recluse,"* *WC* 16 (1985): 153.

7. Robert Ryan, *Keats: The Religious Sense* (Princeton: Princeton University Press, 1976), 150.

8. Dictated 21 July 1832; cited from Duncan Wu, ed. *Romanticism: An Anthology* (Malden, MA: Blackwell Publishers, 1998), 548.

9. Stephen Gill, *William Wordsworth: A Life* (Oxford: Oxford University Press, 1990), 239. My fifth chapter discusses *The Prelude* as a religious poem.

10. See Hoxie Neal Fairchild's discussion in *HNF* 3.208–9. In *RR*, Robert Ryan provides both a synopsis of contemporary responses to *The Excursion* (101–2), and an excellent discussion of the text's ironic interplay of different—and, for Ryan, ultimately unreconciled—religious viewpoints (101–13). The nineteenth-century reception of *The Excursion* as a Christian poem is discussed in my conclusion.

11. Harold Bloom, *The Visionary Company: A Reading of English Romantic Poetry*, revised and enlarged edition (1961; Ithaca: Cornell University Press, 1971), 126–27, 126. The only criticism known to me which directly challenges a radically secularizing approach to the Prospectus is Ryan's treatment in *RR*, 34–36.

12. *HG*, 257, 259. Although I accept Beth Darlington's dating (*HG*, 22), Jonathan Wordsworth attributes the Prospectus to 1800 in "On Man, on Nature, and on Human Life," *RES*, n.s., 31 (1980): 26–29. Wu dates the earliest surviving draft of the Prospectus to 1799 (Wu, 330).

13. Remarking that "Wordsworth's point is that human religious language, however sublime in power, must always be inadequate to express the inexpressible" (*RR*, 35), Ryan cites Wordsworth's statement in the "Preface of 1815" that "the anthropomorphitism of the Pagan religion subjected the minds of the greatest poets in those countries too much to the bondage of definite form; from which the Hebrews were preserved by their abhorrence of idolatry" (*WPr* 3.34). Wordsworth's subsequent praise of Milton for Hebrew-like aversion to a literalizing definite form ("he was a Hebrew in soul"—*WPr* 3.35) may help explain his invocation of Milton for his liberalizing religious project in *The Recluse*.

14. Paul D. Sheats, *The Making of Wordsworth's Poetry 1785–1798* (Cambridge: Harvard University Press, 1973), 212–13.

15. Thomas McFarland, "On Man, on Nature, and on Human Life," *SIR* 21 (1982): 614. McFarland's case for the limitations of the Prospectus as a philosophical document, let me add, does not demonstrate any rejection of Christianity on Wordsworth's part. The poet's belief in God is not really an issue for McFarland, who concentrates on the consequences of the way in which the Prospectus conceptually positions (or fails to position) the idea of God. McFarland argues not that Wordsworth's viewpoint is secular, in brief, but that he had little native talent for systematic thinking.

16. Thomas McFarland, *Coleridge and the Pantheist Tradition* (Oxford: Clarendon Press, 1969), 162. McFarland's point is discussed in chapter 1; this paragraph summarizes an argument presented in more detail in that opening chapter.

17. For 1798–1802 closings ranging from a simple "God bless you" (to Cottle) to the variant, "Adieu God bless you" (to Coleridge) to "God for ever bless thee, my dear Mary" (to Mary Hutchinson) to "Heaven for ever bless you!" (to Sara Hutchinson), see *LEY*, 215, 218, 227, 257, 263, 265, 280, 333, 337, 361, 367. While these closings demonstrate little about Wordsworth's mind and faith, they strike me as sincerely meant, and as such they at least indicate the poet's belief in a Deity capable of blessing human lives.

18. For the "Ode to Duty," often dated 1806, see Jared Curtis's claim that the poem was "probably basically composed, except stanza 1, early in 1804, by March 6" (*PTV*, 104).

19. Lionel Trilling, "Wordsworth and the Iron Time," in *Wordsworth: A Collection of Critical Essays*, ed. M. H. Abrams (Englewood Cliffs: Prentice Hall, 1972), 46. For Trilling, Wordsworth seems Christian by virtue of his "concern for the life of humbleness and quiet, his search for peace, his sense of the burdens of this life, those which are inherent in the flesh and spirit of man. Then there is his belief that the bonds of society ought to be inner and habitual. . . . Christian too seems his responsiveness to the idea that there is virtue in the discharge of duties which are of the great world and therefore dangerous to simple peace. . . . There is his impulse to submit to the conditions of life under a guidance that is at once certain and mysterious; his sense of the possibility and actuality of enlightenment, it need scarcely be said, is one of the characteristic things abut him. . . . And then, above all, there is his consciousness of the *neighbor*, his impulse to bring into the circle of significant life those of the neighbors who are simple and outside the circle of social pride, and those who in the judgment of the world are queer and strange and useless" (46).

20. Judith W. Page finds the reference to Abraham's bosom disturbingly eschatological. She argues that the phrase, in psychological and biographical context, shows Wordsworth "evading his responsibilities to his illegitimate daughter Caroline. He uses conventional religious language to sanction his actions, and he finally places Caroline in the hands of God—a substitute father for the father Wordsworth knows he will never be," in *Wordsworth and the Cultivation of Women* (Berkeley: University of California Press, 1994), 64. While I am indebted to Page's analysis, the celebration of childhood innocence in "It is a Beauteous Evening" strikes me as less dark, and the "Abraham's bosom" allusion less problematic as a protective gesture, than she finds them to be.

21. Raimonda Modiano, "Blood Sacrifice, Gift Economy, and the Edenic World: Wordsworth's 'Home at Grasmere,'" *SIR* 32 (1993): 495, 499.

22. See, for example, D. C. Allen's remarks on the traditional associations of Christ with the deer in *Image and Meaning: Metaphoric Traditions in Renaissance Poetry*, new enlarged ed. (Baltimore: Johns Hopkins University Press, 1968), 173–76.

23. Gill describes Wordsworth's late 1799 tour of Grasmere prior to relocating there as "one of the key experiences of his life. As he had drafted his recent autobiographical poetry, memories of his childhood in the Lakes had surfaced from their deepest recesses. Now by returning to the scenes of their origin he was consciously putting them to the proof, testing them as a basis for a life that might be lived" (Gill, 167).

24. As Mary Moorman notes, in *William Wordsworth: A Biography: The Early Years, 1770–1803* (Oxford: Clarendon Press, 1957), 2–4.

25. Edmund Burke, *Reflections on the Revolution in France*, ed. J. G. A. Pocock (Indianapolis and Cambridge: Hackett Publishing Company, 1987), 80.

26. Robert Ryan similarly attributes Wordsworth's growing religious conventionality in these years not to an intellectual revolution "but rather . . . a quiet personal reintegration into the local and national religious community from which he had kept his distance for a decade" (*RR*, 96).

27. Ryan, *RR*, 96. The sonnet Ryan alludes to is "Thanksgiving after Childbirth," from the *Ecclesiastical Sonnets* (*PW* 3.397).

28. James Chandler, *Wordsworth's Second Nature: A Study of the Poetry and Politics* (Chicago: University of Chicago Press, 1984), 235.

29. Sheats, 249. The most influential contributions to the secondary literature on Wordsworth and death are noted by Alan Bewell, *Wordsworth and the Enlightenment: Nature, Man, and Society in the Experimental Poetry* (New Haven: Yale University Press, 1989), 308 n.1, to which should be added Bewell's own work on the anthropologically conceived "history of death" in Wordsworth.

30. McFarland, *Coleridge and the Pantheist Tradition*, 88.

31. Bloom, 139. Many scholars note the deathly intimations of "Tintern Abbey," but I am particularly indebted to Esther Schor on the displacement of elegy in Wordsworth's poem, in *Bearing the Dead: The British Culture of Mourning from the Enlightenment to Victoria* (Princeton: Princeton University Press, 1994), 127–31.

32. Alan Grob, "Wordsworth's *Immortality* Ode and the Search for Identity," *ELH* (1965): 46, 48.

33. Thomas M. Raysor, "The Themes of Immortality and Natural Piety in Wordsworth's Immortality Ode," *PMLA* 69 (1954): 862. Raysor's very sensible complete statement is, "And I feel that some evidence, and rather full evidence, should be offered before one assumes that Wordsworth at any time gave up completely the concept of a finite personal soul after death, or accepted the idea of the annihilation of personal identity and self-consciousness by absorption into the infinite. Perhaps he ought to have done so, if he had followed his thought to the end, but Wordsworth was far from a systematic idealist philosopher. He was a poet who used philosophical or religious concepts only as they formed part of his intuitive experience" (Raysor, 862). Assent to the ontological nullification of the self would have followed not from a systematic idealism in Wordsworth's case but from a pantheism which he never held in rigorously systematic fash-

ion, and which he had certainly abandoned by 1802. Wordsworth's later views of immortality are interestingly summarized in John Wyatt, *Wordsworth and the Geologists*, Cambridge Studies in Romanticism 16 (Cambridge: Cambridge University Press, 1995), 143–47.

34. Jonathan Wordsworth, *William Wordsworth: The Borders of Vision* (Oxford: Clarendon Press, 1982), 321. Jonathan Wordsworth makes this concession in the course of arguing that the equation of "soul" and "imagination" in the Snowdon episode of *The Prelude* "seems to have been more considered" (*Borders of Vision*, 321). In my judgment, the identification became more considered only in spring, 1804, although Wordsworth neither then nor thereafter used the terms with unfailing philosophical discrimination.

35. Priestley, *Memoirs of Dr. Joseph Priestley*, in *The Theological and Miscellaneous Works of Joseph Priestley*, ed. John Towill Rutt, 25 vols. in 26 (London: G. Smallfield, 1817–1832), 1. part 1.202–203. Noting Kant's closing emphases on "the freedom of the will, the immortality of the soul, and the existence of God" in the *Critique of Pure Reason*, McFarland remarks that "it takes only a little reflection to realize that all three are a single collocation, and that if one exists, all must exist," in *Originality & Imagination* (Baltimore: Johns Hopkins University Press, 19185), ix. The mutual implication of the concepts of God and soul tends against the likelihood—exceptions such as Priestley notwithstanding—that Wordsworth, simply as a theist, ever abandoned his belief in the soul's immortality.

36. Geoffrey Hartman, "Wordsworth, Inscriptions, and Romantic Nature Poetry," in *From Sensibility to Romanticism: Essays Presented to Frederick A. Pottle*, ed. Frederick W. Hilles and Harold Bloom (New York: Oxford University Press), 401.

37. See Schor, 151–95; Lora Clymer, "Graved in Tropes: The Figural Logic of Epitaphs and Elegies in Blair, Gray, Cowper, and Wordsworth," *ELH* 62 (1995): 347–86; and, for the social implications of death in the early Wordsworth, Kurt Fosso's excellent "Community and Mourning in William Wordsworth's *The Ruined Cottage*, 1797–1798," *SP* 92 (1995): 329–45.

NOTES TO CHAPTER 4.
WORDSWORTH AND THE IMMORTAL SOUL

1. Lionel Trilling, "The Immortality Ode," in *English Romantic Poets: Modern Essays in Criticism*, 2nd ed., ed. M. H. Abrams (New York: Oxford University Press, 1975), 164. John Hodgson justly remarks that "the great majority" of modern critics have taken the Ode "as an essentially humanist document," while suggesting himself, in keeping with the

majority conviction, that "the ode carefully records the tentativeness and the skepticism of [Wordsworth's] faith and speculations" in 1804, in *Wordsworth's Philosophical Poetry, 1797–1814* (Lincoln: University of Nebraska Press, 1980), 104, 105. The Wordsworth poems discussed in this chapter are cited as they appear in *PTV* unless a parenthetical identification indicates otherwise.

2. Anya Taylor, "Religious Readings of the Immortality Ode," *SEL* 26 (1986): 633–54. Of interpretations which take the poem's affirmation of immortality at face value, those I have found most helpful include Thomas M. Raysor's counterstatement to Trilling, "The Themes of Immortality and Natural Piety in Wordsworth's Immortality Ode," *PMLA* 69 (1954): 861–75; Alan Grob, "Wordsworth's *Immortality Ode* and the Search for Identity," *ELH* 32 (1965): 32–61; E. D. Hirsch, *Wordsworth and Schelling: a Typological Study of Romanticism* (New Haven: Yale University Press, 1960); and Joseph C. Sitterson, Jr., "The Genre and Place of the Intimations Ode," *PMLA* 101 (1986): 24–37.

3. "The historical rise of imagination's importance witnessed a transfer of mental energy from the weakening concept of soul to an alternative vehicle," Thomas McFarland comments; "imagination, and its twin Romantic ideal, originality, were then, and still are, transformations of the human intensity earlier conveyed by soul," in *Originality and Imagination* (Baltimore: Johns Hopkins University Press, 1985), xii. Also see John O. Lyons, *The Invention of the Self: The Hinge of Consciousness in the Eighteenth Century* (Carbondale: Southern Illinois University Press, 1978), 18–27.

4. The varying conceptions of childhood implicated in the dispute between Pelagius and Saint Augustine over the nature of original sin are discussed, and that dispute summarized, by Robert Pattison, in *The Child Figure in English Literature* (Athens: University of Georgia Press, 1978), 10–20. In a related vein, see Gene W. Ruoff's summary of the Church's reception, and eventual rejection, of Origen's theory of a preexistent soul, in *Wordsworth and Coleridge: The Making of the Major Lyrics, 1802–1804* (New Brunswick: Rutgers University Press, 1989), 252–58.

5. R. R. Palmer, *Catholics and Unbelievers in Eighteenth Century France* (Princeton: Princeton University Press, 1939), 136. Palmer concentrates on the French Catholic critique of sensationalism, but the most prominent French defense the soul was probably Rousseau's Savoyard Vicar section of *Emile or On Education*. intro., and trans. Allan Bloom (New York: Basic Books, 1979), 266–313, particularly 278–84.

6. David Hume, *A Treatise of Human Nature*, ed. L. A. Selby-Bigge, 2nd ed., rev. P. H. Nidditch (Oxford: Clarendon, 1978), 254.

7. Coward and Toland are among the writers mentioned in John Redwood's discussion of rationalist attacks on the soul, in *Reason, Ridicule, and Religion: The Age of Enlightenment in England, 1660–1750* (Cambridge: Harvard University Press, 1976), 140–53.

8. Samuel Clarke, *A Discourse Concerning the Being and Attributes of God*, 8th ed. (London: J. and J. Knapaton, 1731), 168.

9. Hoxie Neal Fairchild discusses Kenrick's poem in *HNF* 2.45–46. In "Young's *Night Thoughts* in Relation to Contemporary Christian Apologetics," *PMLA* 49 (1934): 66–67, Isabel St. John Bliss suggests that Gastrell's book exerted a particular influence on Young, but her reconstruction of the religious background of *Night Thoughts* usefully reconfirms the centrality of the issue of the soul's immortality throughout eighteenth-century theological speculation and dispute. Gastrell's *A Defense of an Argument Made Use of in a Letter to Mr. Dodwel, to Prove the Immateriality and Immortality of the Soul* even formed part of a series entitled, Tracts on the Immortality of the Soul.

10. As H. W. Piper shows, in "Coleridge and the Unitarian Consensus," Richard Granvil and Molly Lefebre, ed. *The Coleridge Connection: Essays for Thomas McFarland* (Houndmills, Basingstoke, Hampshire: Macmillan, 1990), 276. Piper discusses Coleridge's use of Baxter for *The Destiny of Nations* in *The Active Universe: Pantheism and the Concept of Imagination in the English Romantic Poets* (London: Athlone Press, 1962), 37–38.

11. That outcry even found poetic expression anticipating Wordsworth's poem, with John Walters writing *An Ode on the Immortality of the Soul: Occasioned by the Opinions of Dr. Priestley* (Wrexham: R. Marsh, 1786). Fairchild mentions this poem in his brief discussion of Walters (*HNF* 2.215–17).

12. Priestley, *Disquisitions*, in *The Theological and Miscellaneous Works of Joseph Priestley*, ed. John Towill Rutt, 25 vols. in 26 (London: G. Smallfield, 1817–1832), 3.286. Priestley's views on the soul are summarized by Erwin N, Hiebert, "The Integration of Revealed Religion and Scientific Materialism in the Thought of Joseph Priestley," in Lester Kieft and Bennett R. Willeford, Jr., ed. *Joseph Priestley: Scientist, Theologian, and Metaphysician* (Lewisburg: Bucknell University Press, 1980), 27–61.

13. For Hartley's denial of the materiality of the soul, see *Observations on Man, His Frame, His Duty, and His Expectations* (1749), Facsimile Reproduction with an Introduction. ed. Theodore L. Huguelet (Gainesville: Scholars' Facsimiles & Reprints, 1966), 1.511–51; for Hartley's defense of immortality, concentrated in the section "Of a Future State after the Expiration of this Life," see *On Man* 2.382–403.

14. Jerome Christensen, *Coleridge's Blessed Machine of Language* (Ithaca: Cornell University Press, 1981), 63–68; J. A. Appleyard, *Coleridge's Philosophy of Literature* (Cambridge: Harvard University Press, 1965), 35–36.

15. John Rea, "Coleridge's Intimations of Immortality From Proclus," *MP* (1928): 201–13. While most Wordsworthians will find Rea's claims for influence vitiated by his 1802 dating of stanzas 5–8 of the Ode, in which the preexistence motif is developed, my own greatest problem with Rea's argument is that it implicitly lends the poem's Platonism more weight than it finally deserves. Although he attributed acquisition of the "Idea" to socialization, Hartley had claimed, for example, that "children begin probably with a definite visible Idea of God; but that by degrees this is quite obliterated, without anything of a stable precise Nature succeeding in its room" until theopathic development eventuates in adult comprehension (*On Man* 1.488).

16. *Biographia Literaria, or Biographical Sketches of My Literary Life and Opinions*, ed. James Engell and W. Jackson Bate, *CWSTC* 7 (Princeton: Princeton University Press, 1983), 2.147.

17. Grob, 35; Helen Vendler, "Lionel Trilling and the *Immortality Ode*," *Salmagundi* 41 (1978): 81; Kenneth R. Lincoln, "Wordsworth's Mortality Ode," *JEGP* 71 (1972): 215.

18. Cleanth Brooks, "Wordsworth and the Paradox of Imagination," in *Wordsworth: A Collection of Critical Essays*, ed. M. H. Abrams (Englewood Cliffs: Prentice Hall, 1972), 180.

19. I cite *Paradise Lost* from *John Milton: Complete Poems and Major Prose*, ed. Merritt Y. Hughes (Indianapolis: Bobbs-Merrill, 1957). For Miltonic resonances in Wordsworth's Ode, see Paul McNally, "Milton and the Immortality Ode," *WC* 11 (1980): 28–33; Anne Williams, "The *Intimations Ode*: Wordsworth's Fortunate Fall," *Romanticism Past and Present* 5 (1981): 1–13; and James W. Pipkin, "Wordsworth's 'Immortality Ode' and the Myth of the Fall," *Renascence* 30 (1978): 91–98.

20. R. P. Graves's comment is cited by Christopher Wordsworth, *Memoirs of William Wordsworth*, 2 vols. (Boston: Ticknor, Reed, and Fields, 1851), 2.490; "Letter from Professor Bonamy Price on the Ode of Immortality," in *Transactions of the Wordsworth Society* 2 (1883): 26; Fenwick note, *PW* 4.463.

21. See Peter J. Manning, "Wordsworth's Intimations Ode and its Epigraphs," *JEGP* 82 (1983): 526–40. Other critics stressing the centrality of father/son relations in the Ode are cited in subsequent notes, but also see Mary Moorman, "Wordsworth and His Children," in Jonathan Wordsworth, ed. *Bicentenary Wordsworth Studies in Memory of John Alban Finch* (Ithaca: Cornell University Press, 1970), 111–41. Jerome

Christensen reads the Ode for its insights into "the potential for tragedy in the relations of child and father," in "'Thoughts That Do Often Lie Too Deep for Tears': Toward a Romantic Concept of Lyrical Drama," WC 12 (1981): 53; Frederick Kirchoff similarly sees the poem constructing a tragic perspective from unresolved Oedipal conflict in "Reconstructions of the Self in Wordsworth's 'Ode: Intimations of Immortality from Recollections of Early Childhood,'" in Lynne Layton and Barbara Ann Schapiro, ed. Narcissism and the Text: Studies in Literature and the Psychology of the Self (New York: New York University Press, 1986), 116–29. For the political implications of Wordsworth's Virgilian epigraph, see Marjorie Levinson, Wordsworth's Great Period Poems (Cambridge: Cambridge University Press, 1986), 92.

22. Ernest Becker, The Denial of Death (New York: Free Press, 1973), 162–63.

23. These considerations may shed light on Moorman's point that "it is the fact, though not easy to explain, that Wordsworth wrote poems about his two daughters, but not about any of his three sons, not even about the treasured second boy, Thomas, whose death in 1812 at the age of six was a well-nigh unbearable blow to him" (Moorman, 117). Mark Reed notes that MS. Y contains some prose describing a baby boy, "no doubt Johnny Wordsworth," in his introduction to 1805 Prelude (1.43), but does not include a transcription.

24. Paul Magnuson has argued influentially that the Ode's "1804 stanzas offer a consolation for loss, but they also offer a new direction for the poem and introduce a myth that is nowhere clearly implied in the opening stanzas. . . . The first line of the poem, 'There was a time,' does not place the vision of celestial light specifically in childhood; that location comes in 1804," in Coleridge and Wordsworth: A Lyrical Dialogue (Princeton: Princeton University Press, 1988), 279. But the myth of stanza five, as Wordsworth introduces it, develops the light imagery and the specific implications of "celestial" and "glory" in the earlier stanzas, just as the children of those stanzas, to whom the speaker turns in pursuing the vanished radiance, tacitly make awareness of the light a characteristic of childhood. I must agree with Grob that the speaker of stanzas 5–11 manages to "find in the aura that had once invested all visual objects a spiritual dimension heretofore incapable of articulation and yet deeply implicit in the poem's initial phase" (Grob, 43).

25. Paul H. Fry, The Poet's Calling in the English Ode (New Haven: Yale University Press, 1980), 140.

26. W. B. Cornochan, "The Child Is Father of the Man," in A Distant Prospect: Eighteenth-Century Views of Childhood, Papers read at a Clark Library Seminar by Patricia Meyer Spacks and W. B. Carnochan (Los Angeles: William Andrews Clark memorial Library, 1982), 45. Garret Stewart

summarizes the view held by most historians of childhood in referring to Romanticism's innovative "emphasis on childhood as a phase rather than a preface to identity," in *Death Sentences: Styles of Dying in British Fiction* (Cambridge: Harvard University Press, 1984), 18.

27. G. Wilson Knight, *The Starlit Dome* (London: Methuen, 1941), 46.

28. As Lucy Newlyn argues brilliantly in *Coleridge, Wordsworth, and the Language of Allusion* (Oxford: Clarendon Press, 1986), 142–64. The motif of filial inheritance recurs in the fascinating essays on Hartley by Judith Plotz, "The *Annus Mirabilis* and the Lost Boy: Hartley's Case," *SIR* 33 (1994): 181–200; and Anya Taylor, "'A Father's Tale': Coleridge Foretells the Life of Hartley," *SIR* (1991): 37–56.

29. Vendler, 75–76. Vendler also observes that throughout the middle stanzas of the Ode "we see the Child wholly in exterior semblance" (Vendler 73). The effort to vicariously recover childhood in stanzas 3–4 of the Ode— and, for that matter, in other 1802 lyrics—gives way to what I read as an adult and parental distance from childhood in the Ode's latter stanzas.

30. Dorothy's 29 April 1802 journal entry recounts how "William lay, & I lay in the trench under the fence—he with his eyes shut & listening to the waterfalls & the Birds. . . . we both lay still, & unseen by one another— he thought that it would be as sweet thus to lie so in the grave, to hear the *peaceful* sounds of the earth & just to know that ones dear friends were near," in Dorothy Wordsworth, *The Grasmere Journals*, ed. Pamela Woof (Oxford: Clarendon Press, 1991), 92.

31. I cite the text of *Hamlet* established by Willard Farnham, in *William Shakespeare: The Complete Works*, Alfred Harbage, gen. ed., rev. ed. (Baltimore: Penguin Books, 1969). The *Hamlet* allusion has been discussed by Christensen, 53–54 and especially 56–57; Daniel W. Ross, "Seeking a Way Home: The Uncanny in Wordsworth's 'Immortality Ode,'" *SEL* 32 (1992): 627–28; and Jonathan Wordsworth, *William Wordsworth: The Borders of Vision* (Oxford: Clarendon, 1982), 64.

32. W. K. Wimsatt, "The Structure of Romantic Nature Imagery," in *Romanticism and Consciousness: Essays in Criticism*, ed. Harold Bloom (New York: Norton, 1970), 87.

33. Manning, "Epigraphs," 533. Manning acknowledges his uncertainty as to "precisely how much weight should be attached to the suggestion of the poet as mother carried by the imagery: certainly the metaphor should not be forced into a rigid identification," but he stresses that "Absent from this tableau . . . is the figure of the father" (Manning, "Epigraphs," 533.n15, 533).

34. John Heath-Stubbs, *The Darkling Plain* (London: Eyre and Spottiswoode, 1950), 33.

35. Willard Spiegelman, *Wordsworth's Heroes* (Berkeley: University of California Press, 1985), 63.

36. For the contrary view that the Ode's religious interests progressively exchange a worldly for a transcendent orientation, see Florence Marsh, "Wordsworth's Ode: Obstinate Questionings," *SIR* 5 (1966): 219–30.

37. Peter J. Manning, "Wordsworth, Margaret, and the Pedlar," *SIR* 15 (1976): 202; Richard J. Onorato, *The Character of the Poet: Wordsworth in "The Prelude"* (Princeton: Princeton University Press, 1971), 38.

38. Norman Sykes, *Church and State in England in the XVIIIth Century* (1934; reprint, Hamden, Connecticut: Archon Books 1962), 419–20.

39. James Montgomery, noting Wordsworth's use of the preexistence motif, wrote that the Ode affirmed "*a doctrine which religion knows not,*" in the *Eclectic Review* 4 (1808): 35–43; cited from *The Romantics Reviewed: Contemporary Reviews of British Romantic Writers*, ed. Donald H. Reiman, 9 vols. (New York: Garland, 1972), Part A, 1.337.

40. "For the nineteenth century," Barbara Garlitz remarks, "the Ode became a gloss on Jesus's words. . . . and its philosophy of childhood a powerful challenge to Calvinism," in "The Immortality Ode: Its Cultural Progeny," *SEL* 6 (1966): 641. Garlitz's account of the Ode's nineteenth-century reception can be supplemented by Katherine Mary Peek, *Wordsworth in England: Studies in the History of His Fame* (1943; New York: Octagon, 1969).

41. From Hopkins' 23 October 1886 letter to Richard Watson Dixon, in *Gerard Manly Hopkins: Selected Letters*, ed. Catherine Phillips (Oxford: Clarendon Press, 1990), 241.

42. Grob, 52. Ruoff remarks of the preexistence myth of the Ode that "Wordsworth's version is the most Westernized, most Christianized form of the doctrine" (Ruoff, 253).

43. See M. H. Abrams discussion of the figure of the child in Romantic literature (*NS*, 379–84).

44. Isaac Watts, "Against Scoffing and Calling Names" (lines 21–22), from *Divine Songs For Children*, in *The Poetical Works of Isaac Watts and Henry Kirke White* (Boston: Houghton, Mifflin and Company, n.d.), 338–39.

45. William Wilberforce, *A Practical View of the Prevailing Religious System of Professed Christians, in the Higher and Middle Classes, Contrasted with Real Christianity*, the Evangelical Library, vol. 2 (New York: The American Tract Society, n.d.), 332.

NOTES TO CHAPTER 5. SOUL'S PROGRESS:
THE FAITH OF *THE PRELUDE*

1. Stephen Gill, *William Wordsworth: A Life* (Oxford: Oxford University Press, 1990), 239. Citations of The Five-Book *Prelude* in this chapter are taken from Wu's edition (*FBP*) and accompanied by notes indicating the corresponding passages in Reed's transcriptions of MSS. W and WW in his Cornell Wordsworth Series edition (1805 *Prelude*). References to Reed are to his introduction to 1805 *Prelude*. For consistency I cite the Cornell versions of the 1805 and 1850 texts of *The Prelude* even when discussing de Selincourt's comparison of the two versions as they appear in his *The Prelude: or, Growth of a Poet's Mind*, 2nd ed., rev. Helen Darbishire (Oxford: Clarendon Press, 1959), hereafter abbreviated *EdS*; differences between the Cornell and Oxford texts are not significant for my argument.

2. For an argument that M. H. Abrams looks for God in the wrong places in Wordsworth's poem, see J. Robert Barth's contribution to a Wordsworth Summer Conference panel discussion on the comparative merits of the 1805 and 1850 texts of *The Prelude*, "Visions and Revisions: The 1850 *Prelude*," *WC* 17 (1986): 19.

3. For Jonathan Wordsworth and Mark Reed's essentially identical reconstructions of the poem's structure and design—reconstructions I accept—see respectively "The Five-Book *Prelude* of Early Spring 1804," *JEGP* 76 (1977): 1–25; and Reed's introduction to 1805 *Prelude*, 27–39. Jarvis presents his views in "The Five-Book *Prelude*: A Reconsideration," *JEGP* 80 (1981): 528–51.

4. Reed, 34. Reed's term "AB" simply refers to his reading-text synthesis of the two existing 1805–1806 fair copies of the Thirteen-Book *Prelude*.

5. Reed, 35. De Selincourt remarked, "there is evidence in MS. W that whilst [Wordsworth] was working on Book IV in February and March 1804 he was probing into the nature of the 'higher mind' and attempting to define it" (*EdS*, 619, n.to 13.1–119).

6. Cited from Wu's appendix in *FBP*, 199 (lines 27–28); see MS. W 38ʳ (1805 *Prelude* 2.288). My final quoted phrase comes from Joseph F. Kishel, "The 'Analogy Passage' from Wordsworth's Five-Book *Prelude*," *SIR* 18 (1979): 281. My understanding of the Analogy Passage depends also on Richard Schell, "Wordsworth's Revisions of the Ascent of Snowdon," *PQ* 54 (1974): 592–603; Kenneth Johnston, *Wordsworth and "The Recluse"* (New Haven: Yale University Press, 1984), 106–10; and Mary Jacobus, *Romanticism, Writing, and Sexual Difference* (Oxford: Clarendon Press, 1989), 276–86.

7. *The Notebooks of Samuel Taylor Coleridge,* ed. Kathleen Coburn, 2 vols., vol. 1: *1794–1804: Text* (New York: Oxford University Press, 1957–1973), entry 1804.

8. See Abrams, *NS,* 29, 74–80, 95–96, and passim; and Jonathan Wordsworth, *William Wordsworth: The Borders of Vision* (Oxford: Clarendon Press, 1982), 231–78.

9. *FBP* 5.269–74; see MS. W 53ᵛ (1805 *Prelude* 2.311–12).

10. Coleridge himself borrowed the phrase from "Tintern Abbey" (line 114) and Wordsworth, as several critics point out, from Milton's *Samson Agonistes* (line 594).

11. For an analogue to my own argument, see Ashton Nichols' account of "Coleridge's 'illness' [as] a powerful force behind the expansion of the two-part text of 1799 into the five-book poem (1804), and later, the autobiographical epic of 1805," in "Coleridge as Catalyst to Autobiography: The Wordsworthian Self as Therapeutic Gift, 1804–5," the fourth chapter of his *The Revolutionary "I": Wordsworth and the Politics of Self-Presentation,* Romanticism in Perspective: Texts, Cultures, Histories (New York: St. Martin's, 1998), 78–101; quotation, 79.

12. *FBP* 5.98–99, 104–5; see MS. W 43ᵛ (1805 *Prelude* 2.295).

13. *FBP* 5.149–66; see MS. W 46ᵛ–47ʳ (1805 *Prelude* 2.299–300).

14. Lucy Newlyn, *Coleridge, Wordsworth, and the Language of Allusion* (Oxford: Clarendon Press, 1986), 187.

15. *FBP* 5.332–40; see MS. W 48ʳ-48ᵛ (1805 *Prelude* 2.302–3).

16. MS W. 48ᵛ (1805 *Prelude* 2.303). Wu notes this variant as an earlier draft in *FBP,* 148n.61.

17. Verse Letter (lines 295–96). Coleridge's phrase is his adaptation, of course, of Wordsworth's description of the Blessed Babe: "From nature largely he receives, nor so / Is satisfied but largely gives again" (*TPP* 2.297–98).

18. *FBP* 5.66–70, 86–94; see MS. W 43ʳ (1805 *Prelude* 2.294–95). In MS. W, the lines I cite are not separated by the passage Wu prints as *FBP* 5.71–85.

19. See MS. WW 28ʳ-28ᵛ (1805 *Prelude* 2.257–58). Jonathan Wordsworth mentions these drafts and notes that composition on Book 6 was underway by late March in "Five-Book *Prelude*" (4, 24). Here too, incidentally, Coleridge's remained a central presence, with Wordsworth using Book 6 to engage and revise the notion of sublimity propounded in Coleridge's "Chamouny; The Hour Before Sun-Rise. A Hymn," as Keith G. Thomas adroitly shows in his "Coleridge, Wordsworth, and the New His-

toricism: 'Chamouny; The Hour before Sun-Rise. A Hymn' and Book 6 of *The Prelude*," in *SIR* 33 (1994): 81–117.

20. Alan Liu, *Wordsworth: The Sense of History* (Stanford: Stanford University Press, 1989), 4.

21. Geoffrey Hartman, *Wordsworth's Poetry 1787–1814* (1964; New Haven: Yale University Press, 1971), 39–69; Liu, 3–31.

22. Coleridge, "Fragment of Theological Lecture," *Lectures 1795 On Politics and Religion*, ed. Lewis Patton and Peter Mann, *CWSTC* 1 (Princeton: Princeton University Press, 1971), 337–39. Although Wordsworth may have been most familiar with Akenside's development of this motif, see Albert O. Wlecke's discussion of John Baillie, author of *An Essay on the Sublime*, and Edward Young, in *Wordsworth and the Sublime* (Berkeley: University of California Press, 1973), 57–59.

23. Alan Bewell, *Wordsworth and the Enlightenment* (New Haven: Yale University Press, 1989), 272–73.

24. Isabel Armstrong, "Wordsworth's Complexity: Repetition and Doubled Syntax in *The Prelude* Book VI," *Oxford Literary Review* (1981): 38. Also see her similar comments on 27–28, 37–41.

25. Harold Bloom, *The Visionary Company: A Reading of English Romantic Poetry*, rev. and enlarged ed. (Ithaca: Cornell University Press, 1971), 151.

26. Nicholas Roe, *Wordsworth and Coleridge: The Radical Years* (Oxford: Clarendon Press, 1988), 219–23.

27. Liu, 23–31. While I concede the Napoleonic palimpsest Liu discovers in Wordsworth's lines, I also argue that the poet's language refers more directly to the Church Militant. Certainly we should recall with Michael Walzer that "the 'militancy' of the church and the spiritual warfare of godly men were ancient Christian themes" (*The Revolution of the Saints: A Study in the Origins of Radical Politics* [Cambridge: Harvard University Press, 1965], 278); and note, as William Haller writes, that Christian moral dedication found perhaps its supreme image in the "soldier who, having been pressed to serve under the banners of the spirit, must enact faithfully his part in the unceasing war of the spiritual against the carnal man" (*The Rise of Puritanism or, The Way to the New Jerusalem as Set Forth in the Pulpit and Press From Thomas Cartwright to John Lilburne and John Milton, 1570–1643* [New York: Columbia University Press, 1938], 142). Wordsworth invokes this widely disseminated iconographic tradition to suggest that the transcendental imagination can circumvent the disjunction of the Church Militant and the Church Triumphal, the soul's struggle against worldliness producing a visionary triumph ordinarily unavailable in life.

28. Jacobus, 268, 269. Deconstructive analysis of the Snowdon passage might begin with the decentering noticed by John Hodgson, who points out that "in relation to the land on which Wordsworth is standing, the mist appears as a sea," while "in relation to 'the real Sea' . . . the mist appears as land" (*Wordsworth's Philosophical Poetry, 1797–1814* [Lincoln: University of Nebraska Press, 1980], 114), so that the mist functions figurally as a Derridean frame or supplement.

29. W. J. B. Owen, "The Perfect Image of a Mighty Mind," *WC* 10 (1979): 8.

30. Robert Langbaum, "The Evolution of Soul in Wordsworth's Poetry," in *The Modern Spirit: Essays on the Continuity of Nineteenth and Twentieth Century Literature* (Oxford: Oxford University Press, 1970), 18–36.

31. See, for instance, Abrams' discussion of "The Poem as Heterocosm" in *The Mirror and the Lamp: Romantic Theory and the Critical Tradition* (1953; New York: Norton, 1958), 272–85.

32. Owen, "The Sublime and the Beautiful in *The Prelude*," *WC* 4 (1973): 67. This article helped establish not only Wordsworth's dependence upon notions of sublimity and beauty in *The Prelude* but his specific debts to Burke. I cite *A Philosophical Enquiry into the Origin of our Ideas of the Sublime and Beautiful*, ed. with an introduction by James T. Boulton (Notre Dame: University of Notre Dame Press, 1958). For Wordsworth's debts to Thomas Burnet, also significant, see Abrams (*NS*, 99–107).

33. Even after the ascendancy of the *Enquiry* in eighteenth-century England, Marjorie Hope Nicolson cautions, "sometimes the Sublime was a 'dreadful' Beauty—the creation of a God of Power; sometimes it was a 'higher' Beauty—the reflection of a God of Benignity," in *Mountain Gloom and Mountain Glory: The Development of the Aesthetics of the Infinite* (Ithaca: Cornell University Press, 1959), 324–25.

34. Akenside, *The Pleasures of Imagination* (3.546–50) in *The Poetical Works of Mark Akenside*, ed. Robin Dix (Madison: Fairleigh Dickinson University Press, 1996).

35. Theresa Kelley, *Wordsworth's Revisionary Aesthetics* (Cambridge: Cambridge University Press, 1988), 18. Although the statement I cite pertains specifically to the geological argument of Wordsworth's *Guide through the District of the Lakes*, Kelley finds the same "aesthetic progress in the [spectator's] mind" in Wordsworth's fragmentary essay on "The Sublime and the Beautiful," and argues, in fact, that "Wordsworth repeatedly describes sublimity and beauty as successive, then competing categories," and that "beauty's capacity to supplant the sublime is the critical point in Wordsworth's aesthetics" (Kelley 8, 3, 42). Bewell also discusses Wordsworth's idea of the sublime-to-beautiful progression in the mind's

responsiveness to nature (Bewell, 140). For the poet's understanding of a "primitive sublime and secondary beautiful" in the context of the geological theory of his day, see John Wyatt, *Wordsworth and the Geologists*, Cambridge Studies in Romanticism 16 (Cambridge: Cambridge University Press, 1995), 44–51.

36. Kelley, 130. Kelley contends, however, that "the Ravine of Arve passage is less indebted to the sublime than it is to the beautiful for its figuration" (Kelley, 10). Those interested should consult her argument that in *Prelude* 6 Wordsworth's beautiful figures successfully contain or domesticate the sublime (Kelley, 105–7).

37. Samuel Holt Monk, *The Sublime: A Study of Critical Theories in XVIII-Century England* (1935; Ann Arbor: University of Michigan Press, 1960), 79.

38. Coleridge's 25 July 1832 Table Talk entry, cited from *Coleridge's Miscellaneous Criticism*, ed. Thomas M. Raysor (Cambridge: Harvard University Press, 1936), 412.

39. Ernest Tuveson, *Millennium and Utopia: A Study in the Background of the Idea of Progress* (Berkeley: University of California Press, 1949), 6.

40. Erich Auerbach summarizes the development of typological theories of exegesis in his essay on "Figura," in *Scenes from the Drama of European Literature* (Gloucester, Massachusetts: Peter Smith, 1973), 11–76. For the endurance of typological paradigms in eighteenth-century literature, see Thomas R. Preston, "From Typology to Literature," *The Eighteenth Century: Theory and Interpretation* 23 (1982): 181–94; and Paul J. Korshin, *Typologies in England, 1650–1800* (Princeton: Princeton University Press, 1982), which even argues that the natural imagery of *Prelude* 6 is typologically organized (Korshin, 98–99).

41. Watts, "The Law and the Gospel" (lines 1–8); cited from *The Poetical Works of Isaac Watts and Henry Kirke White* (Boston: Houghton, Mifflin, and Company, n.d.), 87–88.

42. David Morris, *The Religious Sublime: Christian Poetry and Critical Tradition in 18th-Century England* (Lexington: University of Kentucky Press, 1972), 128. Morris usefully emphasizes how frequently passages of Old Testament sublimity—as in Warton's impressive "The dread Jehovah comes," his version of Isaiah 13—were topics of biblical paraphrase in eighteenth-century British poetry.

43. Morton Paley, "Tyger of Wrath," *PMLA* 81 (1966): 542. Through its breadth of citation, Paley's article brilliantly reconstructs the late eighteenth-century cultural ambience in which the Old Testament, sublimity, and terror could seem mutually analogous facets of a single prophetic vision.

44. Bewell's commentary on *Peter Bell* anticipates my account of *The Prelude* by correlating Peter's progress beyond superstitious fear with an anthropological progression "in which fear and ignorance are a necessary part of the development of religious ideas," and in which the poem's third Part, "as quite literally a 'gospel of nature,' can thus stand to the violent 'world of death' from which Peter has emerged in the same manner as New Testament love stands to Old Testament prophecy" (Bewell, 123, 141).

45. This historical transition, unsurprisingly, was commonly invoked to explain the moral development of the individual Christian: in a sermon "On the Discoveries of Faith," Wesley wrote, for instance, that "even one who has gone thus far in religion, who obeys God out of fear, is not in any wise to be despised, seeing 'the fear of the Lord is the beginning of wisdom.' Nevertheless he should be exhorted not to stop there. . . . Exhort him to press on by all possible means, till he passes 'from faith to faith'; from the faith of a *servant* to the faith of a *son*; from the spirit of bondage unto fear, to the spirit of childlike love," in *The Works of John Wesley*, vol. 4: *Sermons, 115–51*, ed. Albert C. Outler and others (Nashville: Abingdon Press, 1984–), 35. Abrams' well-known discussion of Christian internalizations of historical paradigms as models for personal spiritual development can be found in the "Christian History and Christian Psycho-Biography" chapter of *NS*, 46–56.

46. Aubrey De Vere, *Essays, Chiefly on Poetry*, 2 vols. (London: Macmillan, 1887), 1.263.

47. Herbert Lindenberger, "For the 1805 *Prelude*," *WC* 17 (1986): 3.

48. Barth, 19. Let me remind readers that Barth himself denies the express Christianity of both the 1805 and 1850 text, remarking that Wordsworth himself "at no point in his life is what I would call a traditional Christian, because he had no belief that is discernible to me—even in *The Excursion*—of central Christian doctrine" (Barth, 21).

49. As Wu contends, following up a suggestion by Owen, in *FBP*, 111n.24.

50. See James Chandler's *Wordsworth's Second Nature: A Study of the Poetry and Politics* (Chicago: University of Chicago Press, 1984), passim; and Johnston's recent *The Hidden Wordsworth: Poet, Lover, Rebel, Spy* (New York: Norton, 1998), especially 669. Johnston's case for Wordsworth's conservatism does not depend upon his speculation that the poet worked in 1798–1799 as a government agent.

NOTES TO CONCLUSION.
THE CHRISTIAN WORDSWORTH

1. Elinor Shaffer, *"Kubla Khan" and "The Fall of Jerusalem": The Mythological School in Biblical Criticism and Secular Literature, 1770–1880* (Cambridge: Cambridge University Press, 1975), 85.

2. From a letter to Grosvenor Bedford included in the Bodleian MSS. English Letters, c.25, f.144, 29 December 1814; cited in Geoffrey Carnall, *Robert Southey and His Age: The Development of a Conservative Mind* (Oxford: Clarendon, 1969), 216–17.

3. Shaffer, 87; Jerome J. McGann, "The Meaning of the Ancient Mariner," *Critical Inquiry* 8 (1981–1982): 35–67.

4. Alan Bewell, *Wordsworth and the Enlightenment: Nature, Man, and Society in the Experimental Poetry* (New Haven: Yale University Press, 1989), 119–41.

5. As in chapter 1, I use the term "Catholic" in the sense defined by Edith C. Batho in *The Later Wordsworth* (Cambridge: Cambridge University Press, 1933), 262.

6. Despite the absence of direct influence, the closeness of Higher Critical and Wordsworthian approaches to religious questions emerges in Hale White's account of his 1852 expulsion from New College, a theological school for the Congregational ministry, due to his efforts to modernize the curriculum. At the time White was suspected of acquiring his subversive sympathies from the Higher Criticism, but as he later wrote in his *The Early Life of Mark Rutherford*, "it was Wordsworth, and not German research which caused my expulsion": cited from Stephen Gill's *Wordsworth and the Victorians* (Oxford: Clarendon, 1998), 53. For defenses of Christianity as a historically progressive faith in the Church tradition most familiar to Wordsworth, see R. S. Crane's "Anglican Apologetics and the Idea of Progress, 1699–1745," in *The Idea of the Humanities and Other Essays Critical and Historical*, 2 vols. (Chicago: University of Chicago Press, 1967), 1.214–87.

7. I refer of course to Lamb's "All the north of England are in turmoil" letter of 15 February 1801 to Thomas Manning recounting Wordsworth's somewhat hectoring, and preceptorial, defense of the second edition of *Lyrical Ballads*, in *The Letters of Charles and Mary Anne Lamb*, ed. Edwin W. Marrs, Jr., 3 vols. (Ithaca: Cornell University Press, 1974–1978), 1.272–74; and to Wordsworth's addendum to Dorothy's 14 June 1802 letter to Mary and Sara Hutchinson, in which he instructs Sara on how properly to read "Resolution and Independence" (*LEY*, 366–67).

8. In the *Essay, Supplementary* Wordsworth observes, for example, that "religious faith is to him who holds it so momentous a thing, and error appears to be attended with such tremendous consequences, that, if opinions touching upon religion occur which the Reader condemns, he not only cannot sympathise with them, however animated the expression, but there is, for the most part, an end to all satisfaction and enjoyment" (*WPr* 3.65).

9. Thomas Pfau, *Wordsworth's Profession: Form, Class, and the Logic of Early Romantic Cultural Production* (Stanford: Stanford University

Press, 1997), 8. Although Pfau rightly underscores the power of resistance exercised by Wordsworth's poetry and the "provisional and malleable" political identities the poetry furnished its audience (Pfau, 11), his identification of that audience as middle class argues, in my judgment, for the overriding conservatism of the poetry's social agency, and thus for the reinscriptive rather than disruptive force of its rhetoric. On a similar note, see Alison Hickey's discussion of the complicity of *The Excursion* with Victorian colonialist ideologies and practices in *Impure Conceits: Rhetoric and Ideology in Wordsworth's "Excursion"* (Stanford: Stanford University Press, 1997), 131–65, and, for Wordsworth's support of Bell's Madras educational system, 108–10.

10. Lamb's review of *The Excursion* in *The Quarterly Review* 12 (October, 1814): 100–111; cited from *The Romantics Reviewed: Contemporary Reviews of British Romantic Writers*, ed. Donald H. Reiman, 9 vols. (New York: Garland, 1972), Part A, vol.2.826–31; cited phrases, 828, 829.

11. Montgomery's reservations about *The Excursion* rest on his conviction that Wordsworth's moral "system" "is *not all*" and that "the love of Nature *alone* cannot ascend from earth to heaven": he adds, however, "We do not mean to infer that Mr. Wordsworth excludes from his system the salvation of man, as revealed in the Scriptures" but only that the poet does not emphasize it enough. Declaring that "the Author, in the exordium of his sixth book, sufficiently proclaims his orthodoxy by a votive panegyric on the Church of England," Montgomery regrets the absence of Gospel references in the text as missed opportunities on the part of a poet who "*could* so sing of Christ's kingdom"—were his poetics Evangelical enough—"as would for ever set the question at rest." See Montgomery's review of *The Excursion* in *Eclectic Review*, 2nd Series, 3 (January, 1815): 13–19; in *The Romantics Reviewed*, Part A, vol. 1.352–65; cited phrases, 355, 356. Gill acknowledges that some readers found the faith of *The Excursion* too doctrinally undeveloped to be Christian—see, for example, his comments on John Wilson's response (*Wordsworth and the Victorians*, 66)—but also generalizes, "Denominational magnifying glasses might find flaws in *The Excursion* or *Ecclesiastical Sketches*, but the overall moral tendency of these poems could hardly be doubted" (*Wordsworth and the Victorians*, 19).

12. John Wilson," Sacred Poetry," in *The Recreations of Christopher North*, 3 vols. (Edinburgh and London: W. Blackwood and Sons, 1842), 2.345.

13. See Gill's discussion of how *The Prelude*—as "a story of one of God's elect"—confirmed the popular Christian reception of Wordsworthian humanitarianism (*Wordsworth and the Victorians*, 30–31).

14. Stephen Gill, *William Wordsworth: The Prelude*, Landmarks of World Literature (Cambridge: Cambridge University Press, 1991), 40.

15. Jon Klancher, *The Making of English Reading Audiences, 1790–1832* (Madison: University of Wisconsin Press, 1987), 33.

16. David Bromwich, *Disowned by Memory: Wordsworth's Poetry of the 1790s* (Chicago: University of Chicago Press, 1998), 40.

17. Jack Stillinger, *Coleridge and Textual Instability: The Multiple Versions of the Major Poems* (New York: Oxford University Press, 1994), 100. Stillinger's discussion and notes mention the leading contributors to the debate about intention in literary studies (see, for example, 105–107 and the accompanying notes). I should mention that Stillinger acknowledges the enduring place of intentionality as a premise for interpretive criticism in the course of an argument for the validity of textual versioning. For a brilliant defense of the dependence of literary historical explanation on an idea of authorial agency and intentionality, see Steven E. Cole's "Evading Politics: The Poverty of Historicizing Romanticism," *SIR* 34 (1995): 29–48.

18. Ryan, 96. This paragraph hurriedly summarizes arguments developed more carefully and at greater length in chapter 1–3.

INDEX